D1713376

THE SCIENCE OF PSYCHOTHERAPY

THE SERIES IN CLINICAL AND COMMUNITY PSYCHOLOGY

CONSULTING EDITORS
Charles D. Spielberger and Irwin G. Sarason

Auerbach and Stolberg   Crisis Intervention with Children and Families
Burchfield   Stress: Psychological and Physiological Interactions
Burstein and Loucks   Rorschach's Test: Scoring and Interpretation
Cohen and Ross   Handbook of Clinical Psychobiology and Pathology, Volume 1
Cohen and Ross   Handbook of Clinical Psychobiology and Pathology, Volume 2
Diamant   Male and Female Homosexuality: Psychological Approaches
Fischer   The Science of Psychotherapy
Froehlich, Smith, Draguns, and Hentschel   Psychological Processes in Cognition and Personality
Hobfoll   Stress, Social Support, and Women
Janisse   Pupillometry: The Psychology of the Pupillary Response
Krohne and Laux   Achievement, Stress, and Anxiety
London   Personality: A New Look at Metatheories
London   The Modes and Morals of Psychotherapy, Second Edition
Manschreck and Kleinman   Renewal in Psychiatry: A Critical Rational Perspective
Morris   Extraversion and Introversion: An Interactional Perspective
Muñoz   Depression Prevention: Research Directions
Olweus   Aggression in the Schools: Bullies and Whipping Boys
Reitan and Davison   Clinical Neuropsychology: Current Status and Applications
Rickel, Gerrard, and Iscoe   Social and Psychological Problems of Women: Prevention and Crisis Intervention
Rofé   Repression and Fear: A New Approach to the Crisis in Psychotherapy
Savin-Williams   Gay and Lesbian Youth: Expressions of Identity
Smoll and Smith   Psychological Perspectives in Youth Sports
Spielberger and Diaz-Guerrero   Cross-Cultural Anxiety, Volume 1
Spielberger and Diaz-Guerrero   Cross-Cultural Anxiety, Volume 2
Spielberger and Diaz-Guerrero   Cross-Cultural Anxiety, Volume 3
Spielberger, Diaz-Guerrero, and Strelau   Cross-Cultural Anxiety, Volume 4
Spielberger and Sarason   Stress and Anxiety, Volume 1
Sarason and Spielberger   Stress and Anxiety, Volume 2
Sarason and Spielberger   Stress and Anxiety, Volume 3
Spielberger and Sarason   Stress and Anxiety, Volume 4
Spielberger and Sarason   Stress and Anxiety, Volume 5
Sarason and Spielberger   Stress and Anxiety, Volume 6
Sarason and Spielberger   Stress and Anxiety, Volume 7
Spielberger, Sarason, and Milgram   Stress and Anxiety, Volume 8
Spielberger, Sarason, and Defares   Stress and Anxiety, Volume 9
Spielberger and Sarason   Stress and Anxiety, Volume 10: A Sourcebook of Theory and Research
Spielberger, Sarason, and Defares   Stress and Anxiety, Volume 11
Spielberger, Sarason, and Strelau   Stress and Anxiety, Volume 12
Spielberger and Sarason   Stress and Anxiety, Volume 13
Strelau, Farley, and Gale   The Biological Bases of Personality and Behavior, Volume 1: Theories, Measurement Techniques, and Development
Strelau, Farley, and Gale   The Biological Bases of Personality and Behavior, Volume 2: Psychophysiology, Performance, and Applications
Suedfeld   Psychology and Torture
Ulmer   On the Development of a Token Economy Mental Hospital Treatment Program
Williams and Westermeyer   Refugee Mental Health in Resettlement Countries

IN PREPARATION

Diamant   Homosexual Issues in the Workplace
Reisman   A History of Clinical Psychology
Spielberger and Vagg   The Assessment and Treatment of Test Anxiety
Spielberger, Sarason, Kulcsár and Van Heck   Stress and Anxiety, Volume 14

THE SCIENCE
OF PSYCHOTHERAPY

Harvey J. Fischer, Ph.D.
Lynbrook, New York

⬤HEMISPHERE PUBLISHING CORPORATION
A member of the Taylor & Francis Group

New York   Washington   Philadelphia   London

THE SCIENCE OF PSYCHOTHERAPY

1 2 3 4 5 6 7 8 9 0 E B E B 9 8 7 6 5 4 3 2 1 0

This book was set in Times Roman by Hemisphere Publishing Corporation. The editors were Lisa A. Warren and Christine P. Landry; the production supervisor was Peggy M. Rote; and the typesetter was A. Wayne Hutchins. Cover design by Sharon M. De Pass. Printing and binding by Edwards Brothers, Inc.

A CIP catalog record for this book is available from the British Library.

Library of Congress Cataloging-in-Publication Data

Fischer, Harvey J.
    The science of psychotherapy / Harvey J. Fischer.
        p. cm. — (The Series in clinical and community psychology)
    Includes bibliographical references.
    Includes index.
    1. Psychotherapy.   2. Psychology.   3. Psychology, Pathological.
I. Title.   II. Series.
    [DNLM: 1. Psychotherapy. WM 420 F5288s]
RC480.89'14—dc20
DNLM/DLC
for Library of Congress   90-4676
ISBN 1-56032-122-9   CIP
ISSN 0146-0846

Contents

Preface

Books about psychology are similar to those about cooking. Many present a particular cuisine reflecting the style of a particular chef, a particular region, or a favorite dish. The consumer has a wide menu to suit individual taste, including the democratic presentation of eclectic recipes. An overview of the literature is bound to produce an experience of confusion and mystery, as well as the impression that psychology is closer to art than science.

The differences among eminent authorities and their schools are maintained as the wisdom of personal experience rather than with an impersonal scientific justification. Although this state of affairs is intellectually unsatisfactory, my chief concern is for people who suffer from psychological disorder. The nonscientific state of psychology offers them a sad outlook for relief.

This book is trailblazing in addressing both academic and clinical topics from a strictly scientific viewpoint. The treatment is philosophically sound, well-researched, balanced, comprehensive, and candid.

In this book I present a reasonable progression from the fundamentals and methods that characterize all sciences to their use as an orientation and textual set in defining the field of scientific psychology. I use commonality of precisely defined terms in applying general scientific principles to the data accumulated by contemporary psychology. This provides a correlation among all aspects of study as well as an immediate applicability to common experience and understanding.

This new approach to psychological data leads to new understandings. Many of these confirm conventional wisdom and are presented in a clearer form and with scientific justification. Other understandings are surprisingly different and contradict current assumptions and require a reorientation. These departures are considered in historical perspective, and the issues involved are evaluated scientifically.

The scientific psychological study of psychopathology introduces, defines, and explains the central role of psychological pain in disorders and their treatment. The scientific definition of psychopathology provides the basis for rational methods of treatment. Therapeutic principles are derived from a contemporary scientific paradigm, and their use is described and illustrated.

Because I discuss the basic assumptions and fundamentals of all sciences, previous knowledge of theory is not required. Illustrations are selected from commonly accessible experience, but these are often presented with an uncommon understanding. The subject matter is treated in a clear, thorough, and incisive manner. Therefore, even though this book is directed toward professionals who are learning and honing their skills, it should be comprehensible to anyone with an interest in science, psychology, or psychopathology.

Harvey J. Fischer, Ph.D.

I

PHILOSOPHY

1

General Philosophical Considerations

PSYCHOANALYSIS TODAY

Various authorities in the field of psychoanalysis have reported over a considerable number of years that there is a serious disagreement about the field's fundamental tenets. This state of affairs was noted by Glover in 1938 (cited in Fine, 1977, p. 58). It continued to be noted by the American Psychoanalytic Association in 1954 and 1957 (cited in Fine, 1977, p. 58), by Hartmann in 1959 (1964, p. 319), and by the International Psychoanalytic Association in 1978 (cited in Wallerstein, 1978, p. 502). The situation today is no better. There continues to be the expression of important questions about the basic assumptions of *psychology as a science* (Manicas & Secord, 1983, p. 399).

It has been remarked that authors in psychoanalysis are particularly prone to present their conclusions as assertions, without a supportive base of convincing data (Gay, 1985; Goodman, 1977). Analysts often rely on citing similarity with Freud's writing as adequate proof of their assertions (Rogow, 1985, p. 26). These tendencies have led many scientists from other fields to view psychoanalysis as a cult. Even among analysts there is disagreement as to whether the field should (Bowlby, 1984, p. 8) or should not (Schafer, 1983, p. 255) be considered a natural science.

This confusion over the theoretical basis of psychoanalysis was recently reported in a survey of both analysts and philosophers (Goleman, 1985). There was consensus that the theoretical confusion was most attributable to the lack of a substantial philosophical foundation. The presence of philosophical defects inevitably makes for disagreement about fundamental tenets and has consequent significant differences of position on treatment (Kohut, 1971, p. 165; Rosen, 1977, p. 305). This same issue concerned Hartmann (1959/1964, p. 319) and Schafer (1976, p. 213).

THE PHILOSOPHY OF REALITY AND SCIENCE

The lack of a substantial philosophical foundation that has troubled psychoanalysts in their efforts at refinement has also been troublesome for philosophers. Philosophers try to define the essence of the nature of *reality* in order to arrive at statements that can be demonstrated as philosophically true, under all conditions. There continues to be contention among philosophers about a proper *philosophy of reality*.

Some philosophers have approached the problem of reality from another direction. They have taken the substantial achievements of the "natural" sciences as an

3

indication that these scientists must be comprehending some truth about the nature of reality. As the saying goes, "The proof is in the pudding." Studying the methods that led to those significant findings, philosophers have attempted to derive their underlying *principles* and assumptions, and have considered the implications of these in constructing a philosophy of reality. This seems to be the nature of the undertakings current in the *philosophy of science*.

The same data of observation used in the sciences are available to philosophers of science and are used by them to draw inferences about a philosophy of science. Because different philosophers hold varying basic assumptions, they understand the same observations with different meanings and present differing proposals. I think that the lack of a singular philosophy of reality results in varieties of assumptions and contention among different understandings.

PHILOSOPHIES OF REALITY

Over the course of centuries many people have devoted themselves to the study of the philosophy of reality. Despite the commonality of having uncommon wisdom, these writers have presented differing and even contradictory proposals as to the essence of reality. In order to comprehend the similarities and differences among these proposals, some system is required to serve that purpose. It seems sensible that the theoretical positions of these writers can be identified and distinguished according to particulars in the individual set of basic assumptions contained in their positions. After arriving at the sets of basic assumptions of various philosophical proposals, it appeared that there were two categories among the sets. One group of sets could be described as being characteristic of *objectivist theories* and the other as characteristic of *subjectivist theories*.

Objectivism

Objectivist theories have come to be the "standard view" in epistemology, which is the study of how best to obtain knowledge of the world (Wurmser, 1977, p. 466). Manicas and Secord (1983) have pointed out in their review that this standard is also known both as "foundationalism" and "logical empiricism." This view holds that the perceptual data of observation are regarded as objective facts and that only such data should be used to draw inferences and to form theoretical propositions. This view assumes a world of universal empirical experience that is acknowledgeable by everyone. All observers, if they proceed carefully enough, can agree that they are seeing the same fact. A fact will appear the same to all trained observers.

These "objective" empirical facts are held to define and represent what "really happens" (Subrin, 1985, p. 80). These facts of observation are held to be "brute data" (Taylor, 1971, p. 8) and cannot be controverted by alternate observation or reasoning. The assumption of brute data allows empiricists to use logical and mathematical methods of inference. All objectivist positions assume that the real world is factually perceptible and that these facts speak for themselves without needing interpretation.

Subjectivism

Objectivism has been challenged by Nietzsche's concept of "perspectivism" (Nehamus, 1986), which assumes that people always have preconceptions that shape profoundly the perceptions of a human observer (Harries, 1986; Kuhn, 1970). Preconceptions constitute a theoretical base for the perceiver so that the act of observation is necessarily laden with theory. Therefore, it is not possible to have a data base that is without theory, and any assertion to the contrary is erroneous. Any single event that is seen from different viewpoints must give rise to different facts of observation (Hunt, 1977, p. 328).

Subjectivists recognize that the apparatus of human perception imposes an inherent shape on the form of an observation. Bertrand Russell (cited in Manicas & Secord, 1984, p. 922) emphasized that molecules have neither color nor noise and that the contents of the real world are prima facie very different from sensory data. The phenomenal world differs from the real world, and subjectivists hold that only subjective experience is knowable (Michels, 1985, p. 517). Some subjectivists maintain that differing views are equally correct and that correctness may be designated in infinite ways (Schafer, 1976, p. 364). For example, any event may be designated as a stimulus, a response, or an environmental reinforcement depending on the arbitrary sequence of analysis chosen by the interest of the observer (Bandura, 1978, p. 347). What may be an object for one observer may be regarded by the person as an aspect of oneself (Boesky, 1980, p. 51).

Subjectivists hold that objective observation is impossible. Each individual uses a unique "template" in making observations and sees the world individualistically. Strict subjectivists hold that subjectivism is not only a necessary condition but also a sufficient condition. There is a galaxy of equally valid notions about reality, and certainty is not possible. Uncertainty is ineradicable in epistemology (Taylor, 1971, p. 6). However, Nietzsche pointed out that one interpretation may somehow be better than others (cited in Harries, 1986). Schafer (1983, p. 290) noted that the superiority of an interpretation can be supported by the specification of the basic assumptions that are used.

VALIDITY

There is continuing concern for the validity of statements about the nature of reality. The ultimate test of a statement would be its consonance with a demonstrated philosophy of reality. As I have noted, there is not yet a singular philosophical position to which one can appeal as an unequivocal standard.

There are various objectivist and subjectivist positions and claims for the validity of statements that have been based on consonance with them. Because both categories contain basic assumptions that are not tenable, the demonstration of consonance carries no necessary implication for validity. As the consequence of lacking an ultimate standard, the testing of propositions has had to take recourse to methods that have an indirect implication for validity.

Heuristic Value

The Greek word *heuristic* is cognate with the English *eureka* and refers to the discovery of understanding about data of observation. In empirical scientific thinking, it is assumed that propositions of understanding about an array of data represent the discovery of an aspect of causal power for those data and that these propositions capture a portion of reality. Such propositions are hypothetical inferences about causal powers, theories that attempt to be explanatory of the phenomena (Bowlby, 1984, p. 8).

One corollary of heuristic thinking is that simpler theories are assumed to be more likely to be truer representations of reality. Another corollary of heuristic thinking refers to the notion of a "confirmatory constellation," with criteria of coherence and the narrative intelligibility of theoretical propositions (Ricoeur, 1977, p. 866). This assumes that the demonstration of a theory's consistency and completeness makes it more likely to be a truer representative of reality (Schafer, 1983, p. 206). However sensible heuristic rules may be, and however practically valuable are such tested propositions, the method itself carries no necessary demonstration of probative value (Wallerstein, 1986, p. 436). Despite the simplicity, consistency, and intelligibility of a theory, it may still be a false representation of reality (Mulaik, 1984, p. 919).

Because heuristic appeals for validity are common, it is important to recognize their delimitation. One may imagine that a blind person has constructed a theory about a room in the form of a maplike image. The map has heuristic virtues and serves the person well in getting around the room. The map contains provision for all of the person's perceptual data and is a practical guide. At the same time, a sighted person knows that this heuristically tested map is not an accurate representation of the fuller reality of the room that is accessible to fuller perception. Thus, notions tested heuristically address only the phenomenal world and suffer the delimitation of all objectivist philosophies of reality.

Consensual Validation

Objectivist positions assume that reality is empirically phenomenal. They hold the corollary that the greater the consensus among observers, the more likely the shared perception will be representative of reality. As a refinement of this notion, it is held that the perceptions of trained observers are more valuable.

The assumption that expert observers can better perceive reality is the foundation for the appeal to validity in the common psychoanalytic practice of referring to the assertions of Freud and other professionally proclaimed experts (Gay, 1985). The delimitation of this method is most apparent in the many instances in which experts disagree (Wallerstein, 1986, p. 415).

The usefulness of pooling the observations of experts depends in great measure on the holding of the same basic assumptions by the entire variety of observers. The precondition of having the same foundation of a particular philosophy of science with its particular set of basic assumptions has to be demonstrated. Meeting these preconditions would constitute a presentation of commonality. However, it would also have to be demonstrated that the common set of basic assumptions is true for that commonality to bear an implication of validity. However sensible the rule of consensual validation may be, and however valuable such tested propositions may be, the method itself is not acceptable to the philosophy of science as a necessary demonstration of validity for reality.

TRANSCENDENTAL REALISM

It has been noted that "in recent decades, a virtual Copernican Revolution has taken place in the philosophy of science" (Manicas & Secord, 1983, p. 399). The delimitations of both objectivist and subjectivist positions are claimed to have been solved. This modern proposal has been identified by the terms "transcendental realism" (Bhaskar, 1975, p. 401), "realist epistemology" (Bohm, Bunze, Polony, Scrivner, & Toulmin), "realistic theory of science" (Harre), and "fallibilist realism" (Campbell).

The term *transcendental* refers to the assumption that the real world is beyond the human ability of subjective phenomenal experience (Nagel, 1986). This proposition accepts a subjectivist position as necessary, and this epistemology of reality is now held by most modern philosophers (Kenny, 1986; Nagel, 1986).

Another basic assumption of transcendental realism is that the causal powers of the real world are perceptible in their effects that can be experienced by human faculties. These effects are a proper object for an epistemological study of reality (Manicas & Secord, 1984, p. 923). The realist position holds the corollary that causal powers may be tentatively mapped by constructing an approximation of the "structure" and "systems of structures" of those powers. This statement expresses the philosophical ontology of realism (Manicas & Secord, 1984, p. 923). It is assumed that the "things" of the real world are complex composites of causal powers, similar to the notion of the atomic composition of all matter. The realist assumption of causality shapes the understanding of reality in that constructions of explanation take that form.

Another assumption of realism departs from subjectivism by holding that although the entities of the real world are not perceivable, they are knowable through the observation of the effects of their causal powers. Phenomenal observations may be used as a basis for the construction of conjectures about causal properties resulting in the accumulation of knowledge about the real world. Thus, realism regards subjectivism as a necessary but not sufficient condition.

Realists maintain that the real world is knowable through the construction of hypothetical entities as analogues of the causal properties that are detectable by observation (Manicas & Secord, 1983, p. 411). These entities represent real properties and constitute a proper form for the theoretical exposition of reality.

Realists assert that reality is knowable in constructions of similarity and approximation. This is contrary to the objectivist assumption that reality is knowable absolutely. Realists hold that reality is knowable only probabilistically. This is the meaning of the realist position of epistemological fallibility. This assumption is reflected in the science of physics by Heisenberg's (1930) *principle of indeterminacy*. The causal powers and structures of the real world are experienced in terms of the perception of patterns, tendencies, and probabilities (Manicas & Secord, 1983, p. 402).

INFERENCE

Background

The process of making inferences from data of observation is referred to by the term *hermeneutics*. Transcendental realism requires hermeneutic procedure in its pursuit of knowledge about reality. However, the term has come to have a pejorative connotation as used by "natural" scientists in criticism of the social sciences, especially psychoanalysis.

For many years the term *hermeneutics* has been used singularly to refer to efforts to interpret Biblical passages. In the same sense, the term is also used to refer to the exegesis of any body of written text. I regard this as a mistake in the narrowness of its connotation and use the term to refer to the generality of any effort to understand, explain, and give meaning to any phenomenal data. In this usage it becomes clear that there are distinctly different hermeneutic processes. They differ in accord with their particular philosophical positions and their corresponding epistemological assumptions.

For subjectivists, hermeneutics is a subjective phenomenological procedure (Wallerstein, 1988, p. 3) and is open to the criticism of "circularity" (Steele, 1979, p. 391). This kind of procedure has become known as "radical hermeneutics" (Habermas, 1973). For objectivists, hermeneutics is an empirical procedure (Arlow, 1982, p. 18) and is open to the criticism that observation cannot be performed without theoretical preconceptions (Packer, 1985, p. 131; Russel, 1988; p. 1083).

Beyond textual exegesis, the development of interest in making inferences about people may be credited to Freud and psychoanalysis. This shift from the static target of a text to the ever-changing behaviors of a living person has added complexity to the task of interpretation.

Some objectivists have tried to simplify this complexity by confining the target of hermeneutic activity to the language structure of the verbal behavior of people. These efforts have followed Heidegger's (1927/1962) assumption that language has an intrinsic objective organization. This thesis was expanded by Chomsky (1965). Most contemporary hermeneutic inquiry makes use of the analysis of language (Gadamer, 1976, p. 13). Other proposals in the attempt to objectify the study of language include the rule of representing a subject's passive voice in an active form (Leavy, 1983, p. 51). Others have expanded the data base of language to include sociocultural significations, as in the later work of Heidegger on semiosis (cited in Barrat & Sloan, 1988, pp. 132–133) and "cognitive science" (Sebeok, 1986).

The importance of singling out language has been questioned by the notation that there is no evidence that language is the only, or even the major, vehicle of thought (Bucci, 1985, p. 583) because cognition is known to occur in nonverbal perceptual processes. Also, the argument has been advanced that actions should be given priority as the object of hermeneutic inquiry because they are observable developmentally before the acquisition of language (Packer, 1988, p. 134).

The fundamental objectivist error of limiting the view of reality to what can be humanly observed leads, in some instances, to unsensible conclusions. It has been asserted that "archaic experiences" have no structure (Spence, 1982, p. 26), and this assumption is commonly held by the psychoanalytic community. This assertion refers to the fact that the observer cannot detect patterns of behavior in infancy despite expertise and carefulness. Such asserters might have taken caution from the unseemly implications of personal infallibility or the larger implications of *chaos theory*. They might also have granted greater recognition to the many reports of other observers who have detected regular patterns in neonates. This assertion, besides suffering from premature declaration and containing untenable objectivist assumptions, also shows a violation of principles of epistemology by confusing observable behavior with abstractions of inference (Brenman, 1952, p. 264). In any event, it is untenable to confine observation to either language or action.

Objectivists commit the error of denying subjectivity a place in its vision of the nature of reality (Kenny, 1986, p. 14). These mental processes constitute part of reality ontologically and are susceptible to understanding and explanation by science (Kenny, 1986, p. 9). Notice of this delimitation has led to the recent resurgence of a strict subjectivism that attempts to justify a distinction between the natural sciences and the social sciences (Messer, Sass, & Woolfolk, 1988; Wallerstein, 1988, p. 8). A subjectivist position commits the error of denying the fact that there is an "out there" in its vision of the nature of reality. There is even a popular combinatory position that holds both an "inner" and "outer" reality (Arlow, 1969, p. 43).

Those who appreciate the delimitation of both objectivist and subjectivist philosophical positions as to reality (Kalt, 1983, p. 196) would like to find a position with an explanatory view of the outside as seen from the inside (Wallerstein, 1988, p. 368). There is a need for a position that goes beyond the perspective of a particular person toward an objective view in achieving understandings that are true under all conditions (Kenny, 1986, p. 14).

Among many writers of varying philosophical positions, there is a general agreement that the making of conjectures is a necessary activity. Most agree with the ancient advice of Thomas Hobbs (cited in Rogow, 1985, p. 26) that "there be subtle conjectures at the secret aims and inward cogitations of such as fall under their pen . . . where conjecture is thoroughly grounded, not forced to serve the purpose of the writer." Among these writers the difference is to be found on the issue of what constitutes a "thorough grounding." Which philosophy of reality, which philosophy of science, should be used as the basis for making conjectures?

HYPOTHETICAL ENTITIES

In accord with the basic assumptions of transcendental realism, data of observation are used to frame conjectures as to causal powers accounting for the phenomenal world. It is required to construct these conjectures in the form of hypothetical entities that are experiential analogues to the knowledge of causal properties. Following this rule achieves the attribute of epistemological symmetry, meaning that statements about hypothetical entities have logical relationships that provide both explanation and prediction (Robinson, 1984, p. 920). The rule of analogic construction provides a basis for the claim of realist epistemology that its hypothetical entities are real enough to have practical value (Manicas & Secord, 1983, p. 411).

Consider an example from astronomy. This scientific discipline has developed its own defined technical terms in order to arrive at useful theories from the data of observation (Goldstein, 1986). Using these defined terms, suppose that detailed observation of the orbits of Planet A and Planet B reveals an aberration in a segment of each of their otherwise smooth pathways. The experience of planetary orbits as smooth patterns has a high degree of probability. The notion of orbits is a constructed hypothetical entity (I do not believe that such a line exists literally in space) that serves as an analogue to the observation of planetary motions. The idea of orbits contains the assumption of another hypothetical proposition: the general *law of gravity*. Each scientific discipline has defined general laws in the attempt to understand general causal properties. It is therefore reasonable to maintain that the law of gravity is applicable to both the observation of regular orbits as well as the aberrations of orbits. With this law as a common denominator, the hypothesis may be generated that there is a hitherto unexperienced object in space that can be labeled *C*.

When the object of knowledge is not sufficiently known to allow for a description in observational terms, that which is known about the effects of causal powers may be represented by the construction of a metaphor. To this extent, a metaphor may serve as an appropriate and useful conceptual device. It is a goal of science to seek further data of observation so that the metaphor can be replaced by a description. Metaphors present a partial knowledge of observable phenomena.

In my example, the rule has been followed to choose a metaphor for the new observations from among the hypothetical entities that already serve to represent knowledge of causal astronomical properties. In seeking a form from among past experiences in which to frame conjecture, people seem to be abiding by the principle that "there is nothing new under the sun" (Ecclesiastes, 1:9). This piece of Biblical wisdom may serve to sift out unwarranted speculations as a general guide. At the same time, this rule would enforce a delimitation on conjecture to only the familiar and traditional. It sets a formidable barrier against the consideration of new propositions, both those with merit and without. People recognize that this rule is not sufficient for the aim of knowing better the transcendent world within which they live. It appears that other considerations are required that would warrant a departure from the "sun principle" in order to increase and refine one's knowledge of the world.

EXPERIENCE

In the example from astronomy I chose to represent the causal property accounting for the observation of orbital aberrations by using the form of another planet. One might have proposed alternate forms, such as a spaceship or an extraterrestrial being. In accord with the law of gravity, it would have to be of great mass and probably of gigantic size. The possibility of overlooking the existence of such objects may seem ridiculous or out of this world. In order to preclude such considerations, I can set the rule that unknown things with known functions should be represented by something known whose functions are analogous. Still, there is the possibility that these ridiculous constructions, or unsuspected others, do exist. From a strictly epistemological point of view, it is arguable as to which proposed hypothetical entity is the best representation.

The central issue of this argument could be clarified if the rule is added that experiential forms when used as hypothetical entities should be labeled with capital letters. They present a speculation as to the form of an unknown entity. I do not know if the entity is really a planet, but it may look like a planet. This guess is represented by the term *Planet C*. Other guesses are represented by the terms *Spaceship* and *Extraterrestrial*. Thus, the argument is seen to be over what name to give to the ideational "baby." This is a matter more of taste than epistemology or science. No astronomer need be hampered in professional work by the name given to a *hypothetical entity*. Each of these names is sufficient to refer to something unknown. Whether one or another name is better suited to the purposes of its user appears to be a matter of personal preference. This might be decided by the guide of whatever feels more comfortable.

The issue of which name is best cannot be decided by reference to the currently available data of observation. However, suppose that the development of finer instruments of observation provides new data. One may discover new effects of causal powers that are attributable to a planet, and this would substantiate that Planet C is the correct choice and that the others are wrong. One may also suppose becoming able to send a space probe into that area and obtain the observation of two small planets. It would then become necessary to devise a new descriptive term that was not anticipated by any prior proposed hypothetical entity.

Arguments about the best name for hypothetical entities seem to arise with the difficulty many people experience in living with uncertainty. Perhaps the need to reduce such a sense of distress intrudes into the scientific task of choosing a functional name for an unknown producer of experienced effects. Realist philosophy requires the assumption of fallibility and necessitates accommodation to the concept that reality is a matter of probability rather than certainty.

In the final analysis, judgments about the nature of transcendent reality are inevitably based on experience. Because experience is individualistic, people arrive at their own version of reality. These may be similar among people in some respects, but there will always be significant differences. It is with such an essentially personal version of reality that people all live. People refer to their knowledge of personal and social experience in the effort to understand the world (Kripke, 1977).

This discussion supports the conclusion that any personal name for a hypothetic entity is epistemologically correct. However, each name has its own connotations and they have the force of basic assumptions in influencing the form of perception. Therefore a careful procedure will choose a name for the hypothesized and unobserved thing that has the particular connotations which represent the known and observed functions.

HARD SCIENCE

Philosophers generally are concerned with a variety of topics that are important to humanity, including esthetics and morality. These are inquiries into what makes for a best world and how the world should be. Philosophers of reality inquire into the nature of reality, and philosophers of science study how best to know reality. Philosophers of science base their conjectures about reality on data of observation. The "hard" sciences appear to merit this adjective because they have developed refinements of instrumentation for the detection of observations that transcend considerably the range of biological sensory faculties. This instrumentation allows a new order of data of observation, together with a precision that also transcends that of biological faculties. It is this instrumentation and precision that characterizes the objectivist distinction between the "hard" and "soft" sciences and seems to confirm their assumption of brute data. Objectivists despair that the social sciences can reach comparable precision (Taylor, 1971, p. 50).

The philosophy of transcendental reality regards data of observation, however esoteric and refined, as the perception of the effects of reality rather than as a perception of reality itself. It is necessary to make inferences from the finest data of observation as to the nature of reality. Thus, all sciences are necessarily interpretive disciplines, with none being "harder" or more "natural" than another. Realist philosophy of science holds that all sciences are interpretive disciplines.

The objectivist position has held sway for centuries and has become familiar and comfortable. There is folk wisdom that a tree is a tree. However, the science of physics has developed instrumentation, such as the electron microscope, and learned that the humanly experienced form of a tree is better described as a system of atomic particles existing in orbits of probability. The most modern guess by physics about the nature of matter is that it exists as cloud systems, with each system having special properties. Thus, observational entities are never literal reproductions of reality.

Another demonstration that hard sciences rely on inferential methodology and a system of basic assumptions is provided by physics. For many years observation was held to support the inference of the principle of the *conservation of parity*, which states that all matter consists of universal complementary opposites. This conclusion seemed to be reasonable and a scientific demonstration of common understanding. However, further observations were found not to conform to that principle. Instead, it has been replaced by the new *principle of chirality*, which states that there is an asymmetrical bias toward left-handedness of matter in reality (Browne, 1986). A recent extension of this new principle has resulted in the development of chaos theory.

In the science of biology, the discredited orthodoxy of the theory of the gradual origin of species has given way to the refined conception of "a world of occasional pulses that drive recalcitrant systems from one stable state to another" (Gould, 1978, p. 275), similar to a "quantum" change.

The data of observation at one time supported the inference that elementary particles of matter were atoms. Newer data supported the inference of electrons, protons, and neutrons. Even newer data suggest more elementary entities named *quarks*, and these seem to occur in four kinds. The hypothesis of quarks has not yet been confirmed by observation, but it represents real causal power better than prior conceptions and has proved valuable.

The hard sciences are able to present a special order of data of observation that far transcends human sensory faculties. Nonetheless, as Max Planck pointed out (cited in Manicas & Secord, 1984, p. 922), modern science interprets those data with the assumption that the real world is independent of perception and that observation is a sampling of the effects of reality.

The notion that the social sciences are a different kind of science than the hard sciences (Wallerstein, 1986, p. 420) is not tenable. Although there is a difference in the areas studied by the various sciences, researchers perform their studies with the same philosophy of science and use the same inferential methodology.

REALIST HERMENEUTICS

I have indicated that the term *hermeneutics* is a general reference to procedures for drawing inference from data of observation. The observation of people in social interaction is used to draw inferences as to a philosophy of ethics. The observation of all things under all conditions is used to draw inferences as to a philosophy of reality. The delineation of methodology to know the nature of reality is the work of the philosophy of science. The philosophy of transcendental reality holds that the philosophy of science is a hermeneutic activity.

Realist philosophy of science holds that the principles defining the activity of drawing inferences about reality should be consonant with its philosophical position. The development of these principles is the definition of *realist hermeneutics*. The principles of realist hermeneutics are equally applicable to the methodology of inference for all sciences, although they differ in the selection of their data of observation depending on their area of interest for study. The requirement of adherence to these principles and rules for making inference describes the "hardness" of scientific methodology and professionalism.

Carefulness

Each science has developed its own terminology for entities of observation defining its particular interest in certain transcendent causal powers and the phenomena indicative of those powers. Each science is keenly aware of the importance of these discriminations and chooses its technical terms carefully to represent these critical distinctions. The precept of disciplined science characterizes the careful discourse of scholars and professionals and distinguishes it from the remarks of laypeople. For example, scholars appreciate the significance of the difference between absolute identity and approximate similarity and are careful in applying that specification (Leavy, 1984, p. 919).

Experience of Understanding

The data of observation for all sciences are the human experiences of the effects of transcendental causal powers. Experience also includes inferences of understanding regarding data of observation. People refine their inferences of understanding over time with further observations. The refinement is accompanied by greater confidence in understanding. For example, certainty is often granted to the understanding that a dropped object will fall.

Some people, especially those with scientific interest, will infer that some general causal power is operative, even though not experientially observable. They may recognize that their understanding is consonant with the scientific law of gravity. This example illustrates the hermeneutic principle that scientific inferences about laws that describe causal powers must be reasonably consonant with both general experiences of understanding and the general experiences of observation from which they are derived.

Experience of Observation

Each science directs its observation toward particular phenomena. The phenomena important for a science are not always accessible to observation by the common human faculties for perception and require the assistance of special instrumentation. Consequently, laypeople do not have ordinary access to the special experiences of a science and lack the necessary basis to make informed judgments of understanding about those special experiences. This illustrates the hermeneutic principle that scientific inferences of understanding causal powers must be reasonably consonant with special experiences of observation from which they are derived.

Entities of Observation

Each science develops for its purpose a classification of observation that distinguishes similarities and differences. The entities of observation that constitute the classification provide an identification for distinctions in observation with precision as to the identicalness and oppositeness. This illustrates the hermeneutic principle that scientific entities of observation are constructed with the demonstration of identity and opposition.

For example, the science of physics has established the classification of matter as an entity of observation. Matter is categorized as molecules, atoms, and electrons. Although all three categories share certain specified observational properties, they are also distinguished by other unique specified properties. This illustrates how sciences develop terminology and classification for their entities of observation.

Hierarchies of Entities of Observation

The demonstration of similarity and difference among the details of observation regarding an event sustains the construction of *entities of observation*. A *class* of entity is sustained by the observation of a set of common details among a variety of details. Within a class, differing subsets of details may be observed. These subsets sustain the construction of subclasses that are defined by the presence of both common and distinguishing details. The set of details defining a class of entity of observation is regarded as the regular vector outcome of a set of causal powers. The presence of other details is taken to indicate the variety of manifestation of a particular set of powers.

Refinement in the observation of details may reveal sub-clusters among the details differing from those common to the class set. This observation sustains the construction of a subclass of that entity. A subclass is defined as possessing the set of details characteristic of a class as well as a cluster of other details that is characteristic for the subclass.

This discussion provides a theoretical justification under the realist philosophy of science for the common practice of sciences to arrange entities of observation in hierarchical order, or taxonomy.

Entities of Inference

Each science has its particular interest in an aspect of transcendent causal powers. Realism requires that inferences about causal powers be formed as analogies to entities of observation of the phenomenal world. Conjectures expressing an experience of understanding the phenomenal world are formed as *entities of inference*. This illustrates the hermeneutic principle that scientific inferences of understanding causal powers must be represented by analogies to the phenomenal objects from which they are derived. The technical terms of science that represent the best inferences about causal powers are chosen carefully to be analogous to the properties of their corresponding phenomenal objects.

The general phenomenal observation of a tree may exemplify this usage. The science of physics regards the perceived tree as indicative of a transcendental reality conceived of as a cloud of particles that has properties similar to that of the phenomenal tree. For the physicist, the hypothetical entity of tree is more real than the phenomenal tree. Even though one may know that the observed tree is not ultimately real, it is correct enough to be useful for ordinary purposes.

Inferential Reasoning

Inferential reasoning is one of the modes people use in the employment of their innate mental faculties. Other modes include free association, joking, socializing, esthetic judgment, and taste. The particular "mental set" distinguishing the mode of inferential reasoning is the concentration of attention on the observation of identity and opposition. This is a use of the mental faculty for detecting similarity and difference, but with the qualification of precision.

This may be illustrated with a geometric example. Angles of 5° and 8° may be observed. Within the general category of angles, the possibilities range from 0° to 360°. The observed difference of 3° can be judged as insignificant, and the two angles may be held to be similar. An observed difference ranging from more than 5° can be judged as significant, and the two angles may be held to be dissimilar. Thus, similarity and difference are judgments according to a standard and is expressible in terms of probability.

Judgments as to identity and opposition employ the same scanning for similarity and difference but use a stricter standard that has a higher probability. Only another angle of 5° can be held with confidence to be similar to an observed angle of 5°. Only an angle that is precisely 185° can be held with confidence to be dissimilar to an observed angle of 5°.

From these considerations one understands that entities of observation can be compared with and held to be identical or opposite according to a specified standard. This method requires the precondition that the entities are demonstrated to belong to the same category for which the standard is a specification. One also understands that the method is a mathematical procedure that provides finesse in applying the template used for observation. The method is a mathematical translation of sensory phenomenal observation.

The meaning derived from an observation depends on the philosophy of science of the observer. For an objectivist, the observation of 5° and another observation of 5° are understood to be absolutely identical. Realists understand that in this instance there is a high degree of probability of identity but that this is not absolutely certain. One also understands that a finding of similarity or difference is suggestive of congruence or opposition but with a lesser degree of probability.

The chief point in the realist insistence on framing statements about identity and opposition in probabilistic form is to emphasize consonance with the realist assumption of transcendental reality. Observational identity is not necessarily indicative of identity in reality. For example, two boxes may be demonstrated to be observationally identical as to wrapping. It is not a necessary conclusion that their contents be identical, although that inference has a degree of probability. Framing the conclusion probabilistically makes it clear that new data of observation may result in a different conclusion, with greater probability.

Induction

Realist hermeneutics defines inferential reasoning as the detection of similarities and differences among entities of observation with degrees of probability for inferences drawn from those observations. Inferential reasoning may be used in both an inductive and deductive mode. I have noted that this distinction is often overlooked, especially in the social sciences. Induction refers to applying inferential reasoning to entities of observation in order to make conjectures about the nature of causal powers inferred to account for the observation. These conjectures constitute *experiences of understanding*.

Because inductive inference is based on observation, the validity of those conjectures depends on the validity of the observations. In this regard, there are two important considerations: First, any singular event may be regarded in a variety of ways, all of which may be valid. *Validity* refers to a judgment for a particular purpose. Each science has defined its significantly useful entities of observation. Thus, only descriptions using a science's entities of observation bear a connotation of validity for that science. As sciences come to perfect their observations, they also perfect their entities of observation, which then require redescription in these terms. All entities of observation are established probabilistically. Second, any singular event can only be regarded as a sample of the effect of causal powers. Therefore, the validity of inductive inferences also depends on the validity of the sampling of the entities of observation from which they were derived. Because sampling is subject to fallibility, inductive inferences are expressed probabilistically. Note that sampling procedures have been studied extensively, together with their different implications for probability, and a large literature may be consulted.

In summary, the inductive method of the mode of inferential reasoning is useful in arriving at theoretical conjectures about those aspects of transcendental real causal powers of special interest to a particular science. The experience of understanding that may be achieved through induction is expressed in terms of the principles and laws pertinent to a particular science. Inductive inferences should be presented together with the entities of observation used.

Deduction

Deduction refers to applying inferential reasoning to *entities of understanding* in order to make conjectures about particular entities of observation. The entities of understanding for any science are its principles and laws that account for the particularities of its entities of observation. Because deductive inferences are based on both principles and observation, the validity of these conjectures depends on both classes of consideration.

Any singular event is regarded as the vector outcome of principles that describe detectable aspects of the effects of transcendental powers. Each principle refers to an aspect of causal power that is of interest to a science and represents an understanding achieved through sampling with an attendant degree of probability. Deductions using a single principle have a lesser degree of probability than those using the entire set of principles of a science.

The validity of deductive conjectures depends on both the validity of the principles being applied and the range of principles being applied. Claims for the validity of deductions are supportable by both of these specifications about principles.

The second class of consideration is the validity of observations. As I have discussed, brute sensory data, even those obtained with instrumental extension, are not acceptable as a scientific representation of reality. Only constructions in the form of entities of observation are held to imply a probability of validity. Claims for the validity of deductions are supportable by the use of established entities of observation.

Any singular event may be regarded as an instance of a variety of entities of observation, depending on the interest of the observer. The realist assumptions of transcendentalism and fallibility define entities of observation as representing probable valid samples of the reality of an event. Therefore, a real understanding of an event is the vector outcome of entities of observation. Deductions using a singular entity of observation have a lesser degree of probability than using the entire set of entities of observation of a science.

This consideration applies the hermeneutic rule that inferences are more probably valid if they are derived from a broader base of relevant observation. The same rule appears in the field of statistics under the term *degrees of freedom*. Deductive inferences should be presented with both the entities of observation and the principles used.

DISCUSSION

The definition of reality as transcendental leads to the understanding that causal powers are knowable probably through observation of their effects. Knowledge of reality is attainable through hermeneutic and statistical methods. Those hermeneutic and statistical methods that are consonant with realist philosophy of science are regarded as scientific.

Each singular aspect of causal power tends to produce a particular effect that is detectable in the observation of the details of an event. This is a basic assumption for realist hermeneutics.

Inductive inferences about the nature of a singular aspect of causal power are sustained by the observation of identical details among a variety within a class of events. Inductive inference seeks to understand the principles and laws describing causal powers that account for the observed phenomenal event. Induction proceeds from the specific to the general.

For example, in the class of events described as "dropping," it is observed that all entities classed as objects fall toward the ground. It is reasonable to induce that a common aspect of causal power is indicated by the observation of this identical detail that all objects fall when dropped. The understanding of this aspect of causal power is expressed in the law of gravity.

Because principles are derived from a class of entities of observation, they can only be held to be descriptive of causal powers attributable to the features of the class of entities from which they were derived. For example, observations of the class of objects called quarks were not used in deriving the inference of the law of gravity, and that law may not be appropriately invoked toward understanding quarks.

Principles are derived from observation and are therefore probabilistic and subject to both refinement and reformulation. They represent the state of the art of a science and are the current best understanding of causal powers pertinent to a science.

Another consideration of the fallibility of principles is their delimitation to only an aspect of causal powers. Their invocation is appropriate only within that delimitation. For example, to say that the World Trade Center is downtown is both true and appropriate for a person from Manhattan. For a Londoner, it is still true but it is now not appropriate.

The set of laws of a science expresses an understanding of the simultaneous effects of causal powers that are evidenced in entities of observation. For example, in physics it is assumed that all molecules will be observed to accord both with the *principle of positional indeterminacy* and the law of gravity.

Improved means of observation may result in the detection of effects attributable to a new aspect of causal power as well as the refinement of already known aspects. This understanding provides a basis for the common opinion that science is never a closed system but is always an open system.

Deductive inference about the nature of a singular observed phenomenal event is sustained by knowledge of the principles and laws of causal powers producing detectable effects in the form of entities of observation. Knowledge of general truths that apply to all members of a class of entities provides understanding of the attributes of a particular member in a particular instance. Deduction proceeds from the general to the specific.

For the purposes of deduction, an individual event is understood as a unique instance of a classification of causal power (Stroud, 1984, p. 921) expressed as a law or principle. Therefore, a precondition for the application of a law is the demonstration that the entity of observation chosen to represent the event is a member of the class of entities from which the law derives. For example, the law of gravity may be used to make inferences from observations of molecules but not quarks.

A singular entity of observation, when considered in various contexts, may be part of the data base of several principles. Therefore, all principles relative to a particular entity must be applied in drawing inference. For example, deductions from the observation of molecules must be consistent with the principle of positional indeterminacy as well as the law of gravity (Stroud, 1984, p. 922).

A singular entity of observation is regarded as the vector outcome of all pertinent principles. The singular entity is regarded as a unique instance of the class of entities, and departures from the norm for those entities constitute a basis for conjectures about the discrepancy. For example, the detection of a perturbation in the orbit of a planet is the detection of a departure from the norm of orbits and the general effect described by the law of gravity. The position of an object at any point in the orbit is the vector outcome of the law of gravity and other aspects of causal powers.

The similarities between the details of a singular entity of observation and the normative characteristics of the class of entities sustain inferences about the regularity of the effects of laws. Significant differences are attributable to principles describing causal powers known to produce those particular effects in entities of observation. For example, when a father is seen to come home with his usual characteristics, he is likely to be greeted as usual by his children. If they detect that he is holding a package with wrapping from a toy store, they are likely to draw an inference. If he is known to follow the principles of never bringing gifts for anyone and of regularly bringing work home from the office, they are likely to conjecture that he is carrying his homework in an unusual bag.

Because deduction uses probabilistic laws, the probability of an inference is delimited by the probability of the laws used. Because deduction is applied to entities of observation that are probabilistic as to reality, the probability of an inference is delimited by the probability of the entity of observation being used. In realist epistemology, brute data are used to construct proper entities of observation in the derivation of principles and laws. It is incorrect to use laws to make inferences from brute data.

REFERENCES

American Psychiatric Association. (1968). *Diagnostic and statistical manual of mental disorders* (2nd ed.). Washington, DC: Author.

Arlow, J. (1969). Fantasy, memory, and reality-testing. *Psychoanalytic Quarterly, 38*, 25–51.

Arlow, J. (1982). Psychoanalytic education: A psychoanalytic perspective. *Annual Review of Psychoanalysis, 10*, 5–20.

Bandura, A. (1978). The self-system in reciprocal determinism. *American Psychologist, 33*, 344–358.

Barrat, B., & Sloan, T. (1988). Critical notes on Packer's hermeneutic inquiry. *American Psychologist, 43*, 131–133.

Bhaskar, R. (1975). *A realist theory of science.* Leeds, England: Leeds Books.

Boesky, D. (1980). Introduction: Symposium on object relations theory and love. *Psychoanalytic Quarterly, 49*, 48–55.

Bohm, D. (1957). *Cause and change in modern physics.* London: Routledge & Kegan Paul.

Bowlby, J. (1984). Psychoanalysis as a natural science. *Psychoanalytic Psychology, 1*, 7–21.

Brenman, M. (1952). On teasing and being teased: And the problem of "moral masochism." *Psychoanalytic Study of the Child, 7*, 264–285.

Browne, M. (1986, November 25). Left-handed universe. *New York Times,* p. C-2.

Bucci, W. (1985). Dual coding: A cognitive model for psychoanalytic research. *Journal of the American Psychoanalytic Association, 33*, 571–607.

Bunge, M. (1959). *Causality.* Cambridge, MA: Harvard University Press.

Campbell, D., & Misanin, J. (1969). Basic drives. In P. Mussen & M. Rosenzweig (Eds.), *Annual Review of Psychology* (Vol. 20, pp. 76–89). Palo Alto, CA: Annual Review Press.

Chomsky, N. (1965). *Aspects of the theory of syntax.* Cambridge, MA: MIT Press.

Fine, R. (1977). Psychoanalysis as a philosophical system. *Journal of Psychohistory, 5*, 1–66.

Gadamer, H. (1976). *Philosophical hermeneutics* (D. Linge, Ed. & Trans.). Berkeley, CA: University of California Press.

Gay, P. (1985). *Freud for historians.* New York: Oxford University Press.

Goldstein, R. (1986, March 23). Hey, let's construct reality. *New York Times Book Review,* pp. 13–14.

Goleman, D. (1985, January 15). Pressure mounts for analysts to prove theory is scientific. *Science Times,* pp. 3–4.

Goodman, S. (1977). (Ed.). *Psychoanalytic education and research.* New York: International University Press.

Gould, S. (1978). *Ever since Darwin.* New York: Norton.

Habermas, J. (1973). *Theory and Practice.* Boston: Beacon Press.

Harre, R. (1970). *The principles of scientific thinking.* Chicago: University of Chicago Press.

Harries, K. (1986, January 19). The world as a work of art. *New York Times Book Review,* pp. 10–11.

Hartmann, H. (1964). Psychoanalysis as a scientific theory. In H. Hartmann (Ed.), *Essays on ego psychology* (pp. 318-350). New York: International University Press. (Original work published 1959)

Heidegger, M. (1962). *Being and time* (J. Macquarrie & E. Robinson, Trans.). New York: Harper & Row. (Original work published 1927)

Heisenberg, W. (1930). *Philosophical problems of quantum mechanics.* Woodbridge, CT: Ox Bow Press.

Hunt, H. (1977). Behavioral perspectives in the treatment of borderline patients. In P. Hartocollis (Ed.), *Borderline personality disorders* (pp. 325-344). New York: International University Press.

Kalt, H. (1983). The two hermeneutics of psychotherapy. *American Journal of Psychoanalysis, 43,* 195-204.

Kenny, A. (1986, February 23). Tackling the big questions. *New York Times Book Review,* pp. 9-10.

Kohut, H. (1971). *The analysis of the self.* New York: International University Press.

Kripke, S. (1977, August 14). Naming and necessity. *New York Times Magazine,* pp. 3-4.

Kuhn, T. (1970). *The structure of scientific revolutions* (2nd ed.). Chicago: University of Chicago Press.

Leavy, S. (1983). Speaking in tongues: Some linguistic approaches to psychoanalysis. *Psychoanalytic Quarterly, 52,* 34-55.

Leavy, S. (1984). Philosophy, psychology, and reality. *American Psychologist, 39,* 917-919.

Manicas, P., & Secord, P. (1983). Implications for psychology of the new philosophy of science. *American Psychologist, 38,* 399-413.

Manicas, P., & Secord, P. (1984). Implications for psychology: Reply to comments. *American Psychologist, 39,* 922-926.

Messer, S., Sass, L., & Woolfolk, R. (Eds.). (1988). *Hermeneutics and psychological theory: Interpretive perspectives on personality, psychotherapy, and psychopathology.* New Brunswick, NJ: Rutgers University Press.

Michels, R. (1985). Introduction to panel: Perspectives on the nature of psychic reality. *Journal of the American Psychoanalytic Association, 33,* 515-519.

Mulaik, S. (1984). Realism, pragmatism, and the implications of the new philosophy of science for psychology. *American Psychologist, 39,* 919-920.

Nagel, T. (1986). *The view from nowhere.* New York: Oxford University Press.

Nehamus, A. (1986). *Nietzsche.* Cambridge, MA: Harvard University Press.

Packer, M. (1985). Hermeneutic inquiry in the study of human conduct. *American Psychologist, 40,* 1081-1093.

Packer, M. (1988). Hermeneutic inquiry: A response to criticism. *American Psychologist, 43,* 133-136.

Pocher, M. (1985). Hermeneutic inquiry in the study of human conduct. *American Psychologist, 40,* 1081-1093.

Polanyi, M. (1967). *The tacit dimension.* London: Routledge & Kegan Paul.

Ricoeur, P. (1977). The question of proof in Freud's psychoanalytic writings. *Journal of the American Psychoanalytic Association, 25,* 835-871.

Robinson, D. (1984). The new philosophy of science: A reply to Manicas and Secord. *American Psychologist, 39,* 920-921.

Rogow, A. (1985, September 8). The world on a couch. *New York Times Book Review,* pp. 4-5.

Rosen, V. (1977). The role of metapsychology in therapeutic intervention. In I. Marcus (Ed.), *Currents in psychoanalysis* (pp. 305-316). New York: International University Press.

Russel, R. (1988). A critical interpretation of Packer's "hermeneutic inquiry." *American Psychologist, 43,* 130-131.

Schafer, R. (1976). *A new language for psychoanalysis.* New Haven, CT: Yale University Press.

Schafer. R. (1983). *The analytic attitude.* New York: Basic Books.

Scriven, M. (1969). Logical positivism and the behavioral sciences. In P. Achinstein & S. Barker (Eds.), *The legacy of logical positivism* (pp. 231-258). Baltimore, MD: Johns Hopkins Press.

Sebeok, T. (1986, March 30). A signifying man. *New York Times Book Review,* pp. 5-6.

Spence, D. (1982). *Narrative truth and historical truth: Meaning and interpretation in psychoanalysis.* New York: Norton.

Steele, R. (1979). Psychoanalysis and hermeneutics. *International Review of Psychoanalysis, 6,* 389-411.

Stroud, W., Jr. (1984). Biographical explanation is low-powered science. *American Psychologist, 39,* 921-922.

Subrin, M. (1985). Review: The analytic attitude. *Psychoanalytic Quarterly, 54,* 77-81.

Taylor, C. (1971). Interpretation and the sciences of man. *Review of Metaphysics, 25*, 3–51.
Toulmin, S. (1953). *The philosophy of science*. New York: Harper & Row.
Wallerstein, R. (1978). Perspectives on psychoanalytic training around the world. *International Journal of Psychoanalysis, 59*, 477–503.
Wallerstein, R. (1986). Psychoanalysis as a science: A response to new challenges. *Psychoanalytic Quarterly, 55*, 414–451.
Wallerstein, R. (1988). Psychoanalysis, psychoanalytic science, and psychoanalytic research. *Journal of the American Psychoanalytic Association, 36*, 389–411.
Wurmser, L. (1977). A defense of the use of metaphor in analytic theory formation. *Psychoanalytic Quarterly, 46*, 466–498.

2

Philosophy of Science of Psychology

GENERAL

The realist philosophy of science is based on the general philosophy of transcendental reality. This holds the basic assumptions that the causal powers of reality are transcendental to perception and that the effects of these powers are perceptible. The realist philosophy of science also holds corollary assumptions. Real causal powers are knowable from their perceived effects by inference. Scientific knowledge is probabilistic and hermeneutically achievable. Science is disciplined interpretation.

SCIENTIFIC HERMENEUTICS

Those rules of procedure for inferential reasoning that derive from the realist philosophy of science constitute scientific hermeneutics.

Similarity and Difference

All scientific inference is based on the detection of similarities and differences among the details of the phenomenal world. Scientific observation is organized into clusters of details with perceived similarity and difference according to the standard of general experience.

Sciences develop special refinement in their means of observation and have access to a unique experience of the phenomenal world. The special experiences of a science are an additional standard for organizing ongoing perceptions into clusters of similarity and difference.

Because phenomenal observations are used as a basis for inference, the probability of inference can be enhanced in two ways: (a) by increasing the precision of observation toward finer details of distinction that bears an implication toward unequivocality and (b) by the ordering of clusters of observed details according to identity and oppositeness that bears a more precise implication than that of similarity and difference. It is in these special ways by which science regards the things of ordinary experience that it comes to a knowledge of the esoteric things in transcendental reality (Manicas & Secord, 1984, p. 924) by means of precision in observation and differentiation.

Entities of Observation

The various sciences are distinguished by their interest in a particular aspect of the complexity of transcendental causal powers. In regard to the complexity of any singular phenomenal event, each science delimits its attention to particular details that are held to be indicative of an aspect of causal power. Particular phenomenal details are of more interest to one science than another.

Clusters of phenomenal details are selected by a science as a basis for inductive inference toward understanding the laws and principles that describe its understanding of aspects of causal power. Each cluster represents a class of effect of that law, and each detail represents a variety of that class.

The understanding of causal power represented by a law allows a parallel descriptive labeling of the cluster in terms of functional analogy. This description constitutes an entity of observation for that science that carries causal connotation.

In the realist philosophy of science, a science expresses its knowledge of an aspect of causal power in terms of laws and principles, and it expresses the perceptible effect of those laws in terms of entities of observation. Sciences are distinguishable by their sets of laws and sets of entities of observation. Within a science's set of entities of observation, they have in common a cluster of details of phenomenal observation, and they are distinguished by the addition of different clusters of details.

Entities of observation are established by refinement of observation, the application of inductive reasoning, labeling by functional analogy, and testing as to similarity and difference. This rigorous procedure justifies their presentation as a probable representation of a real effect of causal power. In scientific hermeneutics, only entities of observation may be used in drawing inferences about reality.

DEDUCTION

In regard to the complexity of any singular phenomenal event, each science delimits its attention to understanding a particular aspect of what is really going on. Each science orders its perception in terms of its set of entities of observation and applies its set of laws to make inferences about the specific event. This procedure describes scientific deduction.

DIFFERENT SCIENCES

The realist philosophy of science regards all sciences as holding in common a realist philosophy of reality. They all use the scientific hermeneutic method of inferring laws describing causal powers, the construction of entities of observation, and the precision of distinguishing similarity and difference.

The same phenomenal event may be of interest to all sciences. They differ in their attention to particular details of the event that are taken to be indicative of certain aspects of transcendent causal power. A science is defined by its interest in a particular type of causal power and by the phenomenal effects and manifestations of that power. Thus, sciences are also distinguishable by the set of phenomenal details, expressed as entities of observation, that are indicative of that type of causal power.

The basic difference among sciences is their interest in particular aspects of reality. The delimitation of interest as to both type of causal power and type of manifestation marks the boundary of that science. Each science pursues its particular interest in a manner disciplined by conformance to the philosophy of science.

It is redundant to speak of a "scientific discipline," although not all professionals may be scientific and disciplined. That goal has been hard to achieve without the definition of a realist philosophy of science.

THE SCIENCE OF PSYCHOLOGY

I have defined that all sciences use the epistemological methodology of the realist philosophy of science. They differ in their interest to study a particular aspect of reality, becoming specialists in that aspect. The specification of a field of interest constitutes the definition of a particular science.

DEFINITION OF PSYCHOLOGY

Behavior

The field of psychology is often defined as the study of human behavior. This definition assumes that manifest behavior is the outcome of a complex transaction among a variety of causal powers: physiological, sociological, psychological, and so on. Thus, the study of behavior bears some validity for psychological inferences in that it is partially indicative of psychological causal powers.

The specification of the study of human behavior is sufficient to distinguish the field from the science of astronomy. However, behavior requires bodily activity, and that is the field of study for all of the life sciences. Thus, the specification of behavior does not distinguish the field of psychology from that of physiology. The study of behavior would require a multidisciplinary effort (Manicas & Secord, 1983, p. 405).

Individuality

It is clear that the interest of psychology is not in the study of every aspect of behavior but only in those behaviors bearing an implication of primarily psychological causation.

In consulting the opinion of eminent psychologists who are experienced in this issue, I found that Brenner (1976, p. 194) specified psychology as the study of the individual. Kernberg (1976, p. 131) stated that its aim is a scientific study of individual uniqueness. Schafer (1976, p. 25) offered that the raw data of psychology are individual meaning and experience. Note that the notion of individuality is intrinsic to psychological terms such as the following: motivation, meaning, self, subjective, and introspective. There may well be a general agreement that psychology has to do with the individualistic aspects of human behavior.

The specification of individuality of behavior is sufficient to make a general distinction between psychology and other life sciences. For example, observation of commonalities in behavior bears the implication of a biological causal power in the behavior of all human beings. A singular biological power accounts for patterns of similarity among the individuals of a species. Behaviors observed to be individualistic are manifestly attributable to a psychological rather than to a biological cause. Thus, psychology studies the individualistic manifestations of behavior.

However, the science of microbiology also has an interest in studying individualistic behavior, as in the study of individual patterns of deoxyribonucleic acid. Other biologists are particularly interested in the individual characteristics of the immune system (Dousset, 1981, p. 1469). The increasing interest of various biological sciences in individualistic activity blurs the use of this specification as a distinction of the interest of psychology.

The Brain

I have stated that interest in psychological causal powers cannot define the observation of behavior as particularly indicative of that power. Even the specification of individuality, although helpful, is not sufficiently distinctive. Among psychologists only those behaviors bearing inference as to an individual's mind are of interest. Such mental behaviors are indicative of the possession of abilities for memory, reason, intelligence, consciousness, imagination, decision making, feeling, and perception.

Behaviors that are identified as remarkable for these particular characteristics are attributable to the central nervous system and the brain. This attribution is supported by a considerable variety and amount of experimental evidence. Understanding of the neurophysiological endowment that enables people to behave with these functional characteristics has been promoted recently by the use of analogy to digital computers (Gardner, 1985). More detailed recent findings in the study of the brain's mental functions has led to an appreciation of the regular, complex interrelationship among these functional characteristics (e.g., the role of motor attitudes in perception [Fenichel, 1945, p. 36], the role of memory in perception [Joseph, 1971, p. 248], the role of chemical messengers in perception [Leff, 1978, p. 64]).

Psychologists have come to a better understanding of the regular complexity involved in the apparently simple phenomenal event of seeing a tree. This outcome is now known to be a particular mental organization of the full range of faculties (Joseph, 1971, p. 258). The pattern into which the mind organizes these components is critical for describing the phenomenal event and indicates the superceding role of the brain's capacity to integrate its various processes (Levy, 1985, p. 43).

These considerations describe the regular complexity involved in the brain's performance of its mental functions. When presented with the photograph of a tree, for a person to see the tree is no simple matter. However, this event is of interest to neurologists and opthamologists as well as to psychologists. These other professions often use tests of mental abilities devised by psychologists from their interest in studying these capacities. Behavior attributable primarily to mental capacities of the brain does not provide a specification sufficient to define the particular field of psychology.

The brain's capacities for memory, perception, reason, and so on, are regularly observable in all human beings. These classes of properties are a commonality for the species and are indicative of biological endowment. The term *mental* is a suitable reference for properties arising from biological endowment. In ordinary usage, *mental* has connotations of biological structure common to a species with regularly observed functional consequences. The same sense is conveyed in the terms *mental faculty*, *mental development*, *mental age*, and *mental deficiency*.

Experience

In the example of perceiving a photograph of a tree, the person may report seeing a tree that seems massive and towering. This event is regarded by both neurologists and psychologists as being important in assessing the individual's complexity of mental faculties. However, the person's choice of adjectives in describing his or her perception will draw the particular interest of the psychologist. These adjectives are selected by psychologists as entities of observation because they are a suitable base of data from which to make inferences about the personal experience of the individual.

The realist philosophy of science holds that it is the interest of psychology to study individual personal experience in order to learn about the transcendent psychological causal powers that result in the unique experience. The centrality of the notion of personal experience is conveyed in the common psychological terms of "meaning," "motivation," "self," and "subjective." This notion is similar to Taylor's (1971, p. 12) proposal that the hermeneutic goal of psychological science is the study of subjective meanings. My proposal differs in emphasizing the study of personal experience.

I have defined psychology as the study of personal experience. I define the science of psychology as using the method of scientific hermeneutics in studying personal experience. I hold that these definitions are consonant with the realist philosophy of reality and the realist philosophy of science.

DISCUSSION

I draw the distinction that psychology is not the study of behavior. Psychology observes behavior and uses these findings to study personal unique experience.

Certain mental faculties have been known to contribute significantly to the performance of individualistic behaviors. For example, imagery and association have been noted frequently to supercede reasoning in human behavior (Shepard, 1978, pp. 127–129). One may regard mental faculties as modes of experiencing. Psychology seeks to identify individualistic modes of mental faculties as a relevant basis for inferences about unique personal experiences.

Because the science of psychology seeks to draw valid inferences about personal experiences, only those observations that can be demonstrated as individualistic constitute proper entities of observation for psychology. The psychologist's "eyewitness" observation of a person's verbal and nonverbal behaviors serves as a basis for the detection of individuality. The psychologist may also use personal history and outside observations of the person in order to detect individuality.

BASIC SCIENCES FOR PSYCHOLOGY

My definition of psychology provides an understanding of why psychologists have taken considerable pains to learn more about the mental capacities of humans. Although the development of such an expertise is, strictly speaking, within the province of biology, this area is a science basic for psychology. The identification and detailing of mental functions in their similarity and regularity is a necessary prerequisite for the recognition of dissimilarity and irregularity in their functioning. This demonstration of individuality is necessary to identify the observational entities of psychology.

Among the known mental functions are memory, intelligence, perception, verbalization, imagery, and control of mobility. Other scientists may study these same matters but not particularly for their implication as to personal experience. Because psychologists need a foundation of knowledge of mental capacities and their development, they have studied this area and often have made significant contributions (e.g., Piaget, 1937/1954, 1962, 1976).

In addition to recognizing the study of mental functions as a basic science, one may include the study of other biological functions in which dissimilarity and irregularity have psychological implications, such as the muscular system.

In addition to the class of biological activities, there is the class of social activities. This class is defined according to the similarities and regularities found common to subgroups of a species in a variety of dimensions. The identification of individualistic variation from these patterns may be indicative of personal experience in the performance of those activities.

It appears valuable to add to the basic sciences for psychology those of sociology (especially the study of morals and values), anthropology, linguistics, and education.

ALLIED FIELDS

The realist philosophical definition of psychology allows opportunity for a reconsideration of the relation of psychology to allied fields. Psychology studies the functional dissimilarities and irregularities of a member of a species in order to learn about the psychological causal power that eventuates in those observations and that are accompanied by personal experience. These findings are expressed in terms of psychological laws and principles. Knowledge of psychological laws may be useful to biologists in assessing the psychological consequences of biological interventions and their causal power.

Sociology studies distinctive functional groups within a species; the similarities and differences among those groups are a basis for inferences about the nature of causal powers accounting for the observations. These considerations may cast light on the inter-subjective and common meanings of social reality (Taylor, 1971, p. 45) that can be represented as social components. Knowledge of psychological laws may be useful in describing social groups and in assessing the psychological consequences of social interventions.

These considerations have an interesting application to the report (Davis, 1978) that both songbirds and whales are observed to vocalize in complicated patterns that show a similarity among all members of a species in addition to both "regional dialects" and "personal signatures." The pattern of commonality might be studied by biologists to learn about the common faculty for vocalization and its biological causal power. Sociologists might study the different dialects and learn about their relation to environmental conditions. Psychologists might study the individual signatures and learn about the personal experience of these animals. The study of personal experience of non-human species has been relatively neglected, apart from anecdotal reports. The owners of pets are a large population who can attest to the individualism existing in many species. The techniques developed from such studies would provide a valuable supplement in learning more about the personal experience of human infants and may well be useful in development, education, and psychotherapy.

REFERENCES

Brenner, C. (1976). *Psychoanalytic technique and psychic conflict.* New York: International University Press.

Davis, F. (1978). *Eloquent animals.* New York: McCann & Geoghegan.

Dousset, J. (1981). The major histocompatibility complex in man. *Science, 213,* 1469–1474.

Fenichel, O. (1945). *The psychoanalytic theory of neurosis.* New York: Norton.

Gardner, H. (1985). *The mind's new science (A history of the cognitive revolution).* New York: Basic Books.

Joseph, E. (1971). Perception, an ego function and reality. In I. Marcus (Ed.), *Currents in psychoanalysis* (pp. 246–264). New York: International University Press.

Kernberg, O. (1976). *Object relations theory and clinical psychoanalysis.* New York: Jason Aronson.

Leff, D. (1978, September). Brain chemistry may influence feelings, behavior. *Smithsonian,* pp. 64–70.

Levy, J. (1985, May). *Psychology Today,* pp. 38–44.

Manicas, P., & Secord, P. (1983). Implications for psychology of the new philosophy of science. *American Psychologist, 38,* 399–413.

Manicas, P., & Secord, P. (1984). Implications for psychology: Reply to comments. *American Psychologist, 39,* 922–926.

Piaget, J. (1954). *The constitution of reality in the child.* New York: Basic Books. (Original work published 1937)

Piaget, J. (1962). *Play, dreams and imitation in childhood.* New York: Norton.

Piaget, J. (1976). *Action and concept in the young child.* Cambridge, MA: Harvard University Press.

Schafer, R. (1976). *A new language for psychoanalysis.* New Haven, CT: Yale University Press.

Shepard, R. (1978). The mental image. *American Psychologist, 33,* 125–137.

Taylor, C. (1971). Interpretation and the sciences of man. *Review of Metaphysics, 25,* 3–51.

II

PSYCHOLOGY

3

Impulses

RELATIVISTIC VIEWPOINT

Surveys of the general state of affairs in psychology (Bourne & Ekstrand, 1973, pp. 15–20) often show a multiplicity of theoretical positions and schools of thought. Empiricism and experimental method were emphasized by Fechner. Wundt added the empirical study of introspection. The functionalists (e.g., James, Cattell, Dewey) brought attention to the importance of adaptation to the environment. The gestaltists (e.g., Kohler, Kafke, Wertheimer) appreciated the significance of a broader field of understanding. The behaviorists (e.g., Watson) stressed the need for precision in the description of activity. Psychoanalysts (e.g., Freud) insisted that internal factors were essential for understanding.

From the vantage point of the new realist philosophy of science, I note that these divergent schools coordinate with either an objectivist or subjectivist philosophical position and suffer from their respective delimitations. The objectivist error is in defining that the object of psychology is to study behavior. Psychologists should espouse that they study *personal experience* and that the observation of behavior is a means to that goal. The subjectivist error is in defining that the report of subjective experience is truthful. Psychologists should posit that "real" experience is transcendent to subjective experience, although the latter is useful to learn about the former.

According to realist philosophy, it is crucial to distinguish between the concept of personal experience and subjective experience. Personal experience is a technical scientific term. It is the name for a hypothetical entity to represent a person's real experience in living that transcends the phenomenon of a person's notions of experience. It is the goal of psychology to discover an individual's personal experience in order to be in a position to understand why the individual acts the way he or she does.

For that purpose psychologists seek to elicit the individual's report of subjective experience as an entity of observation. Even if the individual is trying to be sincere, there may be gross inaccuracy due to careless thinking, prejudiced opinion, the vicissitudes of memory, or difficulties in communication. In any event, it is the report that is taken as an entity of observation. From this observation, probabilistic inferences may be made concerning the person's true subjective experience and individualistic behaviors and toward understanding the individual's personal experience.

Another entity of observation for psychology is the individual's behavior. More precisely, psychologists seek to select for observation those behaviors that are indicative of the person's individuality. Such observations allow the drawing of inferences as to the individual's probable subjective experience, true subjective experience, and the state of his or her personal experience.

This application of realist philosophy to psychological matters has eventuated in a particular viewpoint, distinct from that of objectivist or subjectivist positions. The crucial distinction between these philosophies concerns the proper position from which to make observations in order to learn about reality. From the realist view, both the observer and the observed are regarded as entities of observation within a larger framework that is transcendent to both of them. This is similar to the Einsteinian notion of relativity. One might characterize this attitude as an attempt to be objective about an individual's unique subjective place in the world.

My use of the word *objective* does not refer to a standard of achieving a certain and unequivocal truth in psychological matters but to achieving a high probability as to the truth. The probabilistic definition of truth finding is a necessary corollary of the realist assumption of the fallibility of perception. This takes into account the modern notion of "participant observation" (Hartmann, 1959/1964b, p. 337), which obviates the prior sharp distinction between the observer and the observed (Rosen, 1977, p. 67). Thus, realist philosophy applied to psychology merits the modernity associated with relativity and new epistemiological concepts. It seems useful and appropriate to designate this view as relativistic psychology.

The application of realist philosophy to psychology has brought a relativistic point of view in psychological matters. This has clarified that the goal of psychology is the discovery of an individual's personal experience. Toward that goal the proper entities of observation are individualistic behavior and subjective experience. The study of these entities provides a reasonable foundation for drawing probabilistic inferences about the nature of personal experience.

ENTITIES OF OBSERVATION

The relativistic point of view has made it clear that psychology seeks to learn the nature of causal powers that eventuate in individualistic mental activity. I have chosen the name *personal experience* to represent this type of causal power because it serves to emphasize an important distinction.

In considering the question of why a person is performing any particular behavior, realist philosophy provides the orientation that this is the result of the simultaneous operation of multiple causal powers. In other words, one assumes that the particular behavior occurs because of the confluence of physical, chemical, biological, sociological, and psychological types of causal powers. Each of these powers plays an essential role in the outcome and is a necessary constituent of the phenomenon. Every particular behavior is determined by the simultaneous contribution of every type of causal power. There is no behavior that lacks a contribution by every aspect of causal power. Thus, strictly speaking, there is no such thing as a biological or psychological phenomenon. There is only a phenomenon in which one takes a biological or psychological interest.

Among the varieties of behavioral phenomena, it seems reasonable to assume that the degree or amount of contribution by various aspects of causal power accounts for that variety. As a corollary to the realist assumption of transcendent complex causal powers, psychologists assume that particular vectors of those powers are more or less influential from time to time in producing a specific outcome. Thus, some behaviors may be identified as primarily physical, chemical, and so forth. Ultimately, this identification is made on the basis of experience and reason.

The different sciences focus their attention on those phenomena that coordinate with their specific interest about aspects of causal power. Therefore, the different sciences may choose different entities of observation. According to realist philosophy, any phenomenon may be used as a basis for drawing inferences about any type of causal power. However, it is more reasonable to choose the entities that exemplify a salient contribution by that aspect of causal power about which each science seeks knowledge. Each science is then characterizable by the entities of observation that it chooses as proper for its purpose. The same activity may be chosen by different sciences with the aim of drawing different implications about aspects of causal power.

This discussion brings me to consider the following question: What are the entities of observation proper to the science of psychology? From the relativistic point of view, the answer is that both individualistic behaviors and individualistic subjective experience are proper observational entities for the science of psychology.

SUBJECTIVE EXPERIENCE

The phenomenon of subjective experience is a proper entity of observation for psychology. When psychology is defined as the study of personal experience, it is reasonable to assume that this type of causal power is a major determinant in the outcome of subjective experience. I have already stated that the proper observational entities for psychology are those indicative of mental functioning and that it is reasonable to assume that subjective experience is a type of mental functioning.

The phenomenon of subjective experience may be chosen for observation by other disciplines. Human engineering may do so in the effort to reduce errors in the reading of meter displays. Marketing research may do so in the effort to develop a generally attractive package.

Psychologists choose to study subjective experience in order to make inferences as to an individual's personal experience. Consequently, they attempt to identify those aspects of subjective experience that show dissimilarity and irregularity. The assumption is that the more unique an aspect of subjective experience is, the more it is indicative of individualistic personal experience. The marketing researcher and the human engineer, in contrast, will seek to identify those aspects of subjective experience that are similar and regular among people. This is reasonable because each is attempting to address people as a whole and in groups.

PERSONAL AND IMPERSONAL
SUBJECTIVE EXPERIENCE

The phenomenon of subjective experience, in accord with realist philosophy, may be conceived of as an outcome of causal powers. These powers may be classified as *personal* and *impersonal*. The impersonal powers result more in observations of regularity and similarity within the subjective experience of people. Irregularity and dissimilarity are more indicative of unique subjective experience for a particular person. Consequently, it is important to draw attention to a distinction within the phenomenon of subjective experience. There is both an aspect common to most people and an aspect unique to each person.

Those aspects of subjective experience common to all people are indicative of common mental properties. One may conceive that a result of the exercise of mental faculties is the function of subjective experience. People have subjective experience because they have the equipment to do so. For example, the common subjective experience in regard to the Müller–Lyer illusion may be understood as a consequence of a common mental faculty.

I have also distinguished an aspect of subjective experience that is individualistic and distinctive for each person. It is this personal aspect of subjective experience that is one of the specific entities of observation for psychology.

Because individualistic aspects are indicated by the observation of personal irregularity and dissimilarity, psychologists study those functions in their impersonal regularity and similarity. The expertise developed in such studies allows contributions to associated disciplines such as biology and sociology.

For psychological purposes, a term is needed to designate the causal power for the general faculty for subjective experience.

INSTINCT

Within the phenomenon of subjective experience I have distinguished one aspect that is common to all members of a species. In any given situation all people will have an aspect of their subjective experience in common. A part of people's subjective experience will appear with regularity for all members and with significant similarity among them.

The observation of regularity and similarity sustains the inference of their origin in a common transcendent causal power. One may conceive of this causal power as being embodied in a hypothetical entity that I categorize as a mental faculty. Thus, I propose that there is a mental faculty giving rise to the phenomenon of subjective experience. This accounts for its regular appearance in all people and the similarities among all people in its appearance.

The term *instinct* is often used as a name for the common mental faculty that is inferred to cause the phenomenon of the commonality of subjective experience. Traditionally instinct has been defined (Bourne & Ekstrand, 1973, p. 180) as referring to innate behavior that is observable in all members of a species and that appears in a specific setting. More precisely, the term does not refer to behavior but to an assumed causal power for the capacity for such behavior. When a behavior is described as instinctual, it means that the behavior is caused by an instinct. Instinct, then, is an explanatory concept (Compton, 1983, p. 367) to account for the observation that in particular kinds of situations, all members of a species tend to act with remarkable regularity and similarity. It is as if all members of a species have experienced a situation similarly. In addition, these behaviors are notable for being performed in an invariate sequence with a fixed pattern (Bourne & Ekstrand, 1973, p. 180) that follows a developmental continuity (Brenner, 1955, p. 33): an epigenic unfolding of these patterns (Jacobson, 1983, p. 544). Within this definition of the meaning of instinct, the term has been applied to such patterns of behavior as migration and nest building (Kimble & Garmezy, 1963, p. 380).

Because instinct refers to behaviors that are remarkable for their regularity and similarity within a species, there is the reasonable assumption that this is indicative of a biological source. When attention is drawn to the additional specification of complexity in the performance of these behaviors, because they are observed to occur in patterns, it becomes clear that the type of biological source that is involved is mental. It is to such mental biological structures that psychologists attribute the capability to perform coordinative functions.

Instinct refers to a type of mental causal power having an outcome in patterns of behavior that are regular for a species. The distinction of mental causal power has important implications. For example, in the phenomenon of migration, it is necessary for there to be the perception of particular environmental factors as well as the registration of some internal state of readiness. These must also be coordinated and organized with the observed performance of a complex pattern of behavior. This particularization of migration clarifies the assertion that we are dealing with a mental causal power, a conception that may be familiar. However, people are not accustomed to recognize that the type of mental faculty is that of subjective experience.

When people say that birds have an instinct for migration, they mean that the birds have a common subjective experience. This common experience includes common perceptions, common readiness, and common directed activity. It can be said that it is a part of the nature of birds that the birds have an instinct for migration. It is in the nature of birds that they have a common experience about what is called *migration*. Psychologists are unaccustomed to recognize that birds have this particular common experience, let alone any subjective experience at all.

However, I am sure that the owners of birds have many anecdotes indicative that birds do have a subjective experience. The same will be said by the owners of dogs and other pets. Thus, there is a fund of general experience to which to refer in order to sustain the assertion that there is a phenomenon of subjective experience among animals.

The specification of common subjective experience as a precondition for instinctual behavior makes clear the necessity for each species to possess common faculties in order to eventuate in a common behavior. In the example of the migration of birds, the birds must all possess the various faculties that enable the action of flight. Similarly, they must all possess faculties for the detection of particular environmental conditions: some type of external sensory faculty.

Consider the example in which birds and bears both have an instinctual response to the perception of snow. Because their responses are different, birds might migrate and bears hibernate. Although they both are able to perceive snow, the "meaning" of snow is significantly different for each of them. The type of activity implied in meaning is regarded as mental and emphasizes that instinct-patterned behaviors include an experiential element.

One factor that may contribute to this different meaning can arise from structural differences among the kinds of sensory apparatus. Compound eyes "see" a different view of the same phenomenon, and this is imposed by the structure of the apparatus.

However, even if the sensory structures of birds and bears were substantially identical, the vastly different instinctual behavior suggests that this difference is better attributed to a "central" characteristic. Birds and bears both see the same snow, but each has its own characteristic and different subjective experience of that snow.

The observation of instinctual phenomena supports the proposition that each species has inherent sensory and experiential structures that enable that kind of activity. Thus, the term *instinct* refers to a commonality of perceptual experience that is characteristic for a species.

This definition of instinct has a biological connotation because it is held to be true for all members of a species despite the existence of social and individual distinctions within a species. Each subgroup performs the same instinctual behavior, as does each individual.

This definition of instinct is essentially similar to that held by Freud. Freud (1938/1964, p. 149) recognized that such phenomena must necessarily be met with "everywhere," meaning for all members of a species. He also recognized that the phenomenon must necessarily entail some type of "endogenous excitation" (Freud, 1915/1957, p. 114) that psychologists have specified as a subjective experience. My understanding of experience is that it includes both an impersonal perceptual causal factor and a personal interpretive factor. This duality in the simultaneous operation of two different causal powers was appreciated by Freud, who thought of instinct as being a "frontier concept" between the physical and the psychological (Freud, 1915/1957, p. 112).

My discussions of instinctual behavior have led to the understanding that in certain environmental conditions, all members of a species have a common experience of that situation and that the species is endowed with a common faculty for experiencing. Consider the application of this understanding to the example of bird migration. Note that the species does not migrate as a whole but tends to do so in groupings. This suggests the additional influence of a social causal power, which would be of particular interest to sociologists. Also note that within any particular migratory flock, the individuals take individual positions. This suggests the influence of a type of causal power of interest to psychologists because it is indicative of an individual variety in the experience of migration.

Consequently, one may understand that in the performance of migration, each bird has a compound experience. One element is in common with all members of the species, and I refer to this as instinctual. Another element varies among the subgroups, and I refer to this as a sociological variation of instinct. Another element varies among the individuals within a subgroup, and I refer to this as a psychological variation of instinct.

Psychologists have an interest in learning about the instincts that are characteristic of a species, together with their sociological variations, in order to be able to identify the individual variations from those patterns. It is the observation of individualistic variation of instinctual patterns that may serve as the basis for making conjectures as to the psychology of the individual—and appreciation of the individual's unique experience of instinctual phenomena.

DRIVE

In discussions of observations of patterned behavior of a species in particular situations, which I attribute to a type of causal power termed *instinctual*, I draw a distinction from considerations referred to as *drives*. Drive also refers to patterned characteristics of a species that are indicative of mental faculties common to all of its members (Compton, 1983, p. 408). However, the concept of drive emphasizes that one of the chief causal powers resulting in that kind of patterned behavior is internal to the organism. Instinctual patterns are defined to include the perception of a particular environmental situation that is external to the organism. Thus, drive patterns may be defined as including the perception of a particular internal situation. Brenner (1955, pp. 26–30) expressed the same point in stating that drive is a hypothesis regarding a state of central excitation. However, it is not that drive refers to an internal impulse toward activity but to a transcendent causal power that eventuates in a specific pattern of activity.

As an example of drive-patterned behavior, consider the observation that some species engage in sexual patterns of behavior in coordination with the menstrual cycle. The biological event of menses is regularly accompanied by patterns of estrous behavior. The pattern is typical for the species, occurring with regularity and similarity for all of its members. The complexity of such patterns is indicative of a mental causal power making for a commonality of experience. This mental power must be accompanied by a sensory faculty for the detection of this particular bodily condition. The estrous drive pattern also requires a sensory faculty for the detection of an external object. These sensory faculties are coordinated by a mental faculty that enables the performance of the patterned activity.

Recall that drive patterns also require the component of a physical state of readiness for their performance. This necessitates the presence of a faculty capable of sensing this type of bodily event. Thus, both drive and instinct patterns include the same class of internal sensory faculty. The difference appears to be that in instinct patterns the experience of an external event plays a precipitating role and the other faculties are necessary preconditions, whereas in drive patterns the experience of an internal event plays the precipitating role.

The instinct pattern of migration is precipitated by the perception of the external event of snow. The drive pattern of estrus is precipitated by the perception of the internal event of menses.

As in the case with instinct patterns, drive patterns also coordinate with the presence of particular bodily conditions. Because species differ significantly as to bodily structures and functions, one should expect to find various drives that are characteristic of a species and different from those of other species.

Although one expects to find drive patterns common to each member of a species, one also expects to find group distinctions within each species as well as individual variations. Psychologists aim toward identifying individualistic variations of drive patterns because these may serve as the basis for making conjectures as to the psychology of the individual: an appreciation of the individual's unique experience of drive phenomena.

NEEDS

In discussions of patterned behavior, there is often raised a distinction from considerations referred to as *need*. This occurs in the context that all species are observed to eat and to breathe, each in their ways characteristic of the species. This distinction emphasizes that need-patterned behavior is significantly different from that of instinct or drive patterns, indicating a different causal power. The conception of need refers to the precipitation of patterned behavior by a causal power internal to the organism, which is the same as that proposed for drives.

The proposition of needs holds that internally caused patterns, such as eating and breathing, are categorically different from estrus because eating is necessary to sustain individual life and estrus is not. However, the consideration of this distinction is clouded because the word *need* has several very different connotations. For technical purposes, I use it here to refer to a condition of categorical necessity in which a presumed causal power results in the same type of behavior being performed by all members of a species. Thus, humans need to breathe.

I distinguish this technical usage of need from instances in which it is used as a simile, giving an imperative overtone to requirements, desirableness, usefulness, or morality (e.g., "I need to get to work on time," "I need to brush my teeth," "I need a pencil," "I need to help my friend").

The technical term *need* is confined in usage to those patterns of behavior for a species that have the specification of constancy. Thus, humans have the need to breathe all of the time. Although this pattern may be influenced and altered by both environmental and internal factors, the general pattern continues to be operative. This is an essential distinction from instincts and drives, where the pattern is not continually operative but is precipitated by specific environmental factors. It is this consideration that sustains the understanding that needs are indicative of necessities in sustaining life.

Biology has long recognized that the need to breathe is a specific variation of the general need for many living species to take in oxygen. The human species is equipped with lungs as a specialized faculty for that purpose. The biological structure is different from that of other species, such as those who take in oxygen through their skin. Because species differ significantly as to bodily structures and functions, one expects to find various forms that affect the need for oxygen. These forms would be characteristic of a species and differ among the species. The fact that faculties for the detection of internal carbon dioxide levels institute the function of breathing does not alter the argument.

Although one expects to find need patterns that are characteristic of a species, one also expects to find group distinctions of need patterns within a species, as well as individual variations within group distinctions. Psychologists aim to identify individualistic variations of need patterns because these may serve as the basis for making conjectures as to the psychology of that individual: an appreciation of the individual's unique experience of need phenomena.

SUMMARY

My discussion of situations in which all members of a species are observed to act with remarkable regularity and similarity has shown that this necessarily includes a commonality of experience. Members of a species have a commonality of subjective experience in certain situations. I have identified and distinguished between three types of impersonal subjective experience: instincts, drives, and needs. Each type is subject to social variation and to individual variation. Instances of individual variation in the performance of instinctual, drive, and need types of activity are proper observational entities for psychology because they constitute a reasonable basis for making inferences about the personal experience of an individual.

Note that the phenomenon of subjective experience is a composite event. It has an aspect that exists in common with all other members of the species. It has an aspect that exists in common with a particular social grouping. It has an aspect that is unique for that individual. Species are endowed with a mental faculty for subjective experience, which accounts for the observation that in certain situations members of a species will behave in a remarkably similar fashion.

IMPULSE

My discussion of regular and similar behavioral patterns in particular situations has shown the distinctions among instinctual, drive, and need patterns. Each of these is characterized by an innate endowment of disposition and a tendency to behave in a particular manner. These observations may be comprehended by the notion that a singular transcendental cause is observed to eventuate in three types of patterns. I use the term *impulse* to refer to this cause because it has the connotation of an incitement to action that is referable both to within and without an organism.

There are instinctual, drive, and need types of impulse. When a person experiences an impulse, there is the tendency to behave in a particular manner. This is observable in instinctual, drive, or need patterns of behavior in accord with specific contingencies. Identified contingencies are continual physiological events (e.g., breathing), episodic physiological events (e.g., estrus), and environmental events (e.g., snow). It is expected that contingencies to impulse activities will be discovered that are both common to and different among the species.

DISCUSSION

The psychological literature often uses the terms *instinct*, *drive*, and *need* interchangeably. "Behavior based on needs is called 'instinctive'" (Kimble & Garmezy, 1963, p. 380) and "the construct of instinctual drives" (Compton, 1983, p. 393) are examples.

On occasion there is the attempt to draw distinctions. Brenner (1982, p. 26) distinguished drive from instinct as being due to a central excitation. Loewald (1971, p. 109) defined instinct as the most primitive element of motivation.

All of those writers recognized the indication of a commonality of disposition or inclination in the observation of remarkable regularity and similarity of certain behaviors. However, Schafer (1976, p. 198) noted that referring to this disposition by terms such as drive does not constitute an explanation, certainly not in the sense that an explanation describes something regarded as unknown by reference to things that are known.

Thus, the current situation regarding impulse patterns is the vague understanding that some disposition is involved that has more of a psychological character than a biological one (Brenner, 1979, p. 553; Loewald, 1971, p. 109). It seems that this is the best understanding currently possible without the benefit of the new realist philosophy of science.

DEFINITIONS

1. *Impulse* refers to the general effect within subjective experience of a transcendental cause in producing for a species similar and regular patterns of behavior that appear in association with particular situations. Impulse assumes common

endowment with faculties for both perception and experience. Impulse is observable in three forms, or types of patterns.

2. *Instinctual impulse* refers to an impulse situation in which the commonality of experience and behavioral tendency for a species is primarily contingent on an environmental event. Birds, for example, on perceiving snow, will experience the instinctual type of impulse called migration.

3. *Need impulse* refers to an impulse situation in which the commonality of experience and behavioral tendency for a species is primarily contingent on a continual physiological event. Mammals, for example, on perceiving deprivation of oxygen, will experience the need type of impulse called breathing.

4. *Drive impulse* refers to an impulse situation in which the commonality of experience and behavioral tendency for a species is primarily contingent on an episodic physiological event. Dogs, for example, on perceiving menses, will experience the drive type of impulse called estrus.

TYPES OF CAUSAL POWERS

1. *Biological:* In all impulse situations, including those showing regular group and individual variations, there is observable significant commonality among all members of that species. This observation sustains the inference that there is at work a type of causal power that produces effects of general biological significance. Thus, all impulse experiences are subject to the general effects of a biological causal power.

2. *Sociological:* In all impulse experiences, although there is a commonality of patterned behavior for all members of a species, there are observable significant distinctions among various groups of that species. This observation sustains the inference that there is at work a type of causal power that produces effects of particular social significance. Thus, all impulse experiences are subject to the effects of a sociological causal power.

3. *Psychological:* In all impulse experiences, although there is commonality of patterned behavior for all members of a species, and although there is a commonality of patterned behavior distinctive for subgroups of a species, there are observable significant distinctions among each of the individuals of that species. This observation suggests that there is at work a type of causal power that produces effects with particular individualistic significance. Thus, all impulse experiences are subject to the effects of a psychological causal power.

In summary, then, all impulse situations (needs, drives, and instincts) are the compound outcome of biological, sociological, and psychological types of transcendent causal powers.

CONSIDERATION OF AN INSTINCT OF AGGRESSION

Theoretical discussions, especially in the psychoanalytic literature, have assumed the existence of an *instinct of aggression*. Hartmann (1950/1964, p. 134) held that aggression is the normal response to external danger. This view is accepted by most psychoanalysts (Brenner, 1977, p. 217), including Schafer (1976, p. 282) and Mahler (1981, p. 625).

Compton (1983, p. 377) pointed out that Freud never accepted aggression as a drive because there was no evidence for universality or a somatic source. Freud did consider the possibility that aggressive behaviors might be a derivative of a "death instinct" (Freud, 1930/1961a, p. 140), but he regarded this notion only as a speculation (Freud, 1938/1964, p. 161).

The postulation of an aggressive drive is an abstraction from experience with aggressive behaviors (Brenner, 1955, p. 30), and the belief that everyone is capable of acting destructively is assumed. However, the possession of a potential does not carry the implication of necessity (Kohut, 1977, p. 111), which is a required condition for any drive. The observation that acting aggressively shows developmental transitions and is a biological event (Brenner, 1955, p. 35) does not have necessary implications as to drive. All behaviors will vary with the changing development of faculties.

Among the aggressive behaviors cited in the postulation of an aggressive drive are those referred to as sadistic (Freud, 1923/1961b, p. 55). Freud (1920/1955, p. 73) regarded sadistic and masochistic behaviors as being independent of and contrary to the generally accepted law that all behavior accords with the *pleasure principle*.

Masochism has long been regarded as a defensive vicissitude of sadism and as a manifestation of aggressive instinct (Reik, 1941, p. 186). This notion has persisted despite published reports that successful treatment has uncovered origins of masochistic behavior among the contexts of a regressive form of loving (Abraham, 1924/1954, p. 464); as a vicissitude of survival (Berliner, 1947); as secondary to frustration (Kernberg, 1975, p. 69); as the result of a disturbed healthy assertiveness (Kohut, 1977, p. 130); and as a consequence of fear (Spiegel, 1978).

The term *masochistic* has become a general label for a variety of behaviors that are apparently in defiance of the pleasure principle (Eisenbud, 1967, p. 5). Instead of interpreting them as manifestations of a death instinct, the law of entropy, or repetition–compulsion, they may be viewed as part of a process that ultimately serves the interests of survival and self: preservation of the ego (Menaker & Menaker, 1965).

Regardless of whether masochistic behavior may be indirectly indicative of the operation of these various issues, it would be an epistemiological mistake to regard masochistic behaviors as the direct manifestation of anything. This would constitute what I have defined as the objectivist error. In fact, the label *masochism* entails the assumption of aggressiveness. It means that one is treating oneself aggressively. This is surely not the case in its original usage in which the goal of the masochist is to experience sexual pleasure.

Because the term *masochism* assumes the operation of an aggressive instinct, I return to that consideration. When the literature refers to aggression as an instinct, it can be understood from my discussions of realism that what is meant is what is defined as an impulse. Furthermore, because aggression is regarded as a constant motivational factor, it can be recognized as a need type of impulse. Proponents of an aggressive impulse (e.g., Lorenz, Ardry) hold that humans are innately territorial and aggressive and take as evidence the observation that animals show these same patterns.

In contradiction, Leakey and Lewin (1977, p. 62) pointed out that the animal kingdom shows a broad range of territoriality and that chimps and gorillas are notably nonterritorial. They also noted that animal aggressiveness is often "ritualized" and a "display" and is not convincing evidence for the presence of hostile motivation (Leakey & Lewin, 1977, p. 60). Patterson (1977, p. 449) contributed that chimps may be difficult but that this is not aggressiveness, whereas gorillas are generally placid and unaggressive. Farb (1978) noticed that chimps rarely use weapons and that when they do, they strike the target only 10% of the time, with no attempt at persistence. In contrast, many instances of altruistic behaviors have been observed in animals (Leak & Christopher, 1982, p. 314).

There seems to be no fund of consistent observations to provide a tenable basis to assume that the animal kingdom has an impulse for aggressiveness. However, it is possible that such an impulse may be found that is characteristic of a particular species. Negating the presence of an aggressive need in gorillas does not rule out the possibility for humans. This possibility is often sustained by the citation that early humans were hunters. However, paleoanthropologists (*APA Monitor*, 1984, p. 17) now consider that the oldest tools found were used for scavenging instead of hunting and that modern hunter–gatherers do not try to exterminate each other.

In the development of small children, patterned aggressiveness is not observable in the first year (Parens, 1979, p. 386), only likes and dislikes. Later on in development, Freud (1920/1955, p. 16) noticed that there was a pattern of assertiveness, but he regarded this as the pursuit of mastery, which is not particularly aggressive.

The citation of cannibalism and war is countered by the finding that cannibalism is a rare occurrence and primarily ritualized and that war is arranged by leaders and is a social phenomenon (Leakey & Lewin, 1977, pp. 63–64).

It seems clear from a realist position that there is no such thing as an aggressive impulse in humans. The evidence cited by proponents does not fit the basic concept of a drive (Compton, 1982, p. 390) and is effectively rebutted by other evidence. Aggressive behavior will have to be viewed as something other than an inevitable instinctual outcome.

This unequivocal theoretical position will come as neither loss nor shock to most practicing psychoanalysts. They have long held that it is necessary to analyze all aggressive behaviors (Greenson, 1967, p. 236) because the behaviors are regarded as being the outcome of a variety of issues. Aggression has been found often to be used as a defense against loss and separation (Grinberg, 1977, p. 125); as a vicissitude in the quest for gratification and security (Greenson, 1967, p. 396); and as a reaction to narcissistic trauma (Kohut, 1977, pp. 114–115).

From the relativist position, aggressive behavior is regarded as a socially defined phenomenon. This position accords with the "social–constructivist" view that emotions such as anger are socially constituted syndromes (Averill, 1983, p. 1146). In any event, psychologists consider this as an observation of manifest data that must then be evaluated in the interest of making conjectures about the personal experience of the subject's performance of that behavior.

CONSIDERATION OF A SEXUAL INSTINCT

The concept of a *sexual instinctual drive* is a basic assumption of psychoanalysis that is used as a fundamental explanatory construct (Compton, 1983, p. 367). The specifications of an innate somatic source, regularity in development, and regularity in function are all meant to support the assertion that every member of the human species is possessed of a sexual instinct.

It has long been observed that adult humans regularly are subject to temptations to perform sexual activity, particularly in order to experience pleasant sensations. It was Freud's conception that children also engage in specific actions in order to experience pleasant sensations, although body parts other than the genitalia may be used, as in thumb sucking (Freud, 1905/1960, p. 47). Thus, the deliberate retention of the feces or urine in order to experience pleasant sensations may be regarded as masturbatory behavior (Freud, 1905/1960, p. 53). This usage involves a broadening of the sense of the term *masturbation* beyond delimitation to the excitation of the genitalia (irrespective of the attainment of orgasm). I redefine masturbation to refer to the excitation of any body part in order to experience pleasant sensations.

There is the general observation that people engage frequently in genital sexual activity, not particularly for procreation but in order to indulge the sensations involved in that activity. Similarly, people are observed to perform other activities in order to indulge in the accompanying sensations. Despite the variety of body parts and external objects used in these activities, there is the central commonality of the stimulation of the experience of sensations. Because the experience of sensation necessarily entails the participation of the neurological sensory apparatus, and because the sensory apparatus is part of one's body, one comprehends that all such activities are masturbatory. However, the label *masturbatory* refers only to the engagement of a part of one's body. It is a term that is general as to the body part involved in the activity, and its chief specification is to the stimulation of sensory experience, regardless of the body part being used.

One can recognize that humans of all ages regularly engage in a variety of activities in which the intent is to stimulate pleasant sensations. There is the general assumption that the wish to experience tangible gratification is one constant factor in human motivation (Bandura, 1978, p. 350).

From the relativistic viewpoint, one may say that the observation of such activities supports the inference that the individual is occupied with a personal experience of pleasure. One also observes that the human species shows a remarkable regularity and similarity in the performance of these patterns of activities. This supports the inference that the experience of pleasure in the performance of these patterns is similar among the variety of individuals. I have defined this phenomenon as an *impersonal subjective experience*, for which I use the term *impulse*. Thus, whenever any of these specified patterns are observed, the individual is experiencing an impulse, the quality of which is pleasure. For example, whenever humans are engaged in thumb sucking, it is tenable to assume that they are experiencing a pleasure impulse and that this is a commonality of experience among all humans. The inference of the operation of this type of transcendental cause in the production of this manifestation does not preclude the probable operation of any other types of transcendental causes in the production of the manifestation.

The identification of this class of behavior, which may be represented by the activity of thumb sucking as indicative of an impulse for pleasure, leads to the assumption of a commonality of subjective experience while the activity is being performed. When a person experiences the impulse for pleasure, there is the tendency for him or her to behave in one of these particular manners. Thumb sucking is one of these particular manners. Thus, the performance of any of these activities is invariably, although not necessarily exclusively, accompanied by the experience of an impulse for pleasure.

I have described three types of patterns of impulse behaviors depending on the specific contingencies with either environmental or physiological events. Observation reveals that thumb sucking occurs in conjunction with a great variety of events, both environmental and physiological. There is no evidence of regularity with which to support the contention that either an instinctual or need type of impulse is in operation. In regard to sexual behaviors specifically, there are observations in which external conditions are apparently provocative of these patterns. However, these are not observed to be regularly provocative for all members of the species, nor even for the same individual over time. In fact, as early as 1897 Freud (1905/1960, p. xii) recognized that sexual behaviors occur normally without the presence of outside stimulation. The cause of the performance of pleasure patterns appears to be associated with events that are internal to the person and episodic in nature. This is similar to the drive type of impulse, although the episodic physiological event, such as menses, is not identified.

To summarize, pleasure-seeking activities may be observed to occur with regularity and similarity among humans. The commonality of pleasure within subjective experience assumes a common endowment with faculties serving that purpose. All humans are endowed with an impulse for pleasure. The pleasure impulse is not contingent on specific episodic physiological events. The pleasure impulse does appear to be contingent on episodic subjective events.

The best understanding of the transcendent cause for the observed regularity of pleasure-seeking activities among humans is that there is such a drive type of impulse. Although this drive is subjective in origin, it is not physiological in the usual sense. There is no consistent evidence to identify the drive with the functioning of any body part (Brenner, 1982, p. 74). Although one can identify "erogenous zones," parts of the body the stimulation of which is often regarded as pleasurable, Freud's (1905/1960, p. 34) assumption that these are also "erotogenic" is not tenable.

Certain body parts are more frequently used in the interest of indulging in a pleasurable sensory experience. The labeling of these parts as erogenous indicates the recognition that they are anatomically and physiologically suited for that purpose. Erogenous also implies that the chief focus of the experience is on the physiological sensations elicitable from these parts. This distinguishes it from other types of pleasurable experience in which the focus may be on social or financial aspects.

It should be clear that although certain body parts can be identified as frequently chosen by people operating with a drive for pleasure, the sensations elicited are not in themselves intrinsically pleasurable. As Freud (1905/1960, p. 78) put it, there are both pleasurable and unpleasurable tensions. It can be said that a singular sensation may be regarded as either pleasurable or unpleasurable. There is no sensation that will be invariably regarded as pleasurable. The sense of pleasure does not inhere to the body part being stimulated.

As an example of this same point, consider the observation that when people are thirsty they frequently choose to drink water. However, one would not conclude that the presentation of water would invariably be regarded with the wish to drink it. People's experience is contrary to this proposition. The regularity of the observation of the choice of water is indicative of the operation of a transcendent cause, but the additional observation that water is not invariably chosen negates the possibility of locating the cause in the water itself.

Therefore, I feel confident in maintaining that the drive for pleasurable experience does not have its locus in erogenous body parts, even though people engaged in masturbation will often use erogenous zones. The same considerations lead to the understanding that the term *autoerotic* refers to an observer's conclusion that a person is stimulating an erogenous zone with the primary intent of eliciting sensations that will be regarded as a pleasurable experience.

Thus far, I have stated that the observation that people often engage in masturbatory activity is not indicative of the locus of a drive for pleasure in any body part nor, for that matter, in any external object. It appears that a person may engage any object in the drive for pleasure, although some objects are chosen frequently.

The terms *erogenous* and *autoerotic* imply the nonuse of other than body parts in the drive for pleasure. This distinction was important in accord with the assumption of the existence of erogenous zones. Because I contend that erogenous zones do not exist, I regard the continued use of these terms unnecessary and misleading.

Regarding specifically copulative sexual activity, many animal species engage in sexual behavior in coordination with estrus. These species evidence a drive for sex associated with the episodic physiological event of estrus. In the human species psychologists have been unable to identify the performance of sexual behavior with any regular and general particular external or physiological condition. The patterns of human sexual behavior do not appear to indicate the existence of a sexual drive as they do in other species. Instead, the human pattern seems to indicate that sexual behavior is performed as one kind of activity that follows an impulse for pleasure.

One may observe that several sexual patterns are generally preferred by particular social groups. However, the variations observable are both more frequent and more remarkable than the similarities. A fair summation seems to be that human sexual behavior is primarily an individualistic matter. Variation among individuals, and with the same individual from time to time, appears to be the rule for humans.

Particular anatomical and physiological faculties are identifiable as frequently used in the performance of sexual behavior. Note that these faculties follow regular and general changes with the growth of all people. However, these regularities are not indicative of the presence of a sexual impulse. Instead, they are indicative of processes of development and maturation that are generally active for all body faculties.

These considerations of sexual instinct have led me to the conclusion that there is no evidence to support the contention that humans are possessed of a sexual instinct. The observation that people often and with great variety perform sexual behavior provides better support for the proposition that humans are possessed of a drive for pleasure.

REFERENCES

Abraham, K. (1954). A short study of the development of the libido. In D. Bryan & A. Strayey (Trans.), *Selected papers of Karl Abraham* (pp. 418–502). New York: Basic Books. (Original work published 1924)

American Psychological Association. (1984, Nov.). *APA Monitor.*

Averill, J. (1983). Studies on anger and aggression: Implications for theories of emotion. *American Psychologist, 38,* 1145–1160.

Bandura, A. (1978). The self-system in reciprocal determinism. *American Psychologist, 33,* 344–358.

Berliner, B. (1947). On some psychodynamics of masochism. *Psychoanalytic Quarterly, 16,* 459–471.

Bourne, L., & Ekstrand, B. (1973). *Psychology: Its principles and meanings.* Hinsdale, IL: Dryden Press.

Brenner, C. (1955). *An elementary textbook of psychoanalysis.* New York: International University Press.

Brenner, C. (1979). The components of psychic conflict and its consequences in mental life. *Psychoanalytic Quarterly, 48,* 547–567.

Brenner, C. (1982). *The mind in conflict.* New York: International University Press.

Compton, A. (1982). On the psychoanalytic theory of instinctual drives. IV: Instinctual drives and the ego-id-superego model. *Psychoanalytic Quarterly, 50,* 363–392.

Compton, A. (1983). The current status of the psychoanalytic theory of instinctual drives: I. Drive concept, classification, and development. *Psychoanalytic Quarterly, 52,* 364–401.

Compton, A. (1983). The current status of the theory of instinctual drives. II: The relation of the drive concept to structures, regulatory principle, and objects. *Psychoanalytic Quarterly, 52,* 402–426.

Eisenbud, R.-J. (1967). Masochism revisited. *Psychoanalytic Review, 54,* 5–26.

Farb, P. (1978). *Humankind.* Boston: Houghton Mifflin.

Freud, S. (1955). Beyond the pleasure principle. In J. Strachey (Ed. & Trans.), *The standard edition of the complete psychological works of Sigmund Freud* (Vol. 18, pp. 1–64). London: Hogarth Press. (Original work published 1920)

Freud, S. (1957). Instincts and their vicissitudes. In J. Strachey (Ed. & Trans.), *The standard edition of the complete psychologial works of Sigmund Freud* (Vol. 14, pp. 111–140). London: Hogarth Press. (Original work published 1915)

Freud, S. (1960). Three essays on the theory of sexuality. In J. Strachey (Ed. & Trans.), *The standard edition of the complete psychological works of Sigmund Freud* (Vol. 7, pp. 123–243). London: Hogarth Press. (Original work published 1905).

Freud, S. (1961a). Civilization and its discontents. In J. Strachey (Ed. & Trans.), *The standard edition of the complete psychological works of Sigmund Freud* (Vol. 21, pp. 57–145). London: Hogarth Press. (Original work published 1930)

Freud, S. (1961b). The ego and the id. In J. Strachey (Ed. & Trans.), *The standard edition of the complete psychologial works of Sigmund Freud* (Vol. 19, pp. 3–66). London: Hogarth Press. (Original work published 1923)

Freud, S. (1964). An outline of psychoanalysis. In J. Strachey (Ed. & Trans.), *The standard edition of the complete psychological works of Sigmund Freud* (Vol. 23, pp. 144–207). London: Hogarth Press. (Original work published 1938)

Greenson, R. (1967). *The technique and practice of psychotherapy.* New York: International University Press.

Grinberg, L. (1977). An approach to the understanding of borderline disorders. P. Hartocollis (Ed.), *Borderline personality disorders* (pp. 123–142). New York: International University Press.

Hartmann, H. (1964a). Comments on the psychoanalytic theory of the ego. In H. Hartmann (Ed.), *Essays on ego psychology* (pp. 113–141). New York: International University Press. (Original work published 1950)

Hartmann, H. (1964b). Psychoanalysis as a scientific theory. In H. Hartmann (Ed.), *Essays on ego psychology* (pp. 318–350). New York: International University Press. (Original work published 1959)

Jacobson, J. (1983). The structural theory and the representational world. *Psychoanalytic Quarterly, 52,* 514–563.

Kernberg, O. (1975). *Borderline conditions and pathological narcissism.* New York: Jason Aronson.

Kimble, G., & Garmezy, N. (1963). *Principles of general psychology.* New York: Ronald Press.

Kohut, H. (1977). *The restoration of the self.* New York: International University Press.

Leak, G., & Christopher, S. (1982). Freudian psychoanalysis and sociobiology. *American Psychologist, 37,* 313–322.

Leakey, R., & Lewin, R. (1977, Aug.). Is it our culture, not our genes, that makes us killers? *Smithsonian,* pp. 56–64.

Loewald, H. (1971). On motivation and instinct theory. *Psychoanalytic Study of the Child, 26,* 91–128.

Mahler, M. (1981). Aggression in the service of separation–individuation. *Psychoanalytic Quarterly, 50,* 625–638.

Patterson, F. (1977, Oct.). Conversations with a gorilla. *National Geographic*, pp. 438–465.
Reik, T. (1941). *Masochism in modern man*. New York: Farrar, Straus.
Rosen, V. (1977). The role of metapsychology in therapeutic intervention. In I. Marcus (Ed.), *Currents in psychoanalysis* (pp. 305–316). New York: International University Press.
Schafer, R. (1976). *A new language for psychoanalysis*. New Haven, CT: Yale University Press.
Spiegel, L. (1978). Moral masochism. *Psychoanalytic Quarterly, 47*, 209–236.

4

The Drive for Pleasure

ORGAN PLEASURE

The observation that humans generally and regularly may be observed to engage in detectable patterns in the performance of sexual activity has been the basis for inference as to the operation of a common causal power.

Freud (1905/1960, p. 157) believed that those body parts that are frequently engaged were endowed with this causal power and were constituted as "erotogenic zones." He also believed that these intrinsic "organ pleasures" (Freud, 1915/1957, p. 126) were hierarchically related to the orgasmic function of the genitalia. This was consistent with his view that the orgasmic experience represented the epitome of pleasurable experience. Freud's conceptions entail two basic assumptions with which I take exception.

First, I question the notion of intrinsic organ pleasure. I place in opposition the observation that many men experience both erection and ejaculation without satisfaction (Kinsey, Pomeroy & Martin, 1948, p. 159). The biological events of erection and ejaculation are evidence that the penis, the major pleasure organ of the male, has been significantly aroused. Nonetheless, despite the arousal of this organ, an experience of pleasure is negated. Thus, the organ is seen to be able to operate in a biological mode that is independent of pleasure. The concept of organ pleasure necessarily implies that stimulation of the organ will inevitably generate a pleasurable experience. My observation demonstrates that this concept is not tenable. Additionally, it has been reported that in many instances of orgasm in women, a pleasurable experience is not a necessary accompaniment (Masters & Johnson, 1966, p. 216; Masters & Johnson, 1970a, p. 31).

Second, I question the notion that the orgasmic experience represents the epitome of pleasurable experience. I place in opposition the observations just cited that demonstrate that for both sexes, an orgasmic event may occur without satisfaction, let alone an "epitome" of pleasure. The modern understanding is that the attainment of a state of biological orgasm is not by itself a sufficient condition for the attainment of a state of pleasure and satisfaction (Hartman & Fithian, 1972, p. 192).

ORGASM

Because references to the psychological consequences of the biological state of orgasm are often both explicitly and implicitly implicated in consideration of pleasurable experience, it appears desirable to refer to further current knowledge.

The state of orgasm in both the human male and female has been physiologically defined as that period when vasocongestion and myotonia are released (Masters & Johnson, 1966, p. 6), with sensations of contraction and throbbing (Masters

& Johnson, 1966, p. 217). Despite anatomical differences, the physiological events in orgasm are primarily parallel for both sexes (Masters & Johnson, 1966, p. 285).

The physical capacity for orgasm is part of human equipment, although its achievement is not invariable for the female (Masters & Johnson, 1966, p. 139) or the male (Weaver, 1970, p. 124). The achievement of orgasm may be observed in preadolescents (Kinsey et al., 1948, p. 159) and children of many cultures (Masters & Johnson, 1966, p. 140).

The observation of ejaculation in the male is often taken as evidence of orgasm (Masters & Johnson, 1966, p. 212). However, orgasm may occur without the emission of semen (Kinsey et al., 1948, p. 158; Ovesey, 1970, p. 100), and emission of semen may occur without erection (Masters & Johnson, 1970a, p. 100). The events of erection, orgasm, and ejaculation may each occur independently. Erection and ejaculation have been identified as neurologically different (Benedek, 1971, p. 43; Wershub, 1967, pp. 43–44). It has been demonstrated that even after the point of ejaculatory inevitability has been reached, if proper stimulation is discontinued the orgasmic experience will be profoundly disturbed and unsatisfactory (Masters & Johnson, 1966, p. 215). In the interest of enhancing their pleasurable experience, many men have learned to practice control of ejaculation (Masters & Johnson, 1966, p. 211), especially by tightening the anal muscles (Kinsey et al., 1948, p. 581). Tightening of the levator ani muscles also retards orgasm in the female and has been implicated in vaginismus (Ellison, 1972, p. 36). Consequently, in discussions involving male orgasm, one should bear in mind distinctions between the events of erection and ejaculation and avoid the assumption that they are simultaneous.

Regarding females, there is much current discussion about the difference between clitoral and vaginal orgasms. It is often cited that the clitoris is richly endowed with nerve endings, whereas the vagina is relatively insensitive (Brody, 1967, p. 44). However, it is known that the muscles underlying the vagina are well equipped with proprioceptors (McGuire & Steinhilber, 1970, p. 110). The physiological event of orgasm may be brought about by the stimulation of a variety of body parts and by the use of a variety of means of stimulation. It has been demonstrated that the physiology of orgasm is identical in any case (Brody, 1967, p. 42; Masters & Johnson, 1966, p. 66).

I have already noted the common observation that orgasm is accompanied by varying degrees of pleasure. This is seemingly contradicted by the observation that the orgasms are nevertheless substantially identical. This contradiction is obviated by the recognition that one is dealing with two different classes of phenomena. Orgasm is a physiological event, whereas the experience of that orgasm is a mental event.

It is often carelessly assumed that there is an inevitable standard pleasure experience that accompanies the state of orgasm (Kinsey et al., 1948, p. 159). This belief in organ pleasure is often held together with the common knowledge that particular circumstances have a profound influence on the experience (e.g., rape, premature ejaculation). It is also known that the physiological event of orgasm may be quite outside any conscious experience (Eissler, 1977, p. 41).

These considerations, together with the Kinsey, Pomeroy, Martin and Gebhard's (1953) finding that a considerable number of females never have orgasm (p. 142) and that 70% of males ejaculate within 5 minutes of intercourse (p.

163), lead me to conclude that the observation of a state of physiological orgasm cannot be taken as a certain indication of pleasurable experience.

Sexuality

I have stated that the observation of orgasm does not necessarily indicate a pleasurable experience, particularly of the kind meant by the term *sexual*. More than 20 discretely measurable physiological events are identifiable in the process of arousal leading to orgasm (Kinsey et al., 1953, p. 649), and they are essentially the same for both sexes. Even if they are all measurably present, an inference of pleasurable experience cannot be taken for granted.

The physiological assertion that orgasm is a state similar for the sexes is often countered by the observation that in coitus—the most frequent form of sexual activity for both sexes (Kinsey et al., 1953, p. 173)—it is found that most males (92%) achieve orgasm and that it is considerably less (Fisher, 1973b, p. 185) for females (58%). Most males achieve their orgasm rapidly, whereas females who do so are significantly slower (Kinsey et al., 1953, p. 164). These observations of significantly different orgasmic functioning between the sexes during coitus are taken as the basis for the inference that orgasm is a different event for males and females.

However, it has been found that the clitoris and labia minora, the biological homologues of the penis (Gould, 1987b, p. 16), are the major organs for sexual arousal in the female (Eissler, 1977, p. 51; Kinsey, Pomeroy, Martin & Gebhard, 1953, p. 158). The usual technique for coition is poorly suited for the stimulation of these organs (Kinsey, Pomeroy, Martin & Gebhard, 1953, p. 164; Masters & Johnson, 1966, p. 133). Therefore, the significant difference between males and females in achieving orgasm during coition is better attributed to the fact that coition is an unsuitable technique for the female achievement of orgasm. When females wish to achieve orgasm they predominantly do so by the technique of manipulation of the clitoris and labia minora. With this technique 95% will achieve orgasm (Kinsey et al., 1953, p. 132) and 70% will do so within 5 minutes (Kinsey et al., 1953, p. 163).

I feel confident in the accuracy of the observation that men and women are substantially similar in both orgasmic function and in the physical endowments to achieve orgasm. Thus, I refer to the orgasmic function of humans, where ejaculation is regarded as a collateral event due to male anatomy.

From the psychological point of view, the observation of orgasm serves as the basis for inferring that the person is probably, although not necessarily, experiencing pleasure.

Arousal

In the achievement of orgasm there is a regular group of physiological changes consequent to stimulation. However, no single element can be taken as a necessary indication of sexual experience because it appears among people—as well as other mammals—in situations in which the experience is identifiable as an instance of fear or anger (Kinsey et al., 1953, p. 134). Therefore, it is a unique combination, a syndrome, of physiological events that is taken as a probable indication of sexual pleasure. The inference of an experience of pleasure is enhanced in probability by a multiplicity of collateral observations. This consideration is reflected in the wisdom of understanding that the genitalia are not the only "sex organs" (Kinsey et al., 1948, p. 573).

In the syndrome of physiological events that are defined in the achievement of orgasm, each element is observed to change its function in a particular manner. Heart rate is increased, blood pressure is increased, and certain parts reflect these increases. The observation of these increased physiological functions is comprehended by the adoption of the term *arousal*. In a state of arousal, each element of the syndrome is observed to change in an increased manner that is detailed by physiological measurement.

For psychological purposes one should be careful to distinguish between a physiological event and the experience of that event. For example, although the labia majora are sensitive to touch, the experience is not ordinarily reported as being particularly pleasurable (Kinsey, Pomeroy, Martin & Gebhard, 1953, p. 159). There is the same finding for the male homologue (Gould, 1987b, p. 16), the scrotum (Kinsey, Pomeroy, Martin & Gebhard, 1953, p. 578). Thus, although body parts may be demonstrated to be in a state of physiological arousal, this state may or may not be experienced as pleasant.

Various situations have been identified as contributing to a state of physiological arousal. Hormonal products have been observed to contribute to the development of this syndrome (Greenblatt, 1972, p. 110). Erection has been observed to accompany rapid eye movement sleep from birth to extreme old age (Fisher, 1973a, p. 181). Teaching Kagel's exercises of the pubococcygeal muscles is found to enhance the development of vasoconstriction (Hartman & Fithian, 1972, p. 87). The teaching of special "sensate focus" is often found to assist the development of arousal (Kalodny, 1970, p. 50). Various techniques may be learned that are effective in the achievement of arousal and orgasm (Hartman & Fithian, 1972, p. 175; Ovesey, 1970, p. 103).

It appears to be abundantly documented that human beings are normally endowed with the physical capacity to achieve physiological states of arousal and orgasm. However, as I have repeatedly pointed out, the presence of arousal, orgasm, or both cannot be taken as a necessary indication of an experience of pleasure.

MASTURBATION

In pursuing my concern to identify indications of an experience of pleasure, I adopt the assumption that when states of arousal and orgasm are achieved through masturbation, they are more likely to be accompanied by an experience of pleasure. Support for this assumption is found in the observations that measurements of maximal physical intensity of orgasm occur when they are achieved through self-regulated techniques (Masters & Johnson, 1966, p. 133) and 92% of females achieve satisfaction through masturbation (Kinsey et al., 1953, p. 498). Although 65% of males have shown failure of arousal (mostly erection) and orgasm during coitus, they were all successful with automanipulation (Masters & Johnson, 1966, pp. 312–313).

An activity may be designated as masturbatory when it effects physiological arousal, regardless of whether orgasm is achieved (Kinsey et al., 1953, p. 133). Autostimulation by use of the hands is the most commonly observed technique (Kinsey et al., 1953, p. 510). I have already pointed out that the body parts most frequently chosen for stimulation to a state of arousal are the labia minora and clitoris among females (Gould, 1987b, p. 16) and the male homologues of the shaft and head of the penis. It is likely that these areas are chosen commonly because they are the sites where arousal to a level of intensity is productive of distinct indications that are identified as a "plateau phase" (Masters & Johnson, 1966, pp. 280–281), with further indications that are identified as an "orgasmic phase" (Masters & Johnson, 1966, pp. 282–283), with particular contractions and sensations of throbbing and "release." Thus, my definition of masturbation is refined to an act of autostimulation in which a plateau phase of arousal has been achieved, regardless of orgasm. This specification takes into account the venerable observation that stimulation of any part of the body may make a significant contribution to erotic experience (Freud, 1905/1960, p. 99), although the genitalia are most often preferred.

No discussion of masturbation can exclude the widespread superstition that this practice leads to both physical and mental bad consequences (Kinsey et al., 1953, p. 170; Masters & Johnson, 1966, p. 201). This opinion continues to exist despite the proclamations of medical authorities that there is no evidence of either physical or mental deleterious effects (Kinsey et al., 1953, p. 170; Masters & Johnson, 1966, p. 202). The current medical view of masturbation is that it is a normal activity of childhood and adolescence.

Levine's (1951, p. 121) work is regarded as a contribution to Freud and the early psychoanalysts. However, although they viewed masturbation as harmless per se, they perpetuated the pejorative flavor in the form that its persistence in later years was a mark of immaturity with inevitable harmful consequences of personal tension and interpersonal difficulties in mating (Reich, 1951, pp. 84–87). This negative view continues despite contrary opinions, such as its beneficial association with later character development (Kramer, 1954, p. 137) and the general findings of Kinsey et al. (1953, p. 170) and Masters and Johnson (1966, p. 201).

The unequivocal popularity of masturbation among the young makes it clear that the pejorative view is held among adults. It is my opinion that this negative view evolves from the commonality of experience that the usual practice of coition is unsatisfactory. Because it is also common opinion that coition is the ideal form of sexual activity, the failure of satisfaction is attributed to a prior indulgence in masturbation. Thus, the pejorative view of masturbation can be recognized as the reciprocal of the idealization of coition.

I should note that the definition of an activity as masturbatory requires the presence of physiological arousal as marked by states of vasocongestion and myotonia. This definition serves to distinguish another class of similar activity that is frequently observed and referred to as "play." Pediatricians have long reported that playing with various parts of the body using several techniques constitutes a normative activity for children (Levine, 1951, p. 124). This indicates the commonality of an experience of pleasure in exploring the various sensations that are produced. The syndrome of a child's engagement in play is marked by a casual attitude in which the child may be easily diverted to another amusement. In the syndrome of masturbatory engagement, the child resists diversion and gives every appearance of being intensely absorbed in the sensations (Levine, 1951, p. 119).

The attitude of concentration on the sensations is an inference that is sustained by the observation of resistance to distraction. In addition, the inference is sustained by the observation that the activities are performed rhythmically (Levine, 1951, p. 120). The same behaviors occur normally in a nonrhythmic, casual fashion. The addition of rhythmicity is indicative of the operation of a mental faculty capable of organizing the activity for a different purpose. Rhythmicity and absorption may be noted in all cases in which there is a state of orgasm (Levine, 1951, p. 119), and the achievement of orgasm is not rare even prior to 3 years of age (Levine, 1951, p. 119). Orgasm has been reported in at least 2% of the general population under the age of 5 (Kinsey et al., 1953, p. 127).

The concentration of attention on the sensations being produced appears to be an essential distinction between manipulation for play and manipulation for arousal. It has often been remarked that the achievement of a state of arousal depends on the focus of attention to bodily sensations (Fisher, 1973b, p. 212). Difficulties in achieving states of arousal are often successfully overcome by the teaching of sensate focus (Kalodny, 1970, p. 50). The observation that a tactile experience involving the genitalia does not necessarily result in physiological arousal (Masters & Johnson, 1970, p. 108) is understood to be due to the different focus of attention. In the light of these considerations, a pattern of behavior may be regarded as masturbatory when there is evidence of a concentration of attention being used in stimulating the body to a plateau phase of arousal.

COITION

It has been found that masturbation occurs among people of all ages and all cultures, as well as among most infrahuman mammalian species (Kinsey et al., 1953, pp. 134–135). If one views the achievement of orgasm as a general indication of an experience of pleasure and satisfaction, one may conclude that masturbation is the preeminent technique for experiencing sensual gratification. Nonetheless, people are observed to prefer to achieve their sensual gratification in relation with other people, primarily through coition (Kinsey et al., 1953, p. 132). I have referred to this phenomenon as the *idealization of coition*.

It appears that the most common justification of idealizing coition is that this method serves the biological function of reproduction. The notion is venerable and has Biblical authority (Genesis 1:28) in the advice to be fruitful and multiply. It is said that it is for this purpose that "male and female created he them" (Genesis 1:27). The division of humanity according to male and female is a specification of difference in the genitalia and constitutes the direct implication of reproduction. The derivation of the word *sexual* is from the concept of division and is used to refer to reproductive activity.

The assumption that the reproductive form is the ideal method for indulging in sensual experience is represented by the establishment of institutions for that purpose. The Reproductive Biology Research Foundation of Masters and Johnson and the Center for Marital and Sexual Studies of Hartman and Fithian are two well-known institutions. The titles *Reproductive* and *Marital* reflect that assistance is offered to "the marital unit" (Masters & Johnson, 1970a, p. 3) so that couples may better enjoy coition (Hartman & Fithian, 1972, p. vii). I have already noted that additional assistance is often offered to females because coition is not particu-

larly suited to achieve arousal in its usual patterns and to males who often experience difficulties in coition that are absent in masturbation (Masters & Johnson,
1966, p. 197). The idealization of coition was made explicit by Freud when he
declared that the "healthy" outcome of the pursuit of pleasure is when it comes
under the sway of the reproductive function (Freud, 1905/1960, p. 63).

Although masturbation clearly appears to be the better method of achieving
sensual arousal and orgasm, both males and females are prepared to make some
sacrifice for the idealization of coitus. They appear generally accepting of the
delimited pleasure available from this culturally prescribed form of activity.

In fact, as has already been documented, the usual form of coition may be fairly
described as "ejaculation centered." Both partners appear accepting of whatever
sensual pleasure is contingent on the achievement of the male's ejaculation through
coition. The common pattern of the rapid achievement of coital ejaculation has
often been described as a "male-dominated" activity (Masters & Johnson, 1970a,
p. 96). However, this interpretation assumes that ejaculation represents a state of
subjective sensual satisfaction for the male, and I have shown that this is not
tenable. The male's ejaculation is the focus of the activity rather than the male's
achievement of sensual gratification in a broader manner. This is also true for the
female, who often develops a pattern of pelvic thrusting during coitus, which
constitutes an active effort to assist the male's ejaculation. The thrusting pattern is
a frequent target of sexual reeducation, and its change is reported to result in the
female's greater appreciation of her own sensual experiences, often for the first
time within the marriage (Masters & Johnson, 1970b, p. 109).

DISCUSSION

My purpose in selecting the foregoing observations was in the interest of exam-
ining the proposition that the regular patterns of sexual activity were indicative of a
common causal power or type of drive. I have come to appreciate the necessity of
distinguishing between two types of sexual activity that differ significantly as to
both physiological and psychological aspects: masturbation and coition.

The activity of masturbation may generally be regarded as regularly associated
with an experience of sensual pleasure. Self-arousal of the body to the degree of an
orgastic state appears to be regularly associated with a maximal experience of
sensual pleasure. I also recognize lesser degrees of arousal that are associated with
lesser degrees of pleasure. Various patterns of masturbatory activity may be used
with various body parts. The patterns are observed to occur with similarity and
regularity among the species. The similarity and regularity are best attributed to
the endowment of the species with structures that are particularly suited to develop
a state of physiological arousal.

The observation of masturbatory activity is regularly indicative of a subjective
experience described as sensual pleasure. Thus, despite the variety of individuals
and situations, it is tenable to hold that in the performance of any masturbatory
activity, there is a commonality of sensually pleasurable experience. I refer to this
particular situation as an impulse for sensual pleasure. It is observations of masturbation that are the evidential basis for the assertion that humans possess a type of
causal power described as an impulse for sensual pleasure.

The initiation of masturbatory behavior has been found not to be contingent on either environmental or physiological events. It is observed to be contingent on episodic subjective events; I identify this type of impulse as a drive. Thus, I am confident to assert that people possess a drive for sensual pleasure that, when activated, will lead to the performance of masturbatory behavior.

The activity of coitus is associated with an experience of sensual pleasure only insofar as a state of arousal is achieved. The general pattern of coital activity is associated with a lesser state of arousal than masturbatory activity for both men and women, regardless of the presence of ejaculation. It is tenable to hold that the observation of arousal in coital activity is regularly indicative of an experience of sensual pleasure, even though the degree of sensual pleasure is regularly less than that achievable through masturbation. It is not tenable to hold that the observation of coitus is regularly indicative of an experience of sensual pleasure if there is no observation of a state of arousal.

I am confident to assert that when the drive for sensual pleasure is activated, it will always lead to masturbatory activity and sometimes to the performance of coitus. Conversely, when masturbatory activity is observed, the activation of the drive for sensual pleasure may always be inferred. When coital activity is observed, the activation of the drive for sensual pleasure may always be inferred, but not its degree. It appears to follow from these considerations that coital activity is an expression of the drive for sensual pleasure only insofar as it is performed as a masturbatory activity.

Instances of the observation of coitus have been reported that are best described as acts of dominance (Eissler, 1977, pp. 44–45) because sensual pleasure is judged to constitute a minor aspect of the experience. More commonly, it is known that coitus performed by both males and females as prostitution has a minor pleasurable aspect (Masters & Johnson, 1966, p. 10), although it is primarily a financial activity.

One may hold that when coital activity is observed, some degree of operation of a drive for sensual pleasure is active, although observable details are indicative of other qualities of transcendent powers that are active within subjective experience, often to a major degree. The drive for sensual pleasure seems generally to play a minor role in the usual pattern of coitus. The quality of these other major powers is indicated by the observation that the usual pattern of coital expression is both learned and psychosocial (Masters & Johnson, 1966, p. 138). These psychosocial factors are observed to significantly affect the physiological event of arousal from enhancement through negation (Masters & Johnson, 1970a, p. 297). Thus, the citation of coitus in an examination of the drive for sensual pleasure appears to be inept, especially because the citation of masturbation is more appropriate. Those who hold a priori a pejorative view of masturbation would be constrained from citing this behavior in the normative context of a drive.

I conclude that people are possessed of a drive for sensual pleasure. The behaviors that evidence this drive are designated as masturbatory. Masturbation stimulates the physiological development of vasocongestion and myotonia that is defined as a state of physiological arousal. The sensations contingent on a state of arousal are generally and regularly experienced as sensually pleasurable.

The designation of the drive for sensual pleasure as sexual is inaccurate. *Sexual* necessarily implies the differentiation between males and females, whereas the evidence for the drive for sensual pleasure is masturbatory and the same for both sexes. The common usage of the term *sexual* may be understood technically in the sense of the terms *erotic* and *sensual*. However, *erotic* is not technically acceptable because it has the implication that the site of the drive is in the sexual organ rather than in the subjective attitude of the person (Fisher, 1973b, p. 5).

In the event of physiological arousal, the position of psychologists leads them to appreciate the role of psychological factors both in its production (such as the concentration of attention) and in the mental factors that constitute the experience of the arousal. These considerations are recognized by psychologists when they observe that the fantasy content in the performance of an activity is of decisive importance for the quality of the experience (Kris, 1951, p. 101) and that the ultimate criterion for sensuality is subjective (Compton, 1983, p. 382).

REFERENCES

Benedek, T. (1971, December). Aphrodisiacs. *Medical Aspects of Human Sexuality*, pp. 42–63.

Brody, J. (1967, November). Frigidity. *Medical Aspects of Human Sexuality*, pp. 42–48.

Compton, A. (1983). The current status of the psychoanalytic theory of drives: I. Drive concept, classification, and development. *Psychoanalytic Quarterly, 52*, 364–401.

Eissler, K. (1977). Comments on penis envy and orgasm in women. *Psychoanalytic Study of the Child, 32*, 29–83.

Ellison, C. (1972, August). Vaginismus. *Medical Aspects of Human Sexuality*, pp. 34–55.

Fisher, S. (1973a, August). Morning erections. *Medical Aspects of Human Sexuality*, p. 181.

Fisher, S. (1973b). *The female orgasm*. New York: Basic Books.

Freud, S. (1960). Three essays on the theory of sexuality. In J. Strachey (Ed. & Trans.), *The standard edition of the complete psychological works of Sigmund Freud* (Vol. 7, pp. 123–243). London: Hogarth Press. (Original work published 1905)

Freud, S. (1957). Instincts and their vicissitudes. In J. Strachey (Ed. & Trans.), *The standard edition of the complete psychological works of Sigmund Freud* (Vol. 14, pp. 111–140). London: Hogarth Press. (Original work published 1915)

Gould, S. (1987a, December). Freud's phylogenetic fantasy. *Natural History*, pp. 10–19.

Gould, S. (1987b, March). Freudian slip. *Natural History*, pp. 14–21.

Greenblatt, R. (1972, January). Endocrinology of sexual behavior. *Medical Aspects of Human Sexuality*, pp. 110–114.

Hartman, W., & Fithian, M. (1972). *Treatment of sexual dysfunction*. Long Beach, CA: Center for Marital and Sexual Studies.

Kalodny, R. (1970, July). Observations on the new Masters and Johnson report. *Medical Aspects of Human Sexuality*, pp. 47–60.

Kinsey, A., Pomeroy, W., & Martin C. (1948). *Sexual behavior in the human male*. Philadelphia, PA: Saunders.

Kinsey, A., Pomeroy, W., Martin, C., & Gebhard, P. (1953). *Sexual behavior in the human female*. Philadelphia, PA: Saunders.

Kramer, P. (1954). Early capacity for orgastic discharge and character formation. *Psychoanalytic Study of the Child, 9*, 124–141.

Kris, E. (1951). Some comments and observations on early autoerotic activities. *Psychoanalytic Study of the Child, 6*, 95–116.

Levine, M. (1951). Pediatric observations on masturbation in children. *Psychoanalytic Study of the Child, 6*, 117–124.

Masters, W., & Johnson, V. (1966). *Human sexual response*. Boston: Little, Brown.

Masters, W., & Johnson, V. (1970a). *Human sexual inadequacy*. Boston: Little, Brown.

Masters, W., & Johnson, V. (1970b, October). On human sexual inadequacy. *Medical Aspects of Human Sexuality*, pp. 108–123.

McGuire, T., & Steinhilber, R. (1970, October). Frigidity, the primary female sexual dysfunction. *Medical Aspects of Human Sexuality*, pp. 108–123.

Ovesey, L. (1970, November). Retarded ejaculation. *Medical Aspects of Human Sexuality*, pp. 98–104.

Reich, A. (1951). The discussion of 1912 on masturbation and our present-day views. *Psychoanalytic Study of the Child, 6*, 80–94.

Weaver, R. (1970, October). Scrotum and testes. *Medical Aspects of Human Sexuality*, pp. 124–143.

Wershub, L. (1967, April). Premature ejaculation as a form of sexual impotence. *Medical Aspects of Human Sexuality*, pp. 43–45.

5

Motivation

IMPULSES

The study of human behavior from a relativist psychological point of view has led me to attempt to identify those qualities of transcendent causal powers that appear to operate commonly among all people and that are indicative of an *impersonal subjective experience*, or *impulse*. If one refers to this notion with the term *motivation*, then it is understood that one is searching for the general motives operative in human behavior. This is the same notion that is addressed by the question, "Why do people do what they do?" If one is able to identify the general motives operative in a person's behavior, then one is in a position to identify the individual variations in that behavior and to make reasonable conjectures about that person's individual experience.

On the basis of previous considerations, the reader may recognize that any impulse constituting part of an individual's experience in any singular instance will be a compound. One aspect of an experience of impulse will be held in common with all members of the species. Another aspect will be held in common with social subgroups of the species. A third aspect may be found that will be individualistic and unique for that person.

I have refined the definition of terms to take into account these distinctions. *Impulse* refers to the generality of motivation within experience regardless of any categorization according to the form of expression or its contingency on any environmental or internal event.

SOURCE

Psychologists attempt to identify the general motivational aspects of human subjective experience. They study behavior seeking to discover patterns that may be indicative of particular qualities of motivation. These qualities represent understanding of why a person initiates an activity, organizes it in a particular pattern, and then stops that activity (Bourne & Ekstrand, 1973, p. 23).

Because observational entities are behaviors performed by people, it is understandable that psychologists have been occupied with investigating the source of the energy that impels the activity. The traditional terms of instinct, drive, and need are all designed to preserve the implication of a "somatic source" (Compton, 1983, p. 71) of this energy that is initiated by somatic changes and is terminated by somatic changes (Compton, 1983, p. 81). The location of such a somatic source is specified in the current belief that "all of psychology is an aspect of the functioning of the central nervous system" (Brenner, 1982, pp. 19–20). However, as I have already pointed out in the mistaken notion of "erogeneity," it is an error to attribute the locus of the energy of an impulse to any organ. This erroneous assumption contributes to the fact that the current state of knowledge about a somatic source for motivation is undecided and that the conjunction of psychological meaning and physical force is not known (Compton, 1983, p. 74). The impasse concerning the source of energy that impels activity, when regarded from the point of view of realist philosophy, appears to arise from some arguable assumptions.

It is reported that activity is observed to be "initiated" and "stopped." This cannot be literally true because initiation necessarily requires a prior nonactive state. One knows only of death as a nonactive state for people and activity cannot be observed after that. "Stopped" requires that a change be to a non-mobile state, or death. Because it is reported that the person is alive before, during, and after the period of observation, it is not possible to observe either initiation or stoppage of activity. Instead, what is being observed is a state of continued activity with changing patterns of that activity.

The entire person is involved in the performance of any activity. It is an artifact of an objectivist philosophical system to conclude that the organ selected for observation is the locus for a quality of energy that is inferred from patterns of that same organ's activity. For example, the reference to the genitalia as a sexual organ shows the prior assumption of a sexual quality of transcendent power. Then, any pattern of genital activity may be taken to be indicative of sexuality. Apart from the epistemological error in such thinking, this example also uses another untenable assumption. My investigations did not support the proposal of a sexual impulse but accounted for the data of observation by the inference of a drive for sensual pleasure.

Activity is not the attribute of any particular organ. Activity is an attribute of all organs and is common among living things. Activity is a term selected by psychology to refer to the general biological capacity for mobility that is characteristic of all living organisms. Therefore, the answer to the question about the somatic source of energy that impels any activity is to be found in the general biological conditions for the state of life.

An observation of activity can only sustain the inference that the person is alive. It is the observation of patterns of activity that can sustain inferences about the qualities of being alive. Psychologists are interested in studying patterns of activity in order to learn about their transcendent causal powers. It is their practice to refer to these causal powers of patterns of activities as motivation. Psychologists seek to understand the general motivations of people that result in their performance of patterns of activity. From such a base of understanding, the psychologist is in a position to identify individual variations of these patterns and to use them to make reasonable inferences about the psychology of that individual.

BEYOND SENSUAL PLEASURE

My previous discussion leads to the assertion that people possess a drive for sensual pleasure. This drive is a constant motivational factor that varies in the intensity of its contribution to the performance of patterns of individualistic behaviors. In Freud's study of what he termed "psychoneurotic" phenomena, he discovered the important role of this drive. The devious pursuit of this motivation was seen to account for the peculiar patterns of behavior that are called psychoneurotic symptoms (Freud, 1915/1957a, pp. 125–127).

SELF-PRESERVATION

Freud's study of psychoneurotic symptoms demonstrated that the drive for pleasure was a sustainable inference that accorded with the data of observation regarding certain patterned regularities among the details of these symptoms. However, he noted that there were other individualistic patterns of details that appeared regularly in these cases but were antithetical to the concept of a drive for pleasure. These details suggested a different causal quality of motivation: they sustained the inference that the quality of motivation was describable as "self-preservation" (Freud, 1915/1957a, p. 124).

The notion that people possess a general motivation to preserve their life is warranted by its acceptance in common experience. The observation of phenomena designated as hunger and thirst—human needs—is regarded as unequivocally indicative of this quality of motivation (Bourne & Ekstrand, 1973, p. 127) and is entitled *primary drives*. Such "primary needs" are seen as obvious evidence of a "drive for self-preservation" (Hartmann, 1955/1964a, p. 316).

The motivational quality of self-preservation is often variously referred to as *primary drive*, *need*, and *drive*. Within the relativist system, the phenomena referred to are classed as impulses (indicative of a general motivation). Within that class, hunger and thirst are identified as examples of a need type of impulse because they refer to continuing physiological events. Thus, people have a continuing need to eat and drink, and this is indicative of an impulse for self-preservation.

Freud's understanding of behaviors motivated by the impulse for self-preservation led him to conceptualize a hypothetical entity as an agency to carry out these behaviors. He named this agency *ego* and used the terms *ego-instincts* and *self-preservative instincts* synonymously (Freud, 1915/1957a, p. 174).

Thus, Freud's study of symptoms presented evidence for the operation of both a drive for sensual pleasure and an impulse for self-preservation, an ego-type activity. He observed that ego-motivations could supercede the motive to pursue sensual pleasure and that this was also notable among normal people. For example, in the distress accompanying organic illness, an ordinarily loving attitude will be decreased as long as there is suffering (Freud, 1914/1957c, p. 82). These patterns of behavior indicated that self-preservation had greater motivational force than the pursuit of pleasure.

Freud noted that although the pursuit of pleasure was a universal and constant motivation, it was not the dominant force. There were many observations indicating that this was set aside by an interest of self-preservation. Further study of these patterns contrary to the pursuit of pleasure led him to conclude that they were variations of the motivation to adapt to reality. It appeared to him that such an "acceptance of reality" also served the purpose of self-preservation (Hartmann, 1956/1964b, p. 254).

PLEASURE PRINCIPLE AND REALITY PRINCIPLE

Various patterns of behavior are identifiable as motivated primarily by the drive for sensual pleasure. Experiences of sensual "unpleasure" are also identifiable in avoidant patterns of behavior. I may state that there is a drive to pursue experiences of sensual pleasure and that there is a drive to avoid experiences of sensual unpleasure. Both of these types of motivation are evidenced in a multiplicity of patterns. Freud found it a convenient condensation to refer comprehensively to this complexity with the term *pleasure principle*. Relativists refer to sensual pleasure or unpleasure motivations as the *pleasure principle*; I use this term in the relativist sense.

Other patterns of behavior are identifiable as motivated primarily by the impulse for self-preservation. Among these patterns there is the class that tends to preserve life by the maintenance of vital bodily functions. There is also the class that tends to maintain life by effecting an adaptation to reality. At the same time, patterns can be identified that indicate an avoidance of detriments to both classes of self-preservation. These classes of motivation are evidenced in a multiplicity of patterns. Freud found it a convenient condensation to refer to this complexity with the comprehensive term *reality principle*. Relativists also designate this complexity of motivation as the *reality principle*; I use the term in the relativist sense.

The hypothetical concepts of the pleasure and reality principles are a convenient and economical way to refer to the considerable multiplicity of overt phenomena that are indicative of the operations of the drive for sensual pleasure and the impulse for self-preservation.

Because it is conceived that the pleasure and reality principles are representative of causal qualities in the performance of all psychological behaviors, one may speak of layers of motivation. Because reality principle considerations tend to supercede pleasure principle considerations in the performance of psychological behaviors, one may speak of a hierarchy of motivations (Hartmann, 1964c, p. xi).

PRIMARY NARCISSISM

The study of people in psychotic states showed the commonality of patterns indicative of subjective experiences described both as an attitude of megalomania and as a distinct withdrawal of interest from the world outside themselves (Abraham, 1908/1953, p. 69). This subjective condition was referred to as *narcissism*. A narcissistic state was recognized as being similar to the mental state that is observed to appear regularly in early childhood. Developmental phases in this normal narcissistic attitude were detailed as early as 1913 by Ferenczi (1953).

It seemed to Freud (1914/1957c) that all people went through a narcissistic phase and that this condition persisted as a strong motivational force throughout normal adult life, although in a "damped down" form (Freud, 1914/1957c, p. 93). The observation that narcissistic patterns are recognizable throughout life led him to conclude that they indicated the presence of a causal power, "some measure of which may be attributed to every living creature" (Freud, 1914/1957c, pp. 73–74).

The notion of any normative subjective experience is comprehended by relativisim as an impersonal subjective experience, or impulse. Thus, the data of observation support the inference that human beings possess a narcissistic impulse.

The study of paraphrenias demonstrated that, at least in these cases, patterns of behavior indicative of a narcissistic impulse were observed to supercede the motivational impulses denoted by both the pleasure and reality principles. These patterns were being performed even though they were contrary to the recognition of illness, death, enjoyment, and the laws of nature and society (Freud, 1914/1957c,

p. 91). Considerations of "self-regard" (Freud, 1914/1957c, p. 98) were seen to have the most powerful motivational force.

The study of cases of melancholia, psychotic depression, demonstrated that they were distinguishable from normal instances of mourning by the chief role of "self-regard" (Freud, 1917/1957b, p. 245), or narcissistic impulse. Narcissistic considerations in these cases operate with such force that the otherwise basic motivation to cling to life can be set aside and suicide attempted (Freud, 1917/1957b, p. 252). This indicates that the narcissistic impulse can supercede both the reality principle and the pleasure principle.

PROBLEMS

Freud (1920/1955) had found other clinical states in which patterns of behavior indicated a motivational power supeceding the pleasure and reality principles. In cases of traumatic neurosis, the person appeared compelled to reexperience recollections that were both unpleasant and recalled a situation of jeopardy to life (Freud, 1920/1955, p. 13). In cases in which children play the game of "gone," they actively reexperience a sense of loss that they must feel as unpleasant, together with an anxiousness for their state of well-being (Freud, 1920/1955, p. 15). In the course of psychoanalytic treatment, it was commonly observed that patients would even use the greatest ingenuity to reexperience events they regarded as unpleasant and fraught with peril for themselves.

It was clear to Freud that the existence of these patterns indicated the presence of a motivational force stronger than those of the familiar pleasure and reality principles (Freud, 1920/1955, p. 23). The quality of this force seemed to indicate the presence of a "compulsion to repeat" (Freud, 1920/1955, pp. 22–23). He did not consider, instead, that these might be vicissitudes in the manifestation of narcissistic impulse because he had already rejected the concept of a separate ego-instinct (Freud, 1920/1955, p. 51).

The observation of narcissistic patterns indicating the experience of a megalomanic sense of self-regard led to the undoubted acceptance of such a state as part of normal development. However, Freud (1914/1957c, p. 77) believed that this could not be an original state because "every individual passes through a period during which he is helpless and has to be looked after" (Freud, 1915/1957a, p. 135). The assumption that everyone enters life with an original experience of helplessness led Freud to look on narcissistic patterns as a secondary, although inevitable, development in which people come to take themselves as an object of their own love (Freud, 1915/1957a, p. 133). Thus, he came to view narcissism as a vicissitude of the pleasure principle within an enlarged redefinition of the reality principle (Freud, 1920/1955, pp. 44–53). Freud continued to maintain the assumption that the infant's original experience is one of helplessness in which the sense of self is not distinguished (Freud, 1930/1961, pp. 66–67) until formed by its need for protection (Freud, 1930/1961, p. 72).

REFERENCES

Abraham, K. (1953). The psychosexual differences between hysteria and dementia praecox. In D. Bryan & A. Stracey (Trans.), *Selected papers* (pp. 64–67). New York: Basic Books. (Original work published 1908)

Bourne, L., & Ekstrand, B. (1973). *Psychology: Its principles and meanings.* Hinsdale, IL: Dryden Press.

Brenner, C. (1982). *The mind in conflict.* New York: International University Press.

Compton, A. (1983). The current status of the psychoanalytic theory of instinctual drives: I. Drive concept, classification, and development. *Psychoanalytic Quarterly, 52,* 364–401.

Ferenczi, S. (1950). Stages in the development of the sense of reality. In E. Jones (Trans.), *Sex in psychoanalysis* (pp. 213–239). New York: Basic Books. (Original work published 1913)

Freud, S. (1955). Beyond the pleasure principle. In J. Strachey (Ed. & Trans.), *The standard edition of the complete psychological works of Sigmund Freud* (Vol. 18, pp. 1–64). London: Hogarth Press. (Original work published 1920)

Freud, S. (1957a). Instincts and their vicissitudes. In J. Strachey (Ed. & Trans.), *The standard edition of the complete psychological works of Sigmund Freud* (Vol. 14, pp. 111–140). London: Hogarth Press. (Original work published 1915)

Freud, S. (1957b). Mourning and melancholia. In J. Strachey (Ed. & Trans.), *The standard edition of the complete psychological works of Sigmund Freud* (Vol. 14, pp. 237–258). London: Hogarth Press. (Original work published 1917)

Freud, S. (1957c). On narcissism: An introduction. In J. Strachey (Ed. & Trans.), *The standard edition of the complete psychological works of Sigmund Freud* (Vol. 14, pp. 211–238). London: Hogarth Press. (Original work published 1914)

Freud, S. (1961). Civilization and its discontents. In J. Strachey (Ed. & Trans.), *The standard edition of the complete psychological works of Sigmund Freud* (Vol. 21, pp. 57–145). London: Hogarth Press. (Original work published 1930)

Hartmann, H. (1964a). Comments on the scientific aspects of psychoanalysis. In H. Hartman (Ed.), *Essays on ego psychology* (pp. 297–317). New York: International University Press. (Original work published 1955)

Hartmann, H. (1964b). Notes on the reality principle. In H. Hartman (Ed.), *Essays on ego psychology* (pp. 241–267). New York: International University Press. (Original work published 1956)

Hartmann, H. (1964c). Introduction. In H. Hartman (Ed.), *Essays on ego psychology* (pp. ix–xv). New York: International University Press.

6

Neonate Experience

CURRENT POSITION

Concerning the question of the state of the neonate's subjective experience, the prevailing assumption is that this must coordinate with the objective fact that the infant is in a position of helplessness (Freud, 1915/1957, p. 135). Thus, it is assumed that the neonate experiences helplessness and anxiety (Freud, 1936/1959, p. 77; Lax, 1977, p. 293).

The assumption of a neonatal experience of helplessness requires the coordinated assumption of a sense of self that can serve as an agency for experiencing. If a sense of self experiences helplessness on entering the world, it is a logical extension to conceive of that self as being in an original vulnerable position. Then, no matter what variety of aspect of reality presents itself to the newborn, the child in such a vulnerable state must necessarily experience helplessness. In keeping with these considerations it is conceived that the infant's self must be rudimentary and unorganized, no more than "scattered deposits of focal points" or "ego-nuclei" (Glover, 1949, pp. 65–66).

In order to maintain the assumption of an experience of helplessness, the sense of self that is conceded to exist must not be experienced as a unitary self (Kohut, 1977, pp. 98–99). That would imply a state of self-confidence that would be contrary to helplessness. Thus, the prevailing assumption is that the neonate's self is monadic but autistic (Mahler, 1968, p. 7) and incapable of maintaining a coherent conception (Volkan, 1976, p. 29) of himself or herself or the objects in the world (Smith, 1978, p. 1050). It is assumed that this is an undifferentiated state (Hartmann, 1952/1964, p. 166; Jacobson, 1983, p. 545; Kernberg, 1976, p. 38; Spitz, 1959) in which the child experiences neediness (Fraiberg, 1977).

PROBLEMS

It is common to observe that within a few weeks after birth, the infant performs coordinated activities that are adaptive to the world. This might be taken to indicate that the infant experiences a sense of capability and effectiveness. It would be reasonable to hold that such capibilities existed prior to the observation of their use (Glover, 1961, p. 87). In order to still maintain the assumption of helplessness, it was further proposed that these activities were being performed in a merely "canalized" manner (Glover, 1961, p. 88) that is devoid of mental content (Greenacre, 1952, p. 35).

There are many reports of observations of the fetus acting in patterned ways, such as sucking, swallowing, having a heartbeat, and kicking (Greenacre, 1952, p. 32), as well as evidence of learning before birth (Restak, 1986; Terhune, 1979, p.

374). The traditional position asserts that these are merely "life movements" (Greenacre, 1952, p. 32), but this assertion is counter to the realist philosophy of science. The observation that these activities are being performed individualistically is taken to be an unequivocal indication of subjective experience. Besides, it is maintained on philosophical grounds that the mental capacity for subjective experience is inherent for human beings. The proposition that any individualistic pattern of behavior can be performed without mental content must be rejected, together with the assertion that this represents life movements.

Conjectures about the experience of the infant during the birth process have been considered. Freud had noted that birth did not appear to be as remarkable an experience for the neonate as it was for the mother and other observers and was not a source of universal and inevitable psychic trauma (Freud, 1936/1959, p. 67). The observation that neonates are less reactive postpartum than they were in utero suggested that the massive sensory input of the birth process produced a sensory fatigue so that their experience was relatively anesthetized (Greenacre, 1952, pp. 14–17). This phenomenon may be parallel to the observation that a state of self-initiated hypertonus appears to have a blocking effect on perceptions by effecting a preoccupation of the musculature (Fenichel, 1937, pp. 37–38).

THE NEWBORN

More sophisticated recent observations have demonstrated that various mental faculties are functioning at a time much earlier than formerly believed (Jacobson, 1983, p. 544). Although Piaget had reported the imitation of facial gestures at 8–12 months, and Emde, Gaensbaur & Harmon (1976) found this at 2–3 months, this behavior was elicited by Meltzoff (1986) at 12–21 days, whereas Hack (1975) demonstrated its presence at the first day (as did Bower, 1976, and Lane, 1985). Imitative behavior is evidence of the ability to coordinate the capacity for the perception of various sensory data, together with the capacity to organize and control the musculature, and the capacity to perceive data with a fine degree of discrimination.

The same coordination of a complexity of mental faculties is demonstrated in the observations of walking movements while the newborn is supported (Bower, 1976) and in the child's being able to reach and to touch visible objects. Data from the sense of hearing are processed with complex coordination, as demonstrated by experiments that show learning in this modality both for the fetus (Terhune, 1979, p. 374) and the newborn (Hack, 1975). Learning experiments using the sensory modality of taste show evidence of the newborn's fine discrimination as well as various individual preferences (Lipsitt, 1986). Studies of the tactile modality also show the use of fine discrimination within complex adaptive patterns (Hack, 1975; Rice, 1975).

There are many reports of the observation of individuality in the behavior patterns of newborns (Terhune, 1979), and these are indicative of concentration, anticipation, and coordination of motor activity (Brazelton & Abs, 1979). Observations of the individuality of neonates has often been observed as being expressed in various exercises of preference and taste. These may well be an extension of the biological foundation of mental faculties. Recent anatomical examinations of the infant brain reveal evidence of an individual uniqueness previously unknown (Restak, 1986). Also, there is evidence to suggest that the immune system is as individualistic as fingerprints (Stockton, 1978).

Observations of the newborn's selective preference to concentrate attention on both the caretaker (Kagan, 1978) and on the faces of humans who are similar to the caretaker (Hack, 1975) demonstrate that the neonate is an organized and organizing being who actively participates with the world (Dowling, 1981, p. 290). The newborn is sensitive to and interacts with his or her human and nonhuman environment (Fast, 1985, pp. 154–155).

HELPLESSNESS

The assumption of the attribute of helplessness to the subjective experience of the neonate has the corollary of a necessary dependence on the caretaking mother and underlines the importance of the mother in the child's psychology. The most eloquent exponent of this view can be found in Mahler (1968, p. 49) and her conception of symbiosis.

However, a study of Mahler's (1968) case illustrations has shown no convincing evidence to support the necessity of her inference as to the nature of the infant's experience (Slap & Levine, 1978, p. 514). Her notion of the neonate's experience seems to be an extension of her assumption that it must be coordinated with the child's perceived physical helplessness.

The correctness of the assumption that the neonate experiences helplessness and is necessarily psychologically dependent on the mother is also belied by another line of observation. The study of a large group of children who were exposed to meager and unstable mothering did not reveal the consequence of significant disturbance (A. Freud & Dann, 1951), which the assumption predicts. Other research showed that infants appeared able to thrive in the face of reduced mothering (Keniston, 1977).

Because there is considerable evidence that an early deprivation of mothering does not necessarily result in a later disorder of either development or function (Kagan, 1985), it is not tenable to assume that mothering is essential to the infant nor that the infant's subjective state is one of helplessness. It appears that *caretaking*, as differentiated from *mothering*, is sufficient for the infant's basic well-being. Babies seem to be endowed with powerful and maturational mental faculties so that neither their biology nor their environment are sufficient to determine their destiny.

SUMMARY

The general psychoanalytic conception that infants are born in a narcissistic state that is characterized by the experience of helplessness is not supported by observation (Peterfreund, 1978; Stechler & Kaplan, 1980). The newborn is not psychologically helpless (Smith, 1978) but capable of complex interactive mental processes (Love, 1985).

Infants have a psychic organization (Dowling, 1981) with functional conceptions of both the self and objects of the environment (Terhune, 1979). The data of observation confirm the basic assumption (if not necessarily the details) of Fairbairn (1952) and Klein (1946). These differ from Fast's (1985) proposition in that they show the neonate to be cognizant of the externality of the environment. The data do not merely indicate prestructural propensities (Shapiro, 1981) but that of fully functional structural patterns. The infant is born with an individualized functional self. The infant is accurately described as a cognitive being (Trotter, 1987, p. 36) with characteristic patterns of individual emotional expression (Izard, cited in Trotter, 1987, p. 40). As Roberts (cited in Trotter, 1987, p. 41), put it, the womb should be regarded more as a school room than as a waiting room.

REFERENCES

Bower, T. (1976, Nov.). Repetitive processes in child development. *Scientific American*, p. 38.
Brazelton, T., & Abs, H. (1979). Four early stages in the development of mother–infant interaction. *Psychoanalytic Study of the Child, 29,* 349–369.
Dowling, S. (1981). Abstract report from the literature on neonatology. *Psychoanalytic Quarterly, 50,* 290–295.
Emde, R., Gaensbaur, T. & Harmon, R. (1976). *Emotional expression in infancy.* New York: International University Press.
Fairbairn, W. (1952). *An object–relations theory of the personality.* New York: Basic Books.
Fast, I. (1985). Infantile narcissism and the active infant. *Psychoanalytic Psychology, 2,* 153–170.
Fenichel, O. (1937). Early stages of ego development. In H. Fenichel (Ed.), *Collected papers, second series* (pp. 25–48). New York: Norton.
Fraiburg, S. (1977). *Every child's birthright.* New York: Basic Books.
Freud, A., & Dann, S. (1951). An experiment in group upbringing. *Psychoanalytic Study of the Child, 6,* 127–169.
Freud, S. (1957). Instincts and their vicissitudes. In J. Strachey (Ed. & Trans.), *The standard edition of the complete psychological works of Sigmund Freud* (Vol. 14, pp. 211–238). London: Hogarth Press. (Original work published 1915)
Freud, S. (1959). The problem of anxiety. In J. Strachey (Ed. & Trans.), *The standard edition of the complete psychological works of Sigmund Freud* (Vol. 20, pp. 77–175). London: Hogarth Press. (Original work published 1936)
Glover, E. (1949). *Psychoanalysis.* New York: Staples Press.
Glover, E. (1961). Some recent trends in psychoanalytic theory. *Psychoanalytic Quarterly, 30,* 86–98.
Greenacre, P. (1952). *Trauma, growth, and personality.* New York: Norton.
Hack, M. (Producer). (1975). *Our amazing newborn* [Film]. Cleveland, OH: Case Western Reserve University.
Hartmann, H. (1964). The mutual influences in the development of ego and id. In H. Hartmann (Ed.), *Essays on ego psychology* (pp. 155–181). New York: International University Press. (Original work published 1952)
Jacobson, J. (1983). The structural theory and the representational world: Developmental and biological considerations. *Psychoanalytic Quarterly, 52,* 543–563.
Kagan, J. (1978). *The growth of the child.* New York: Norton.
Kagan, J. (1985, December 11). *The nature of the child.* New York: Basic Books.
Keniston, K. (1977). First attachments. *New York Times Book Review,* p. 11.
Kernberg, O. (1976). *Object relations theory and clinical psychoanalysis.* New York: Jason Aronson.
Klein, M. (1946). *The Psycho-analysis of children.* London: Hogarth Press.
Kohut, H. (1977). *The restoration of the self.* New York: International University Press.
Lane, E. (1985, June 11). Making faces with baby. *Discovery,* pp. 1–5.
Lax, R. (1977). The role of internalization in the development of certain aspects of female masochism. *International Journal of Psychoanalysis, 58,* 289–300.
Lipsitt, L. (1986). Learning in infancy: Cognitive development in babies. *Journal of Pediatrics, 109,* 172–182.
Mahler, M. (1968). *On human symbiosis and the vicissitudes of individuation.* New York: International University Press.
Meltzoff, A. (1986). Immediate and deferred imitation in 14- and 24-month old infants. *Child Development, 56,* 62–72.

Peterfreund, E. (1978). Some critical comments on the psychoanalytic conceptions of infancy. *International Journal of Psychoanalysis, 59*, 427–441.

Restak, R. (1986). *The infant mind*. Garden City, NY: Doubleday.

Rice, R. (1975, Nov.). Premature infants respond to sensory stimulation. *APA Monitor*, pp. 8–9.

Shapiro, T. (1981). On the quest for the origins of conflict. *Psychoanalytic Quarterly, 50*, 1–21.

Slap, J., & Levine, F. (1978). On hybrid concepts in psychoanalysis. *Psychoanalytic Quarterly, 47*, 499–523.

Smith, M. (1978). Perspectives on selfhood. *American Psychologist, 33*, 1053–1063.

Spitz, R. (1959). *A genetic field theory of ego formation*. New York: International University Press.

Stechler, G., & Kaplan, S. (1980). The development of self. *Psychoanalytic Study of the Child, 35*, 85–105.

Stockton, W. (1978, April 2). A new clue in the cancer mystery. *New York Times Magazine*, pp. 18–20.

Terhune, C. (1979). The role of hearing in early ego formation. *Psychoanalytic Study of the Child, 29*, 371–383.

Trotter, R. (1987, May). You've come a long way baby. *Psychology Today*, pp. 35–45.

Volkan, V. (1976). *Primitive internalized object relations*. New York: International University Press.

7

Self-Images and Object-Images

SELF

Although people are motivated by the pleasure and reality principles, these may be superceded by another quality of motivation. I have referred to this quality as a narcissistic impulse. Having discarded the objection posed by the assumption of an initial experience of helplessness, I am now able to consider that the narcissistic impulse represents an original quality of subjective experience. It is my purpose to seek data of observation to provide a base for reasonable inference as to the nature of the experience of a narcissistic impulse.

I have remarked that in the course of performing all of the varieties of activities of living, humans also experience these activities. Thus, humans are endowed with a mental faculty for experiencing. I found it useful to distinguish between a class of impersonal experience with the components of commonality among all members of a species and commonality among social groups. This made it clear that in addition to impersonal experience, there was also an individual experience. The term *experience* refers to a complex subjective phenomenon. The mental faculty for experiencing has aspects that are generally human, social, and individualistic.

The phenomenon of experience is compounded with pleasure, reality, and narcissistic motivational qualities, all of which have general, social, and individual aspects. I now consider the choice of a term for that mental faculty that can account for these patterns of observation.

The traditional term used in this regard is the *ego*. However, Freud often used it in two senses (Strachey, 1937): to refer to a person's self as different from other people (Strachey, 1937, pp. 7–8) and as an agency of the mind with a group of characteristic functions (Strachey, 1937, pp. 8–9). As Schafer put it, there is a purposive agent (Schafer, 1976, p. 104) and a relationship-forming agency (Schafer, 1976, p. 119).

Hartmann (1950/1964) recognized this confusion. He summed up the pattern of observations as indicating that "the opposite of object-cathexis is not ego-cathexis, but cathexis of one's own person, i.e., self-cathexis" (Hartmann, 1950/1964, p. 127). In relationship with other people, all of a person's mental faculties are involved, not merely that subgroup referred to as *ego*. There is general recognition today that it is inappropriate to use *ego* to refer to the aggregate of mental faculties and that the term *self* is better (Gedo & Goldberg, 1973; Meissner, 1986). There is also a general shift in psychoanalysis today away from the structural model of id–ego–superego to the model of the object relations of a "self" (Eagle, 1986, p. 92).

In neo-Freudian psychoanalysis, the term *self* refers to a system of mental faculties in which there is a complex interaction (Rangell, 1982, p. 727) eventuating in a singular pattern of activity. This is different from the relatively unitary sense of the term *self* used by Adler, Jung, Horney, Sullivan, and Rogers (Ticho,

1978, p. 717). The empirical sense of self, or self-conceptions (Smith, 1975), is the notion emphasized by those writers.

Among Freudians, a sharp distinction is made in two uses of the term *self*. First, there is the reference to a representational concept (Boesky, 1980, p. 574) of subjective experience. Second, there is the reference to a hypothetical construct that is an inference abstracted from data of observation (Boesky, 1980, p. 581). In the relativist system, *self* is also used in two ways: to refer to descriptions of a quality of experience and to refer to a hypothetical construct that accounts for a pattern of observations. (I use the term mostly in the latter sense.) For example, "self" reports are used as part of a pattern of observations in inferring a "self." One's own subjective notions of self, or sense of identity, may not coincide with the psychologist's constructions of that person's self or identity (Meissner, 1981, p. 80).

The term *self* refers to the conception of a mental faculty that has the functions of maintaining relationships with objects (people and things) and acting as a purposive agent. However, these considerations are entirely different from those of the relativist philosophical position. The relativist psychologist is not particularly concerned with making inferences from observations as to the presence and manner of performance of mental faculties. Instead, it is his or her particular purpose to attempt to learn about the experience of the person who is performing those mental activities.

SUMMARY

The general current usage of the term *self* refers to a hypothetical entity that is conceived as the total of mental faculties operating as an integrated system of capabilities and having a developmental history (Meissner, 1981, p. 82). Therefore, all humans are born with a self, and its component mental faculties are possessed in common with all people.

Id, Ego, and Superego

In Hartmann's (1950/1964, p. 127) clarification that the entire person participates in relationships, he emphasized that among the components of the system of mental faculties there are those that are designated as *ego*. This implies that the self has ego, id, and superego aspects. This classification or sorting of mental faculties has been found useful in the conduct of psychoanalytic psychotherapy (Brenner, 1976, p. 3).

Among the mental faculties that Freud (1923/1961) attributed to the ego class (used here as a hypothetical construct) are consciousness, mobility, censorship (pp. 15–16), perception, memory (p. 27), body image (p. 31), intellectual functioning (p. 32), criticality (p. 33), the maintenance of ideals (p. 34) with moral and esthetic values (p. 47), and a social sense (p. 49). He conceived that the commonality of this ego class was their use in dealing with the external world (p. 30). Those mental faculties that are used in dealing with social aspects are distinguished as the class called *superego* (p. 49). Those that deal with impulses are designated as *id* (p. 51).

A central notion in the Freudian view of the psychological aspects of behavior is that each activity is the resultant compromise formation among the competing demands of each of the mental faculties (Brenner, 1976, p. 4). It is held that sorting according to id–ego–superego is helpful in identifying the chief components that are in conflict in the performance of maladaptive behaviors.

However, it was noted that ego-type functions were often found to be in opposition among themselves (Hartmann, 1950/1964, p. 138) and that all combinations of id–ego–superego conflicts could be observed (Schafer, 1976, p. 63). Furthermore, it was found that changes in ego functions were accompanied by changes in id and superego functions (Friedman, 1978, p. 533), so that this distinction was unclear and of doubtful use.

The notion that intrapsychic conflict can be comprehended by the classification of mental faculties into id–ego–superego is not substantiated by observation (Shapiro, 1981, p. 11) and appears to be an inference determined primarily by erroneous assumptions.

As Hartmann (1950/1964, p. 139) pointed out, being rational and realistic are not faculties but characteristics of judgment about someone's use of mental faculties. Schafer (1976) extended this understanding so that any singular faculty may be seen to be used variously in an id, ego, or superego manner (Schafer, 1976, pp. 206, 208, 283).

If one considers the control of mobility as a class of ego activities, it is apparent that activity may be organized to deal adaptively with the external world. One may also observe that mobility can be controlled in an impulsive manner as well as in a manner that gives appropriate weight to social considerations. Therefore, there are no faculties that serve only ego interests, or id interests, or superego interests.

The data of observation are better accounted for by the conception that the person's self, the total of mental faculties, may be used in various patterns. These patterns may be regarded as primarily of an ego, id, or superego type, but this is a matter of judgment by the observer. Judgments by a trained observer as to adaptive efficiency in the use of mental faculties have a value in making inferences about the adaptive status of the person's self system. Judgments according to a standard of adaptation have implications for the state of health of the self system that depend on assumptions that link mental health with adaptation. However, like all value judgments, their foundation for a claim to reality is dependent on the expertise of the observer and is delimited by the high degree of uncertainty intrinsic to such a method.

The same pattern of behavior may be classed as id, ego, or superego according to which features receive emphasis by the particular observer. Although this procedure is not entirely arbitrary, especially if carried out by an expert, the reliability of any such distinction is questionable. Even if the reliability of the method were established to a high degree, it is not useful for psychological purposes. Psychologists aim to know the experience of the person who performs the pattern, and these categories do not deal with this dimension.

In addition, note that this method makes the objectivist assumption that certain patterns are obvious instances of maladaptation and necessarily reflect a disorder in the self system. Even if there were agreement that the pattern violates commonly accepted social standards, the person may reveal a non-obvious reason that may lead to a reevaluation as adaptive. For example, the person may be performing the apparently maladaptive activity for a considerable sum of money. Conversely, there is the warning that an apparently "normal" and adaptive pattern can be performed even though the self system is generally in a condition of marked psychopathology (Brenner, 1976, p. 27). Therefore, I have demonstrated that judgments about the adaptability of self system patterns is independent of the state of order obtaining within the self system.

The foundation of concerns about the adaptability of patterns of the self system seem to arise from a sociological interest rather than a psychological one. It appears that the categorization of mental faculties according to the concepts of id, ego, and superego developed from the sociological definition of psychopathology as "abnormal," deviating from the observed norm. However, this categorization may prove useful in the sociological examination of human behavior.

REFERENCES

Boesky, D. (1980). Introduction: Symposium on object relations theory and love. *Psychoanalytic Quarterly, 49*, 48–55.

Brenner, C. (1976). *Psychoanalytic technique and psychic conflict.* New York: International University Press.

Eagle, M. (1986). Recent developments in psychoanalysis: A critical evaluation. *Psychoanalytic Psychology, 3*, 93–100.

Freud, S. (1961). The ego and the id. In J. Strachey (Ed. & Trans.), *The standard edition of the complete psychological works of Sigmund Freud* (Vol. 19, pp. 3–66). London: Hogarth Press. (Original work published 1923)

Friedman, L. (1978). Trends in the psychoanalytic theory of treatment. *Psychoanalytic Quarterly, 47*, 514–567.

Gedo, J., & Goldberg, A. (1973). *Models of the mind: A psychoanalytic theory.* Chicago: University of Chicago Press.

Hartmann, H. (1964). Comments on the psychoanalytic theory of the ego. In H. Hartmann (Ed.), *Essays on ego psychology* (pp. 113–141). New York: International University Press. (Original work published 1950)

Meissner, W. (1981). A note on narcissism. *Psychoanalytic Quarterly, 50*, 77–89.

Meissner, W. (1986). Can psychoanalysis find its self? *Journal of the American Psychoanalytic Association, 34*, 726–728.

Rangell, L. (1982). Discussion: Psychoanalytic theories of the self. *Journal of the American Psychoanalytic Association, 30*, 726–728.

Schafer, R. (1976). *A new language for psychoanalysis.* New Haven, CT: Yale University Press.

Shapiro, T. (1981). On the quest for the origins of conflict. *Psychoanalytic Quarterly, 50*, 1–21.

Smith, M. (1978). Perspectives on selfhood. *American Psychologist, 33*, 1053–1063.

Strachey, J. (1937). Symposium on the therapeutic results of psychoanalysis. *International Journal of Psychoanalysis, 18*, 139–145.

Ticho, E. (1975). The development of superego autonomy. *Psychoanalytic Review, 59*, 218–233.

8

Object Relations

IMAGES OF SELF AND OBJECT

The self system of mental faculties is a major hypothetical construct in considerations of realist philosophy as applied to matters of psychology. At the same time, note that the term most popularly used to refer to the same conception is that of *object relations*. A review of the history of this term will clarify the issues involved.

These psychological issues center around the mental faculty of perception. I no longer accept the objectivist concept that a mental picture (I use vision as an example for considerations of all sensory faculties) is a "photographic" reproduction of reality. The objectivist position has been effectively negated by the work of Einstein and Planck (Wurmser, 1977, p. 484). In quantum mechanics, there is no "tree" until someone sees it. What is really there are particles of matter in waves of probability. People's senses act as detectors and counters that send electrochemical information to the brain, where it is transformed into something similar to a visual display. The "screen" displays "dots" of data in accord with the capacities of brain structure. Although this type of understanding may turn out to be inaccurate in its details as further research brings forth new information, it seems unequivocal that the display is not an objective replication of external reality.

Consequently, what a person "sees" is an interpretation of "dots." It is customary to refer to this "vision" as a *mnemic image*. This term recognizes the difference between the shape of external reality and the shape that a person sees. The mnemic image represents the world as the person has come to see it. It is the world in which the person lives. In line with my previous philosophical discussion, one would expect to find that some aspects of the mnemic image will be held in common with social groups and that other aspects will be individualistic.

The concept of mnemic image refers to the person's subjective experience of the world as constructed in a special form, or picture. The image is an empirical representation of how the world looks to the person at that time. The person may report a description of that mnemic image, and that report is part of the data of observation. The report cannot be accepted at face value, and the observer must intervene with the subject in order to arrive at a construction of the person's mnemic image that can be considered as reasonably valid and reliable. The observer may attempt to help the person report the empiric experience with accuracy and clarity. These intervention activities are undertaken in a process of clarification.

Regarding a subject's report of an experience with some object in the world other than one's own person, the ostensible empirical subjective image of that object may be referred to as a *reported object-image*. Although the person may report, for example, seeing a snake, the psychologist wishes to learn about the person's experience in seeing the snake. Therefore, it is always necessary for psychologists to inquire further into what else the person has to say (Brenner, 1976, p. 127) in order to gather a base of data from which to make inferences about the person's experience.

The psychological observer intervenes with clarification. Among others, Kernberg (1977, pp. 94–95) has explicated the method of clarification that includes drawing attention to details and considering those implications that are particularly sustaining or contradictory. The observer's goal is to arrive at a description of the person's experience of an object-image that can be sustained as trustworthy. I refer to the observer's conclusion about the person's real experience of the object as an *object-image*. I use the term to denote a construction by the observer, and it may or may not agree with the person's experiential object-image.

I have distinguished two different phenomena. There is the person's report of an experienced object-image, which is regarded by the observer as part of the raw data of observation. Then there is the observer's assertion as to the person's real object-image, which is regarded as a scientifically sustainable inference that is ascribed to the person as an accurate representation of that person's subjective experience. In this example, there is reason to conclude that the person's experience is accurately represented by the statement that the person holds the object-image of a dangerous snake, whether or not the person consciously regards the snake as dangerous.

CLASSICAL USAGE

With Freud's (1923/1961) change to what he called the structural theory, there was increasing recognition of the usefulness of constructed object-images in studying the psychology of behavior (Compton, 1982, p. 382). The use of constructed self-images had been an ongoing practice, but it appeared with the titles of "ego psychology" and "defense analysis." The unfortunate practice of using the term *ego* to refer to the system of mental faculties instead of the term *self* clouded its use as a reference to the self-image but was continued by Freud (1936/1959, p. 103). Despite Hartmann's (1950/1964, pp. 127, 139) correction, one may see this misusage even today. He had made it clear that the psychological understanding of a pattern of behavior is best framed in terms of self-images and coordinated object-images, each of which had their id, ego, and superego aspects.

However, these constructs were not generally and systematically used. This was probably attributable to the confusion regarding narcissistic phenomena in which the observation of a high degree of self-regard was at odds with the assumption of an original helpless sense of self.

LATER CONTRIBUTIONS

In addition to considering what may be the best framework to adopt in attempting to understand the psychology of why people do what they do, many psychologists have a particular interest in states of disordered psychology. Those who study disorder seek to delineate the essence of the pathology and not to be misled by its symptoms. In the example of measles, although there are striking dermatological manifestations, the essence of the pathology is not located in the dermatological system. In the same way, the locus of the essence of psychopathology is sought within the psychological "system."

From his clinical experience, Winnicott (1955) observed as a commonality among his patients that they acted as though they maintained both a "false self" and a "true self." This conception is consonant with Freud's (1938/1964) later impression that a splitting of the ego (self) is the general condition of all psychopathology. Freud was using the term *ego* in the systematic sense, which I refer to by the term *self*. Winnicott proposed that the locus of psychopathology was to be found within the self system.

Fairbairn (1952) had a different conception that came out of his experience with patients. It seemed to him that the commonality among his patients was that they held particular object-images while performing their disturbed behavior. He proposed that the locus of psychopathology was to be found in the system of object-images.

Advocates of both propositions were in vogue for a time, but neither met with general acceptance. The views of Guntrip (1971), who proposed the derivative concept that object-images were the foundation for self-images, were also popular. He laid the locus of the origin of psychopathology in the system of object-images and the expression of pathology in the system of self-images. It is tempting to speculate that the position of a combination of the views of Winnicott and Fairbairn has something to do with Guntrip's having been in treatment with both of them (Guntrip, 1975).

THE MOTHER-IMAGE

Guntrip's view that the accident of the mother's state of health is crucial for the origin of psychopathology that develops within the system of self-images is a popular position today. The foremost exponent of this view is Mahler and her conception that the self-system has a "mirroring frame of reference" (Mahler, 1968, p. 37). The same notion is conveyed by the collateral terms *projective indentification* and *self-objects*.

Although few people question the impact of the mothering person on a child, I have already reviewed a body of data of observation that indicate that the impact is considerably less on the psychology of the child than on his or her biology. The view of the caretaker's importance for psychological development depends on the assumption of an original state of psychological helplessness, and this has been demonstrated to be untenable and contradicted by the data of observation.

This view also fails to make the vital distinction between the object-image of the mother as seen by the observer and the object-image of the mother as seen by the child. The use of the term *separation* refers to the physical and spatial distance between the mother and child and jumps to the assumption that it must be accompanied by a psychological separation: a subjective sense of estrangement in regard to the object-image (Boesky, 1980, p. 52).

Mahler's (1968) notion of "symbiosis" may sometimes have been an adequate description of the observer's judgment about the mother's attitude toward the child, but it is misleading as an indication of the subjective experience of the child (Modell, 1968; Volkan, 1976).

RECENT CONTRIBUTIONS

Kohut (1971) reported that his studies led him to conclude that the locus of pathology was in the self-system and could be identified as two types of "splitting" of that system (Kohut, 1971, p. 185). The experience of the person in performing pathological behaviors could be comprehended as a type of self-image in relation with a type of object-image. These descriptions constitute "transference dispositions" (Kohut, 1977, p. 173) and refer to characteristic and predictable patterns of behavior. His observations led him to infer that splits in the self-system had to do with the qualities of grandiosity and exhibitionism (Kohut, 1977, p. 186). However, because he also held the assumption of helplessness (Kohut, 1977, p. 100), he could not accept these qualities as part of the original self-system.

Kernberg (1977, p. 278) proposed that his observations supported placing the locus of pathology among systems of self- and object-images. The experience of the person performing pathological behaviors could be comprehended as maintaining multiple sets of self- and object-images (Kernberg, 1976, p. 24) so that inharmonious behavior was an inevitable outcome. In each transference disposition there is the specification of a role adopted by the person together with the complimentary role in which the object is cast (Sandler, 1981). Kernberg made it clear that although the same person was performing these various patterns of activity, it was as if different roles were being adopted. He proposed to take into account these qualities in a systematic fashion by suggesting that the appropriate form of hypothetical entity to represent these observations should be "S-O-A Units" (Kernberg, 1976, p. 86), in which S refers to self, O refers to object, and A refers to the attitude or affect taken by that self-image toward that object-image.

There appears to be no particular appreciation in the current literature of this theoretical proposal. However, realist philosophy regards a conceptual advance in the construction of hypothetical entities as no small matter. Let me illustrate the issue by considering an example of the observation of a person who looks at a lamp and cries out fearfully. The problem is to construct a hypothetical entity in self- and object-image terms so that the exact individualistic pattern of behavior that is being observed is a logical and reasonable outcome of that construction.

If one follows Winnicott's (1955) theoretical position and uses his emphasis on the self-image, one would specify the characteristic that the self is afraid of lamps. However, this is unlikely to be true because it implies that the person would experience fearfulness toward all lamps, and this would not be confirmed by experience. By using the self-image alone, it is possible to capture something of the essence of what is going on, but it is not specific enough to constitute an unequivocal statement. Use of the self-image is held to be necessary but not sufficient.

If one follows Fairbairn's (1952) theoretical position and uses his emphasis on the object-image, one would specify the characteristic with which the object is endowed that makes it reasonable for the self to regard it fearfully. For example, there are snakes in the lamp. However, it is unlikely that experience would confirm an invariably fearful attitude toward all snakes at all times. In using the self-image, it is possible to capture something of the essence of what is going on, but it is not specific enough to constitute an unequivocal statement. Use of the object-image is held to be necessary but not sufficient.

If one follows Kernberg's (1976) theoretical position and uses S–O–A units, one would specify that the self regards the object fearfully, regardless of whether snakes are attributed to the lamp. The emphasis in this formula is on the specification of the affect or emotional attitude of the self toward the object. The affect of fear is neither an attribute of the self-image (as in Winnicott, 1955) nor of the object-image (as in Fairbairn, 1952) but is defined as the derivative of an independent constituent of experience. Kernberg (1976, p. 104) viewed affect as an inborn disposition to experience events in terms of pleasure–unpleasure. However, general experience will not confirm the presence in people of an inborn disposition to regard either lamps or snakes fearfully. In specifying the affect of the self toward the object, it is possible to capture something of the essence of what is going on, but it is not specific enough to constitute an unequivocal statement. The use of affect to define the hypothetical entity is held to be necessary but not sufficient.

SUMMARY

The realist philosophy has led me to frame my conjectures about a person's subjective experience in terms of a self-system. The small review of the history of object-relations theory that I have just evaluated makes it clear that it is necessary also to include the constructions of both object-images and affects in any consideration of subjective experience. Therefore, in the observation of a person's performance of a pattern of behavior, I frame my inferences in terms of these three necessary components. However, I differ with Kernberg's (1976) use of the term *affect*. He defined this motivational term with the assumption of a physiological source, which I have found to be untenable. Instead, I hold that affect refers to a hypothetical entity that represents the compound of transcendental motivational powers, which I have identified as having pleasure, reality, and narcissistic qualities.

In order to arrive at an adequate construction about a person's experience, I find it necessary to frame my conjectures in terms of self-image, object-image, and the motivational qualities of pleasure, reality, and narcissism. If a specification can be made as to each of these "dimensions," this construction will account for the details observable in the pattern of behavior in a manner that is logical and reasonably consistent with experience.

REFERENCES

Boesky, D. (1980). Introduction: Symposium on object relations theory and love. *Psychoanalytic Quarterly, 49*, 48–55.

Brenner, C. (1976). *Psychoanalytic technique and psychic conflict*. New York: International University Press.

Compton, A. (1982). On the psychoanalytic theory of instinctual drives. IV: Instinctual drives and the ego–id–superego model. *Psychoanalytic Quarterly, 50*, 363–392.

Fairbairn, W. (1952). *An object-relations theory of the personality*. New York: Basic Books.

Freud, S. (1959). The problem of anxiety. In J. Strachey (Ed. & Trans.), *The standard edition of the complete psychological works of Sigmund Freud* (Vol. 20, pp. 77–175). London: Hogarth Press. (Original work published 1936)

Freud, S. (1961). The ego and the id. In J. Strachey (Ed. & Trans.), *The standard edition of the complete psychological works of Sigmund Freud* (Vol. 19, pp. 3–66). London: Hogarth Press. (Original work published 1923)

Freud, S. (1964). Splitting of the ego in the process of defense. In J. Strachey (Ed. & Trans.), *The standard edition of the complete psychological works of Sigmund Freud* (Vol. 23, pp. 273–278). London: Hogarth Press. (Original work published 1938)

Guntrip, H. (1971). *Psychoanalytic theory, therapy, and the self.* New York: Basic Books.

Guntrip, H. (1975). My experience of analysis with Fairbairn and Winnicott. *International Review of Psychoanalysis, 2,* 145–156.

Hartmann, H. (1964). Comments on the psychoanalytic theory of the ego. In H. Hartmann (Ed.), *Essays in ego psychology,* (pp. 113–141). New York: International University Press. (Original work published 1950)

Kernberg, O. (1976). *Object relations theory and clinical psychoanalysis.* New York: Jason Aronson.

Kernberg, O. (1977). The structural diagnosis of borderline personality. In P. Hartocollis (Ed.), *Borderline personality disorders* (pp. 87–122). New York: International University Press.

Kohut, H. (1971). *The analysis of the self.* New York: International University Press.

Kohut, H. (1977). *The restoration of the self.* New York: International University Press.

Mahler, M. (1968). *On human symbiosis and the vicissitudes of individuation.* New York: International University Press.

Modell, A. (1968). *Object love and reality.* New York: International University Press.

Sandler, J. (1981). Character traits and object relationships. *Psychoanalytic Quarterly, 50,* 694–708.

Volkan, V. (1976). *Primitive internalized object relations.* New York: International University Press.

Winnicott, D. (1955). The depressive position in normal emotional development. *British Journal of Medical Psychology, 28,* 89–100.

Wurmser, L. (1977). A defense of the use of metaphor in analytic theory. *Psychoanalytic Quarterly, 46,* 466–498.

9

Narcissistic Impulse

I have established the reasonable probability that in all human behavior, there is a transcendent operative motive that has the quality of a narcissistic impulse. I have noted that the narcissistic impulse occupies the chief position among motivational qualities and can supercede both the pleasure principle and the reality principle. I now consider the narcissistic impulse.

LIFE PRESERVATION

I have already reviewed those considerations that led me to conclude that there is a quality of motivation described as "an instinct for self-preservation" that constitutes a part of the general motivational quality described as the reality principle. This discussion also included the observation that the motivation to cling to life can be superceded by narcissistic interests, as in the case of committing suicide to avoid a shameful experience.

The notion of *self-preservation* is commonly understood to refer to the motivation to protect and maintain one's biological existence. However, my example demonstrates that this can be set aside in favor of *narcissistic self-interests*. It is intrinsically confusing to use the term *self* for both of these independent qualities. The confusion has been perpetuated by Freud's (1923/1961, p. 26) dictum that "the ego is first and foremost a body-ego." He was using "ego" in the sense of a "self-system."

It is important to make clear the distinction between one's biological existence and the experience of one's mental existence. The sense of biological existence is represented by the term *body-image*, whereas the sense of mental existence is represented by the term *self-image*. Then, using the terms of my hypothetical entities: the self-image regards its body-image as an object-image. One's body is experienced as an object by the self-image. The sense of self is independent of the sense of one's own body, even though that body is often regarded as a "most favored" object. Bearing these distinctions in mind, it becomes clear that people are motivated to preserve their biological existence and that this is best represented by the term *life preservation*. Considerations of life preservation are comprehended by the motivational quality of the reality principle.

SELF-PRESERVATION

I have noted that life preservation can be superceded by considerations having to do with the preservation of the sense of self, or self-interests. Those instances that indicate a narcissistic impulse were observed by Freud (1920/1955, p. 23) to supercede the pleasure and reality principles, but its implication was at odds with the assumption of original helplessness. Nonetheless, Freud (1936/1959, p. 66) later came to recognize that these cases were a demonstration of the power of narcissistic motivation.

My previous review of narcissistic clinical states, in which the pleasure and reality principles are observed to be superceded, showed that there appeared to be a commonality in the subjective experience of those states that was described as a "megalomanic" sense of self-regard. The term *megalomania* was used by Abraham (1908/1953a) to refer to an inference about the subjective experience of such persons. He inferred that they seemed to be primarily concerned and interested in themselves (Abraham, 1908/1953a, p. 72), that they regarded the world as something to control and to dominate (Abraham, 1924/1953b, pp. 429–430), and that they had an inflated opinion of themselves (Abraham, 1924/1953b, p. 456). Freud added the conclusions that megalomanic people seemed to believe in the omnipotence of their thoughts (Freud, 1914/1957, p. 75) and their sense of personal grandiosity (Freud, 1914/19 , p. 75), as well as a mastering view of the world (Freud, 1920/1955, p. 21).

The megalomanic attitude identifiable in these adult clinical cases was recognized as being similar to that found in early childhood (Abraham, 1908/1953a, p. 73). The same attitude was identifiable in normal adults, although in a "damped down" form (Freud, 1914/1957, p. 93). An examination of people's cultural and ethical ideals led to the conjecture that these ideals were sustained by narcissistic values and served to continue indirectly the childhood belief in the sense of one's self-perfection. It seemed that such a "primary narcissism" develops various forms as the person deals in life with the world (Freud, 1914/1957, p. 57). These forms appeared to be compromise formations between narcissistic interests and the pleasure and reality principles. These observations provide a foundation for the assertion that people are generally motivated to preserve a megalomanic, or narcissistic, sense of self.

NARCISSISTIC IMPULSE

There has been a broad base of observations over a period of years that has led many observers to conclude that all people have an attitude that may be described as megalomanic. People seem primarily to regard the world from a megalomanic point of view, and it is held that this is an accurate representation of their experience.

The term *megalomanic* seems to have been chosen by Abraham (1908/1953a) and Freud (1914/1957) for its synechdocal value. Cases of megalomanic psychosis exhibit the indicated quality in a marked and dramatic fashion, being the outstanding feature of that particular pattern of behavior. However, they came to recognize that the same quality appearing in psychosis in an exacerbated form also appears normally from childhood onward. Thus, Abraham and Freud increasingly referred to this quality with the term *narcissism*. This has more of a neutral implication as to psychopathology and is more suitable to refer to a normative and natural process.

Various patterns of behavior have been repeatedly identified as indicating a narcissistic attitude. Many observers have been impressed by certain properties of a narcissistic attitude, most notably by that of the belief in one's sense of omnipotence (Beiser, 1978; Dorpat, 1977; Fenichel, 1937/1954; Freud, 1914/1957, p. 98; Pumpian-Midlin, 1977; Reich, 1953; Schafer, 1976). The similar property of a sense of one's grandiosity has been the impression of many other observers (Abraham, 1924/1953b; Kernberg, 1975; Kohut, 1971, p. 34). The same property is indicated in the use of other terms such as the belief in hallucinatory wish fulfillment (Mahler, 1968, p. 229), the attainment of unmitigated gratification (Lample-de-Groot, 1962; Sobo, 1977, p. 163), the sense of perfection (Rothstein, 1980; Sobo, 1977), the conviction of an ability for mastery (Freud, 1920/1955, p. 16), the sense of personal autonomy (Gedo, 1936, p. 173), and the sense of one's uniqueness (Bergmann, 1980, p. 75). The same attitude is implied by the more objectivist terms of exhibitionistic and voyeuristic patterns (Kohut, 1977, p. 186) and self-centeredness (Gruber & Vanecke, 1978).

These patterns of behavior may be grouped together as various direct expressions of a narcissistic attitude. Other patterns of behavior appear to be manifestly contrary to the possession of such an attitude. These have been closely investigated, and patterns of their details have been observed that sustain the inference of the presence of a narcissistic attitude. This detection has been accomplished in overtly masochistic patterns (Lax, 1977, p. 293; Spiegel, 1978, p. 223), overt patterns of self-destruction (Kernberg, 1975, p. 125), and overt patterns of helplessness (Dorpat, 1977, p. 23). These modern findings extend Abraham's early observations that narcissistic attitudes are held by people who present delusions of persecution (Abraham, 1908/1953a, p. 75), delusions of inferiority (Abraham, 1924/1953b, p. 455), and in cases of melancholic psychosis (Abraham, 1924/1953b, p. 456). This led to his general conclusion that a narcissistic attitude may be found in both direct and indirect forms of expression (Abraham, 1924/1953b, p. 456).

Those patterns of behavior that have indicated to the observer that the individual possesses a marked "ego-ideal" appear to be an objectivist reference to the maintenance of a narcissistic attitude (Reich, 1953). Schafer (1976, p. 52) has recognized that the same narcissistic attitude is referred to by various terms: neurotic pride, egocentricity, inflated narcissism, manic defense, and infantile ego-ideal.

In recent years it has become fashionable to refer to a narcissistic attitude with the term *self-esteem* (Arlow, 1980, p. iii; Bandura, 1978, p. 349), which has the attitudinal properties of the sense of worthiness, pride, and competence (Brenner, 1979, p. 194). This demonstrates a movement in the field from the negative pathological associations of megalomania to the positive normative association of self-esteem in reference to a narcissistic attitude. Because both the negative and positive judgments in these cases are related to a criterion of mental health, it seems better to continue to use the more neutral term of narcissistic attitude, at least until such time as mental health has been adequately defined. At present, there is no theory of psychopathology that is generally accepted (Allman & Jaffe, 1978, p. 65).

NARCISSISTIC ATTITUDE

Many patterns of behavior indicate that an individual possesses a narcissistic attitude. This attitude has been detected in every stage of life and in every degree of mental health. It has also been noted that infants may be characterized generally as possessing an attitude remarkable for its narcissistic qualities (Peterfreund, 1978; Stechler & Kaplan, 1980). I posit that the narcissistic quality of infantile experience that is indicated by observation is an extension of a prior state of affairs that has only become apparent by later observation. Thus, I have confidence in the assertion that people are born with a narcissistic attitude.

In accord with the relativist position for the science of psychology, I assert that there is a narcissistic impulse. This impulse is possessed by all people and is a quality of motivation in all human behavior. It is one of the reasons why people do what they do. Because it may supercede both the pleasure and reality principles in motivation, it is the chief reason why people do what they do. It is expected that some aspects of the narcissistic impulse will be found invariably to be common among all members of the species. Other variations will be found as a commonality among social subgroups, and still other variations will be unique and distinctive for each individual. From the relativist position I state that people are born with a self-image that has the primary affect disposition of a narcissistic attitude.

REFERENCES

Abraham, K. (1953a). The psychosexual differences between hysteria and dementia praecox. In H. Hartmann (Ed.), *Selected papers* (pp. 64–79). New York: Basic Books. (Original work published 1908)

Abraham, K. (1953b). A short study of the development of the libido. In H. Hartmann (Ed.), *Selected papers* (pp. 418–501). New York: Basic Books. (Original work published 1924)

Allman, L., & Jaffe, D. (1978). *Abnormal psychology in the life cycle.* New York: Harper & Row.

Arlow, J. (1980). Object concept and object choice. *Psychoanalytic Quarterly, 49,* 109–133.

Bandura, A. (1978). The self-system in reciprocal determinism. *American Psychologist, 33,* 344–358.

Beiser, H. (1978). The problem of infantile omnipotence. *Annals of Psychoanalysis, 7,* 113–131.

Bergmann, M. (1980). On the intrapsychic function of falling in love. *Psychoanalytic Quarterly, 49,* 56–77.

Brenner, C. (1979). Depressive affect, anxiety, and psychic conflict in the phallic-oedipal phase. *Psychoanalytic Quarterly, 48,* 177–197.

Dorpat, T. (1977). Depressive affect. *Psychoanalytic Study of the Child, 32,* 3–27.

Fenichel, O. (1954). Early stages of ego development. In H. Fenichel (Ed.), *Collected papers, second series* (pp. 25–48). New York: Norton. (Original work published 1937)

Freud, S. (1955). Beyond the pleasure principle. In J. Strachey (Ed. & Trans.), *The standard edition of the complete psychological works of Sigmund Freud* (Vol. 18, pp. 1–64). London: Hogarth Press. (Original work published 1920)

Freud, S. (1958). On narcissism: An introduction. In J. Strachey (Ed. & Trans.), *The standard edition of the complete psychological works of Sigmund Freud* (Vol. 14, pp. 67–102). London: Hogarth Press. (Original work published 1914)

Freud, S. (1959). The problem of anxiety. In J. Strachey (Ed. & Trans.), *The standard edition of the complete psychological works of Sigmund Freud* (Vol. 20, pp. 77–175). London: Hogarth Press. (Original work published 1936)

Freud, S. (1961). The ego and the id. In J. Strachey (Ed. & Trans.), *The standard edition of the complete psychological works of Sigmund Freud* (Vol. 19, pp. 3–66). London: Hogarth Press. (Original work published 1923)

Gedo, J. (1936). *Beyond interpretation.* New York: International University Press.

Gruber, H., & Vanecke, J. (Eds.). (1978). *The essential Piaget.* New York: Basic Books.

Kernberg, O. (1975). *Borderline conditions and pathological narcissism.* New York: Jason Aronson.

Kohut, H. (1971). *The analysis of the self.* New York: International University Press.

Kohut, H. (1977). *The restoration of the self.* New York: International University Press.

Lample-de-Groot, J. (1962). Ego ideal and superego. *Psychoanalytic Study of the Child, 17,* 94–106.

Lax, R. (1977). The role of internalization in the development of certain aspects of female masochism. *International Journal of Psychoanalysis, 58,* 289–300.

Mahler, M. (1968). *On human symbiosis and the vicissitudes of individuation*. New York: International University Press.

Peterfreund, E. (1978). Some critical comments on the psychoanalytic conceptions of infancy. *International Journal of Psychoanalysis, 59*, 427–441.

Pumpian-Midlin, E. (1977). Vicissitudes of infantile omnipotence. In I. Marcus (Ed.), *Currents in psychoanalysis* (pp. 231–241). New York: International University Press.

Reich, A. (1953). Narcissistic object choice in women. *Journal of the American Psychoanalytic Association, 1*, 22–44.

Rothstein, A. (1980). *The narcissistic pursuit of perfection*. New York: International University Press.

Schafer, R. (1976). *A new language for psychoanalysis*. New Haven, CT: Yale University Press.

Sobo, S. (1977). Narcissism is a function of culture. *Psychoanalytic Study of the Child, 32*, 155–172.

Spiegel, L. (1978). Moral Masochism. *Psychoanalytic Quarterly, 47*, 209–236.

Stechler, G., & Kaplan, S. (1980). The development of self. *Psychoanalytic Study of the Child, 35*, 85–105.

10

Narcissistic Attitude

I have presented the proposition that all human beings are born with the experience of a sense of self and that this self-image is characterized by a narcissistic impulse and attitude. This proposition represents a conclusion drawn from and sustained by observations of children and adults in states of both apparent mental health and pathology. The proposition may be additionally supported by observations that humans' closest relations, the primates, also have a sense of self. That the narcissistic impulse is a transcendent causal power common to the human species implies a general biological distribution and disposition. The identification of a similar causal power in a related species would suggest that differences between those species would be better attributed to something other than the presence or absence of a biological capacity to experience the world from a narcissistic attitude, or in the possession of a sense of self.

By teaching gorillas and chimpanzees American Sign Language (AMESLAN), Patterson (1978) had access to the report of their subjective experience. They learned a vocabulary of signs designating objects, types of activities, past and present, and various emotional moods (Patterson, 1978, p. 438). The primates described new objects by combining signs and used other combinations to designate conceptual notions (Patterson, 1978, p. 461). The patterns of usage were indicative of an understanding of past and present tense, a sense of humor, empathy, and personal preferences (Patterson, 1978, p. 438). They appeared to learn when taught right and wrong and showed touchiness about accepting blame, being argumentative, acting insulted, and lying (Patterson, 1978, p. 438). They also expressed a sense of self-esteem (Patterson, 1978, p. 465) and conversed both with humans and among themselves (Patterson, 1978, p. 451).

Davis (1978) studied the interchanges of sound signals within various species (birds, whales, etc.) and discovered patterns that were individualistic. These were indicative of psychological functioning, but the absence of a medium of communication was a barrier to speculation as to content. She appreciated the unique opportunity in the use of AMESLAN to learn about the individualistic experience of primates. This was carried forward by Goldikas (1980), who taught sign language to orangutans and arrived at findings similar to those of Patterson (1978). Other similar findings have been reported by the Yerkes Primate Research Center (Gould, 1978), documenting that chimps have human mental faculties with complex and sophisticated usage. These also included the expression of mood, desire, and lying, all of which demonstrate self-awareness.

A general review of ethnological studies of animals led Jacobson (1983) to conclude that the epigenetic unfolding of developmental patterns is homologous between humans and animals.

Because recent studies such as these have detected the presence in animals of mental faculties, it is now consistent with experience to propose that among those faculties is a sense of self. In addition, the observation of pride, self-esteem, insult, and lying are indicative that the sense of self among primates is characterizable as narcissistic.

In summary, then, people are born with a capacity to experience that takes place in the form of a sense of self and is constructed as a self-image coordinated with an object-image. The chief interests of the self in regarding objects are identified by the terms *pleasure principle*, *reality principle*, and *narcissism*. Thus, a person's experience of the world of objects is a compound of these simultaneous interests, and any individualistic behavior may be understood as a compromise formation, or vector outcome.

PRIMARY AND SECONDARY PROCESS

Observation of people over their course from infancy through adulthood has shown several distinctions in patterns of behavior. Those patterns that are indicative of psychological functioning have been distinguished as to mode by the terms *primary process* versus *secondary process* and the *pleasure principle* versus the *reality principle*.

Freud (1900/1953) originated the term *primary process* to refer to a mode of thinking that he distinguished from what is considered normal for adults. He observed "condensation" (Freud, 1900/1953, p. 595), in which the intensity of a train of thought is compressed in a sensory manner, as in ancient drawings of kings of extraordinary size. He observed the formation of "collective figures" (Freud, 1900/1953, p. 596), in which the features of several individuals are condensed into one, as in the mythological figure of a griffin. He observed the transfer of intensity to other ideas that were related only in verbal similarity (Freud, 1900/1953, p. 596), as is resorted to in constructing puns. He observed the toleration of mutually contradictory thoughts and "mobility of cathexis" (Freud, 1900/1953, p. 597) in which personal emotionality predominates over rational thought processes. He reported that the primary process mode of thinking was central in the production of neurotic symptoms (Freud, 1900/1953, p. 597) and dreams. Because he viewed this mode as being chronologically prior to the reasonable one, he designated it as "primary" (Freud, 1900/1953, p. 603). The observation of two different modes of thinking, rational and irrational, was the foundation for the inference that this was a reflection of the existence of two different mental faculties. The second one, showing a concern for "reality," appeared only during the course of development and seemed to gain increasingly in importance, especially in that function termed the *testing of reality*.

However, the inference of different faculties as an accounting for these observations was seriously questioned. In a study of artistic activity, Ehrenzweig (1953) reported that the same common faculties were being organized in different modes. Arlow (1958) noted that id, ego, and superego aspects were found in both sets of observations. Holt (1967) found that the patterns called primary process were not random but reflected a specific system. Noy (1969) stated that both processes used the same faculties that he saw as differing in content. The difference in context was explored by McLaughlin (1978) in relation to cerebral hemispheres. Noy's (1979) reviews of such studies concluded that these patterns used the same mental faculties (Noy, 1979, p. 169) and showed equal structure and development (Noy, 1979, p. 177). Because the prior theory of special faculties proved untenable, he noted that the observation of patterns termed *primary process* lacked an accounting (Noy, 1979, p. 170). It seemed to him that there was a viable distinction in that the secondary process patterns could be characterized as "reality-oriented" and primary process patterns as "self-centered" (Noy, 1979, p. 172).

Within the relativist theory of psychology one can appreciate the centrality of the narcissistic impulse and its frequent predomination over both the pleasure and reality principles. From that point of view, it becomes apparent that the patterns referred to as expressions of a special primary process are better attributed to the narcissistic attitude. Thus, one understands that one is observing a person pursuing narcissistic interests. Manifestations of a special "process" are not being observed, as would be a conclusion from an objectivist viewpoint. Similarly, one is not observing secondary process but a person pursuing the reality principle.

One cannot hold the assumption that primary process is the first mode of infantile development (McLaughlin, 1978, p. 263) because primary process cannot be held to be real. The infant is motivated primarily by narcissistic impulse, even though the pleasure and reality principles may be effective in some form according to the child's stage of development.

Primary process patterns were characterized by Noy (1969) as being "infantile and magical" attempts to deal with an expanding self, which explains an infant's self-centeredness (Noy, 1969, p. 176). However, his viewpoint contains the assumption of initial helplessness, which I have stated is untenable. The infantile and magical characteristics are the infant's attempts to express and maintain a narcissistic attitude.

The characteristic of self-centeredness is often noted in the observation of behavior motivated primarily by narcissism. I have assumed that everyone is born with a narcissistic attitude. Therefore, I view self-centeredness as an inevitable characteristic of human life. As a necessary and common characteristic of all people, it cannot per se serve as a distinction among them. It may be supposed that the term *self-centered* arises from the viewer's judgment that the person is violating considerations of the reality principle. With the assumption that it is in the person's self-interest to accord with "reality," it then appears that the person is acting against self-interest. However, a person's self-interests include, besides the reality principle, the pleasure principle and narcissism. Thus, to notice that a person's behavior violates reality should lead to the observation that either pleasure or narcissistic interests are predominant. To notice what "is not" is less good than noticing what "is."

Those instances of unrealistic thinking that had been taken as indicative of a special faculty can now be seen as the exercise of usual mental faculties with the preponderant motivations of the pleasure principle and narcissism. Similarly, instances of realistic thinking can be seen as the exercise of usual mental faculties with the preponderant motivation of the reality principle.

PLEASURE PRINCIPLE AND REALITY PRINCIPLE

Distinction in the mode of psychological function has been noted between infancy and adulthood as to the predominance of the pleasure principle in childhood and the predominance of the reality principle in adults. Relativist psychologists regard this understanding as accurate, insofar as it goes. However, because this does not take into account an essential factor, it is misleading as to its suggestion of reality. The narcissistic impulse, as psychologists have come to learn about it through studies of the narcissistic attitude, is an essential dimension of human experience. Thus, I correct that initial statement and suggest that an infant's behavior is mainly determined by pleasure and narcissistic interests and that the course of development shows the increasing importance of reality interests.

REFERENCES

Arlow, J. (1958). Report of panel: The psychoanalytic theory of thinking. *Journal of the American Psychoanalytic Association, 6,* 143–153.
Davis, F. (1978). *Eloquent animals.* New York: McCann & Geoghegan.
Ehrenzweig, A. (1953). *The Psycho-analysis of artistic vision and hearing.* London: Routledge & Kegan Paul.
Freud, S. (1953). The interpretation of dreams (Pt. 2). In J. Strachey (Ed. & Trans.), *The standard edition of the complete psychological works of Sigmund Freud* (Vol. 5, pp. 339–627). London: Hogarth Press. (Original work published 1900)
Goldikas, B. (1980, June). Living with the great orange apes. *National Geographic,* pp. 830–853.
Gould, S. (1978). *Ever since Darwin.* New York: Norton.
Holt, R. (1967). The development of the primary process: A structural view. In R. Holt (Ed.), *Motives and thought* (pp. 345–383). New York: International University Press.
Jacobson, J. (1983). The structural theory and the representational world. *Psychoanalytic Quarterly, 52,* 514–563.
McLaughlin, J. (1978). Primary and secondary process in the context of cerebral hemisphere specialization. *Psychoanalytic Quarterly, 47,* 237–266.
Noy, P. (1969). A revision of the psychoanalytic theory of the primary process. *International Journal of Psychoanalysis, 50,* 155–178.
Noy, P. (1979). The psychoanalytic theory of cognitive development. *Psychoanalytic Study of the Child, 34,* 169–216.
Patterson, F. (1978, October). Conversations with a gorilla. *National Geographic,* pp. 438–465.

11

Development

NARCISSISTIC IMPULSE

In studying the words and behavior of young children, Freud (1914/1957) believed it incontestable that they possessed a primary and normal narcissistic attitude. There was abundant evidence that they believed in the power of their thoughts and other consequences of the premise of a grandiose notion of self (Freud, 1914/1957, p. 75). They behaved with an "unshakable confidence in the possibility of controlling the world" (Freud, 1913/1955, p. 89). Because I am unhindered by Freud's assumption of infantile helplessness, I hold that the narcissistic description of childhood experience is equally true for infantile experience. I hold that narcissism is primary both in temporality, as being an original condition, and in importance, as being the predominant motivational factor.

There is general agreement that infantile behavior is predominated by the pleasure principle, especially in the exercise of sensual experience (Freud, 1905/1960) in the use of one's own body (Freud, 1905/1960, p. 73). A close examination of such autoerotic behavior (e.g., in the sensual sucking of the thumb) shows that this conduct makes the child independent of the external world in satisfying his or her wish for indulgence (Freud, 1905/1960, p. 48). Thus, the child's pursuit of the pleasure principle is directed by narcissistic considerations. The apparently blissful consequences of autoerotic activity bespeak the fully satisfactory result of doing what one wants, when one wants it, and in just the way one wants it. The narcissistic attitude has been described as "I want what I want when I want it." I would add, "and the way I want it."

GRANDIOSITY

This narcissistic attitude is called "megalomania" with opprobrium and "self-esteem" with approbation. In the infant this attitude is not limited by considerations of illness or death, nor by the laws of society that restrict one's will or enjoyment. An adult may well envy the position of "His Majesty the Baby" (Freud, 1914/1957, p. 91). The study of normal adults reveals that they continue to harbor a narcissistic attitude, although in a "damped down" form (Freud, 1914/1957, p. 93). Thus, one important dimension in understanding the psychological development of human experience may be described as the "taming" of the sense of grandiosity. This may also be described as the development of the increasing importance of the reality principle.

The normal course of the psychological development of human experience is toward the increasing importance of the reality principle as a motivational factor in the performance of individualistic activity. From the point of view of reality, the narcissistic attitude appears grandiose, and this may be used as a general description of narcissism. Thus, people are born with a grandiose self-image that is destined to be tamed.

TAMING OF GRANDIOSITY

Fetal Experience

I have previously considered observations of individualistic activity during the intrauterine state and that this evidences a psychological life at this time. I have shown that psychological experience is composed of pleasure, reality, and narcissistic motivations. An effective form with which to express conjectures as to individual experience is by means of self- and object-images. With these conceptual tools, I now consider intrauterine experience.

I have noted Freud's (1914/1957) opinion that there can be no initial experience of grandiosity because, even with the best maternal care, there is no absence of frustration. However, Ferenczi (1913/1950, p. 213) proposed that the realities of life in the womb may well provide support for an experience of omnipotence because all needs are automatically gratified. One may agree that because those needs for life support are automatically gratified, no experience of frustration can arise in that setting. However, this is a biologically delimited point of view that assumes that the fetus is a "tabula rasa" on which the environment writes. The observation of intrauterine individualistic patterns of activity is a frequent evidence of psychological functioning. Ferenczi (1913/1950, p. 219) observed that "it would be foolish to believe that the mind begins to function only at the moment of birth." It is my contention that the sense of grandiosity is innate and not merely a conclusion from the child's observation. Furthermore, the fetus experiences the facts of its intrauterine environment from a narcissistic point of view.

When observing an individualistic intrauterine activity, one understands that the infant is performing a directed activity. The motivation for this is probably in accord with the pleasure principle: perhaps the exercise of what is regarded as sensually pleasurable, or perhaps the effort to relieve what is regarded as sensually unpleasurable.

My viewpoint is that individualistic activity is evidence for the assumption of a mental faculty for valuing. The perception of variation is not itself a valuing (Bandura, 1978, p. 349). Thus, to notice that two objects are not identical does not imply a consideration as to the nature of that difference. Two trees may be perceived as different but without the additional valuation that they differ according to color.

The recognition of the importance of this distinction led Bandura (1978, p. 349) to propose that when people perform a valuation according to some standard, they do so in terms of high regard, neutrality, or devaluation. I prefer to refer to this notion with an analogy to chemical valences. Therefore, people may value something as plus, zero, or minus. My preference for this form is not to gain an aura of arithmetic certainty because I use the form in the sense of a nonparametric statistical device. This implies the observation of differences as to category rather than quantity. Thus, the valences would represent three different patterns of valuing activity: "I like it," "I don't care," and "I dislike it." My preference to use mathematical symbols is in the effort to make clear the essential incompleteness of such observations, in that the standard used in the valuation is omitted. To represent what is really happening, it is insufficient to specify the valence without specifying the standard being used. That would be like reporting an adjective without its corresponding noun: "I like it." Although such reporting may be observed frequently, one should recognize that information is being presented in a vague form, possibly deliberately.

With the conceptual tool of valencing, Bandura (1978, p. 351) gave his attention to the range of what he termed the "self-regulation of behavior"; I prefer to use "patterns of individualistic behavior." It was his opinion that in all such instances, the person was actively processing perceptual information by valencing according to the standards of his or her own welfare and self-esteem. I prefer the relativist understanding that people valence all perceptual data according to the pleasure principle, the reality principle, and narcissism.

Returning to my consideration of the nature of intrauterine experience, the observation of individualistic activity may be taken as an indication of the consequence of valuing. It reflects that either a plus or minus judgment has been made by the child according to the three major motivations of human experience. A study of the details of a particular pattern of individualistic activity may provide a basis for reasonable speculation as to its particular motivation. At the same time, an experience of "I don't care particularly" may exist when observation fails to detect individualistic mental activity. Of course, I recognize the additional possibility that caring activities may be subject to refraining.

Neonate Experience

Although it is a fact that life support is automatically maintained in the intrauterine environment, this observation does not address the issue of the fetus' experience of that fact. Observations of the fetus in order to study the role of grandiosity in its experience is currently limited. Observation of the newborn is more feasible, and findings during that phase may serve as a foundation for making inferences as to fetal experience.

Many observers have identified certain patterns of behavior of newborns that give the unequivocal impression that they are displeased with their environment. It has been noted that their displeasure appears to be soothed by particular nursing activities. I propose that a study of the details of such soothing activities provides a basis for making reasonable inferences as to what experience of the infant is being soothed.

Feeding

Among the common nursing activities instituted in the attempt to soothe the neonate's state of distress is the offer to feed it by the breast or bottle. This often seems to produce the desired effect. The conclusion that this proves that the infant was hungry, in the sense of a physiologically needful state, is by no means as certain as is often assumed. For example, it has long been demonstrated (Gesell & Ilg, 1937) that a reflexive pattern of sucking activity is activated by touching the infant's cheek. The accumulation of liquid in the mouth will lead to reflexive swallowing. Therefore, the observer will see the child drinking even in the ab-

96 THE SCIENCE OF PSYCHOTHERAPY

sence of a hungry state. The observation of soothing subsequent to feeding may indicate the easement of a hungry state. This is one of several possibilities.

It has long been noted that the activity of sucking on the bottle or the breast involves an experience independent of any need for nourishment. The activity of sucking often takes place in the context of sensual gratification (Freud, 1905/1960, pp. 45–46) and the pleasure principle aspect of human motivation. Sucking is often undertaken by the infant with any body part within reach of the mouth and results in an evident experience of considerable satisfaction and relaxation. Therefore, it is also possible that the observation of soothing subsequent to feeding may indicate the easement of pleasure principle motivation.

The study of infants appearing soothed by feeding will show a general commonality among the patterns of their feeding behaviors. At the same time, one may note individual variations as to timing, manner, intensity, and associated activities. The personal variations in the performance of such common infantile patterns has been noted as being remarkably indicative of the individuality of newborns (Terhune, 1979, p. 371). Therefore, not all of the details of feeding patterns may be ascribed to the pleasure principle or to reflexive actions. Some individuality is indicative of the narcissistic motivation: "I want what I want when I want it, and in the way I want it." It seems reasonable to hold that feeding is successful in soothing when the infant experiences gratification of both pleasure and narcissistic motivations.

Nonfeeding

The state of displeasure evidenced by infants appears also to be soothed by certain nonfeeding nursing activities (Ferenczi, 1913/1950, p. 221). Frequent among these are providing warm coverings to simulate the intrauterine body temperature, rocking to simulate the pregnant mother's movements, and crooning to simulate heart-beat sounds and the muffled noises of the environment.

These observations have provided the basis for the inference that the infant's displeasure indicates its experience of preference for the environment of the womb. This seems barely credible because it assumes that perceptual data are being valenced by the neonate in relation to the reality principle with an assessment of the environment. One may readily grant the collateral assumption that the neonate has the operative mental faculties to perceive the environment, as demonstrated by many studies (e.g., Brazelton & Als, 1979, p. 352). However, the primary assumption is contrary to the understanding that reality considerations are at their weakest at birth and that it requires considerable maturation and efforts of education until reality begins to play an important role in the conduct of a child.

The proposition that the neonate is valencing perceptual data in relation to the pleasure principle is more credible because there are many studies supporting the inference that fetal patterns of behavior are in accord with the pleasure principle. For example, as early as the 31st intrauterine week, the fetus shows a regular preference for its mother's voice among the range of ambient sounds (Terhune, 1979, p. 374). It is credible that the neonate experiences some sensual pleasure on perceiving an increase in skin warmth, the kinesthetic consequence of rocking, and hearing cooing sounds. However, there are two objections to the proposition that pleasure motivation is the chief determinant in such "soothed" patterns. When unscrupulous nurses put crying children to sleep by stroking their genitalia (Freud, 1905/1960, p. 46), the children may be observed to perform active masturbatory patterns. The soothed patterns in question do not show sexual excitation. Instead, one observes a quieting pattern, and this is frequent. Thus, there is no evidence that the child is pursuing a sensation that is positively valenced as to pleasure when soothed patterns are observed.

The possibility that the child is pursuing the easement of sensations that are negatively valenced as to pleasure is credible. However, patterns of distress and soothing are not particularly related to the usual range of ambient temperature. Parents have observed, sometimes to their exasperation, that warmth, rocking, and crooning are unreliably effective in producing soothing. Newborns possess sufficient faculties to perceive the sensory differences consequent to these nursing activities (Brazelton & Als, 1979, p. 351), which they amply demonstrate in their calmer states. For example, there is the sophisticated use of these faculties in newborns' imitation of facial and manual gestures (Meltzoff & Moore, 1977, p. 77) and in synchronizing their movements to adult speech (Condon & Sander, 1974, p. 100). What is being observed in cases in which usually soothing activities are ineffective is a condition in which infants are rejecting sensory stimuli that they usually valence positively. There is considerable experimental evidence of newborns' capacity to resist the intrusion of negatively valenced stimuli, including their ability to "turn off" the intrusion of positively valenced stimuli (Brazelton & Als, 1979, pp. 355–359).

The persistence of a state of upset after ruling out negatively valenced sensory stimuli (such as loud noises and a sticking pin), and the infant's persistence in the rejection of positively valenced stimuli (such as warmth, rocking, and crooning), is indicative of narcissistic disturbance.

From the relativist point of view, the observation of a neonate in a state of upset is understood as the child's experience of disturbance according to either, or both, the pleasure principle and narcissism.

It has been remarked that neonates' first sleep (subsequent to their displeasure on being brought into a new environment) shows their satisfaction with efforts to simulate a restoration of the womb environment (Ferenczi, 1913/1950, p. 227). I have shown that newborns are quite capable of distinguishing environments according to their sensory dissimilarity. Still, newborns appear quieted. One can now understand that infants' experience of satisfaction is in the restoration of their sense of grandiosity. The sensory intrusions of being born seem less of an occasion of the newborns' upset than their experience of insult to their sense of grandiosity.

The term *insult* is used in the medical sense of a general reference to any environmental condition that disturbs the normal state. The term is also appropriate psychologically as a general reference to any environmental condition that is experienced as disturbing to the normal sense of grandiosity, the same as is meant in the common expression "to feel insulted."

CHILDHOOD EXPERIENCE

My inquiry into the nature of fetal and neonate experience has led to the understanding that individualistic behaviors during these phases are indicative of the primary role of pleasure principle and narcissistic motivations. The role of the reality principle was appreciated in the observation of children's many patterns of adaptation in which self-regulation of behavior was coordinated with object-images of their environment.

By the age of 4–6 weeks, infants show a quantum difference in their patterns adaptive to reality, especially in social activities. There is an increased sophistication in their repertoire of facial expressions and range of vocalizations, gestures, and postures, as well as the maintenance of what is often described as a "brightly alert set" toward the mother (Brazelton & Als, 1979, pp. 361–365). This change has been interpreted as evidence of the attainment of a new state of sensorimotor development (Resch, 1979, p. 427) and the arrival of a biological foundation for the "hatching out" of a sense of individuality (Mahler, 1974, p. 92).

This "hatching" interpretation is based on the assumption that the children were previously in a "vegetative state" in which their psychological state is taken to be an extension of their "absolute biological dependence" on their mother (Mahler, 1974, pp. 92–93). However, I have several times reviewed evidence showing that this assumption is erroneous. All of the faculties indicated by acting in a brightly alert manner have been demonstrated as operative in the newborn. The brightening is not evidence for the functioning of new faculties, but is evidence for a change in motivation in the use of already existing faculties.

The brightening is an indication that the reality principle is playing a significantly greater role in the motivation of children to regulate their behavior individualistically. Although children have been observed to have done the same sort of things previously, they may now be observed more often and for longer periods of time.

I agree with Mahler (1974) as to the importance of mothering activities to bring about this quantum change in the child's motivation. However, my understanding is that to the extent that the mothering is experienced by the child as positively valenced according with pleasure and narcissism, the child positively valences the mother-image and has an increasing motivation to care about that image. To the extent that mothering is satisfying to the child's pleasure and narcissistic interests, it seems reasonable to assume that this provides a basis for the child's development of a socialization aspect of reality adaptations.

At the same time, I wish to recognize the fact that mothering is not an absolute necessity in the development of the child's social motivations nor in the child's maintenance of a state of mental health. Depending on how it is carried out, mothering may facilitate or hamper the child's development of social motivation.

I conceive that the motive to adapt to the people in one's environment is only one aspect of environmental adaptation. Other object-images of the environment will be valenced according to pleasure and narcissism and provide a foundation for the development of increasing interest in reality, both in attraction and aversion. Although there is evidence that infants show a preference for human objects (Brazelton & Als, 1979, p. 356; Mahler & McDevitt, 1982; Terhune, 1979, p. 375), non-human object-images are also important to children.

THE MOTHER-IMAGE

There is to any observer an obvious importance of mothering activities for the physical well-being of a child. However, the child's experience of these activities is quite a different matter. All too often, even in the professional literature, there is the erroneous assumption that the child's mother-image must reflect this state of physical dependency and loom as an inflated figure possessed of omnipotence rather than a merely most favored object. Because this erroneous notion seems so entrenched, it appears advisable to present more evidence in the attempt to correct this belief.

Winnicott (1953) drew attention to the regular appearance in childhood of patterns of behavior indicating that children regarded particular objects as being more important to them than their mothers. Bowlby (1969) pointed out that such "transitional objects," such as an attachment to a favorite blanket, serve the child more than adequately compared with the mother's actual presence. In studying the tactile dimension of these patterns, Hong (1978) was able to demonstrate that they were related to other object-images of the environment and not to the mother-image. The importance to the child of environmental object-images other than the mother-image was recognized as a process whose importance was observed to continue regularly into adolescence (Downey, 1978) and was perceptible in his or her patterns involving living space, clothing, and artistic media.

From the relativist point of view, such "transitional phenomena" are regarded as indicating the child's valencing positively an object-image primarily according to narcissistic interest. The child treats the object in a manner to maintain its sense of grandiosity, regardless of considerations of pleasure or reality.

GOOD-BAD

I have shown how children's individualistic activities may be understood as self-generated, primarily motivated by pleasure and narcissism. I have also shown the development of children's reality motivation, primarily in their adaptations in dealing with people. The increasing importance of the social aspect of reality is exemplified in the observation that infants in a state of upset will, on hearing their mother's voice, quiet themselves (Terhune, 1979, p. 380). Thus, social considerations now appear important enough to infants to refrain from an activity that was motivated by pleasure and narcissism. Children begin to "live" a bit less in their private world and a bit more in the social world (Lichtenberg, 1975, p. 401).

That observation does not constitute evidence for a special "social power" inherent in the mother. I have discussed how the mother-image has become increasingly valued in accord with pleasure and narcissistic considerations. Therefore, this observation is an example of children's learning that among the universe of objects, there are those that are valuable for pleasure and narcissistic gratification. Children learn that there are new alternatives in achieving pleasure and narcissistic gratification.

Children value certain object-images in achieving pleasure and narcissistic gratification, especially the mother-image, as a consequence of mothering activities that have this effect. The "specially favored" view of the mother-image is based on its appearance as an ally in the self-motivations of indulging in sensual gratification and the sense of grandiosity. It seems that children have learned to appreciate this particular object for its value in pursuing self-centered interests.

When infants are experiencing pleasure and narcissistic gratification, they regard the mother-image as valuable. One may observe this state when children are active participants in playing with their mother. When infants are satisfied in their pleasure and narcissistic motivation, they no longer regard the mother as valuable. One may observe this experiential state when infants go to sleep with a blissful expression in the middle of the mother's play. A fair summary of the infants' attitude may be, "You have value for me only when I want you." This may be described as a positive valencing of the mother followed by a zero valencing.

Although one may regard this infantile attitude as selfish, one should also recognize that this is sufficient reason for children to moderate their behavior (e.g., in quieting on hearing the mother's voice). Therefore, this is an instance of self-regulation for social considerations, even though social consideration is tangential. This constitutes a small but significant degree of social influence, and one may observe its exercise in every mother who coos, "I'm coming, darling." She sends her voice ahead as an initial ministration.

It is from such humble beginnings that the doctrines of a culture come to play an increasingly important role in children's adaptation to their culture (Fine, 1975, p. 147). The ethics, standards, customs, and characteristics of a society may be observed as they are reflected in the personal morals of individuals raised in that society (Beres, 1965, p. 4). Of course, infants' initial experience with the standards of their culture is with their reflection in their parents' patterns of conduct, their personal morality.

The mother's morality is defined by her sense of how a good mother should behave, what is "good" and "bad" according to that standard. The current ethical standards of a mother's society are further shaped by the mother's personal experiences to form her personal moral standard. It is this personal morality with which the child first comes into contact. Therefore, within the child's small society, "good" and "bad" refer to what that particular mother approves or rebukes, supports or opposes.

Within the world of infants' experience, they learn that certain of their behaviors are encouraged and others are impeded. I choose to represent these experiences by the terms *good* and *bad* in order to emphasize the standards of a particular mother. Within any local society, some considerable commonality will be found among the moral standards of its individuals, together with individual variations. Thus, children's sense of what is good and bad will be similar to the ethics of their society but more precisely determined by the peculiarities of their mother's personal morality.

Good–bad emphasizes the familial origins of the development of social motivations in the self-regulation of behavior from the point of view of the experience of the child. At the same time, this understanding provides a foundation for viewing those psychological disorders characterized as being troubled in this specific dimension (Hartocollis, 1977, p. 506; Kernberg, 1975, p. 49).

It can now be understood that infants conduct their individualistic behaviors with pleasure and narcissistic motivations. I refer to those infants as children when they moderate those patterns for social considerations. This is initiated within the context of their mother's morality. To the extent that children come into contact with the personal morality of other human objects that they have valued, the children's sense of good–bad will be extended.

The standard psychoanalytic understanding of this development in children's motivation in performing individualistic behavior is that there is an initial governance by the pleasure principle that comes under the sway of the reality principle.

Relativist psychology holds that children are initially motivated by the pleasure principle and narcissism and become increasingly swayed by social considerations to modify their conduct.

Normal human children, in the course of development, can be observed to make social judgments and to refrain on that account from doing what they would otherwise have done. Children can anticipate social reward and punishment in the experiential form of the sense of being good or bad. There is general psychoanalytic agreement that these patterns are indicative of children's possession of a superego (Tyson & Tyson, 1984, p. 78), which implies a special mental faculty.

Relativist psychology holds that these patterns do not evidence a special faculty but represent a change in motivation in the use of existing faculties. The patterns sustain the inference that children have come to moderate their pleasure and narcissistic motivations for social reasons in accord with their sense of good and bad.

One may see the interplay of these motivations in those patterns of behavior called temper tantrums. They appear so regularly between the ages of 2 and 7 that they are regarded as normative (Isaacs, 1948, p. 129). They appear in situations in which children are frustrated in pleasure or experience a narcissistic insult, although it is suspected that this insult is the chief factor. Studies have reported that their experience during tantrums includes the sense of being persecuted and the anticipation of the loss of benefits (Isaacs, 1948, p. 130). Such children are experiencing a conflict between narcissistic and social motivations. They wish to refrain from acting narcissistically in order to obtain social benefits and, in other situations, have shown the capacity to do so. In the tantrum situation, children appear to be suffering significantly more hurt of narcissistic insult and the consequent determination to withdraw from the source of that hurt. They feel the necessity to protect their injured grandiosity but, at the same time, they do not wish to give up social benefits. A restraint of narcissism accompanied by the enjoyment of social benefit is experienced as good. The converse explains why children feel bad during tantrums. The banging of one's self that is often observed in the pattern called tantrums is seen as an attempt by the child to struggle against acting narcissistically. In these cases, narcissistic motivation has been exacerbated by the experience of insult and is no longer manageable by usual means.

I may summarize the understanding of how children come to develop the motivation to adapt themselves to social reality. They are presented with a version of the ethical standard of their local society in the personal moral patterns of their mother-image. They come to value the mother as a provider of pleasure and narcissistic gratification and are thereby motivated to attempt to conform to her preferences and repugnances as modes of conduct. The children's experience of social reality is in terms of good–bad. They valence their own forms of conduct according to the social standard of their mother: as positive-good, negative-bad, or zero-amoral.

NARCISSISTIC MODULATION

Because of the consequence of social reality, children become motivated to alter their conduct. These new forms of behavior may appear to the observer as indicative of a tempering of the children's grandiose attitude to the formation of a more realistic attitude (Frankel & Sherick, 1977, p. 279).

However, it has long been noted that a grandiose attitude continues throughout adulthood, but in indirect forms, such as indicated by the terms *ego-ideal* and *ideals* of family, class, and nation (Freud, 1930/1961, p. 95). The persistence of an underlying sense of grandiosity is also indicated by beliefs in magic and the attribution of omnipotence to gods (Freud, 1913/1955, p. 88), as well as the popularity of an exclusive marital relationship (Kernberg, 1980, p. 81) that is "forsaking all others."

These observations support the contention that the original grandiose attitude is neither relinquished nor tempered. Thus, it is more credible to assume that children might have tempered their overt behavior but not their covert attitude. From social considerations, the grandiose attitude has gone "underground."

This understanding appears to account very well for the general clinical observation that "however sublimated, the basic drives remain subject to regression" (Beres, 1980, p. 21). In this usage, the term *regression* refers to the reappearance of primitive forms of behavior that are taken to be characteristic of an elementary stage in the development of a faculty. However, studies have shown that the development of faculties is accurately described as continuous and additive and that apparent "reversals" and "regressions" are indicative of changes in motivation to use those faculties (Bower, 1976). Therefore, however tempered by considerations of social reality, the individual remains capable of acting in an untempered manner.

These new tempered forms of behavior may be understood as compromises children have fashioned between their previously untempered expressions of grandiosity and those expressions either encouraged or opposed by social reality. The new sets of patterns of behavior may give an observer the impression that children have changed their character. They appear to have given up their grandiose self-conception and now control their behavior in consideration of the rights and wrongs established by the mother's morality (Frankel & Sherick, 1977, p. 267). This may be observed when children toddle toward an attractive object, stop, wave their hand negatively, and say, "no, no, don't touch."

SOCIAL SELF-IMAGE

The new patterns of behavior are distinguishable from previous ones by the contribution of social motivational power to children's experience. The difference is not attributable to the perception of a human object nor to the valuing of that object because both of these may be demonstrated in neonates. The significant difference in children's experience is the sense of good–bad and right–wrong as an additional motive for behavior.

The hypothetical entities of relativist psychology represent this change as children's construction of a socialized self-image. *Infants'* behavior is characterized as being performed by a pleasure and narcissistic self-image. *Children's* behavior is now characterized as being performed by a pleasure, narcissistic, and social self-image. Children's experience of transcendent social motivational power is in the sense of good–bad.

It has been noted that infancy is a "prenefarious" stage of development (Jones, 1950, p. 146). This conception refers to the time before the formation of a social self-image and its attendant sense of good–bad.

Relativistic understandings of childhood observations are consistent with the general understanding that developmental processes are continuous and additive. A narcissistic attitude is the chief characteristic of the psychology of infants even in their pursuit of pleasure and is descriptive of the basic nature of human beings. This attitude, with its attendant grandiose self-image, is never abandoned or altered. The observation of new patterns of behavior that characterize phases of development do not indicate a change of attitude but of motivation.

It is as if children have decided to put on a socialized costume for its advantages in dealing with people. This represents a change in what children decide to show of themselves. This change is not genotypical but phenotypical. Nonetheless, this is a "real" change, a real change in motivation and a real change in experience.

My assessment of this social change is that it is only "skin deep." Still, the appearance of a social "skin" where there was none before is a remarkable development. Errors may arise in holding any belief that assumes that socialization is more than skin deep.

The understanding that socialization, despite its importance and value, is only a veneer, came to Freud (1915/1957) when he studied the social changes coincident with a state of war. People with the highest ethics and reasonableness were seen to behave as though they had completely abandoned what had appeared to have become essential characteristics of their self-image. Freud concluded that the appearance of an ethical and reasonable self-image was an illusion he suffered: "that people had not sunk so low as we had feared, because they had never risen so high as we believed" (Freud, 1915/1957, p. 285).

Nations, as well as individuals, may be observed to set aside in their motivation both moral restraint and community of interests (Freud, 1915/1957, p. 288). Narcissistic motivation has been recognized by some historians as a powerful factor in understanding the behavior of nations, classes, and groups (Gay, 1985). It is my understanding that people will moderate their behavior according to good–bad social criteria only insofar and for as long as cultural behavior is advantageous for narcissistic purposes (Freud, 1915/1957, p. 284).

REFERENCES

Bandura, A. (1978). The self-system in reciprocal determinism. *American Psychologist, 33*, 344–358.

Beres, D. (1965). Psychoanalytic notes on the history of morality. *Journal of the American Psychoanalytic Association, 13*, 3–37.

Beres, D. (1980). Certainty: A failed quest? *Psychoanalytic Quarterly, 49*, 1–26.

Bower, T. (1976). Repetitive process in child development. *Scientific American, 38*, 38–41.

Bowlby, J. (1969). *Attachment and loss* (Vol. 1). New York: Basic Books.

Brazelton, T., & Als, H. (1979). Four early stages in the development of mother–infant interaction. *Psychoanalytic Study of the Child, 34*, 349–369.

Condon, W., & Sander, L. (1974). Neonate movement is synchronized with adult speech. *Science, 183*, 99–101.

Downey, T. (1978). Transitional phenomena in the analysis of early adolescent males. *Psychoanalytic Study of the Child, 33*, 19–46.

Ferenczi, S. (1950). Stages in the development of the sense of reality. In E. Jones (Trans.), *Sex in psychoanalysis* (pp. 213–239). New York: Basic Books. (Original work published 1913)

Fine, R. (1975). *Psychoanalytic psychology*. New York: Jason Aronson.

Frankel, S., & Sherick, I. (1977). Observations on the development of normal envy. *Psychoanalytic Study of the Child, 32*, 257–281.

Freud, S. (1955). Animism, magic and the omnipotence of thoughts. Pp. 78–89 in *Totem and taboo*. In J. Strachey (Ed. & Trans.), *The standard edition of the complete psychological works of Sigmund Freud* (Vol. 13, pp. 1–161). London: Hogarth Press. (Original work published 1923)

Freud, S. (1957). Thoughts for the time on war and death. In J. Strachey (Ed. & Trans.), *The standard edition of the complete psychological works of Sigmund Freud* (Vol. 14, pp. 273-302). London: Hogarth Press. (Original work published 1915)

Freud, S. (1958). On narcissism: An introduction. In J. Strachey (Ed. & Trans.), *The standard edition of the complete psychological works of Sigmund Freud* (Vol. 14, pp. 67-102). London: Hogarth Press. (Original work published 1914)

Freud, S. (1960). Three essays on the theory of sexuality. In J. Strachey (Ed. & Trans.), *The standard edition of the complete psychological works of Sigmund Freud* (Vol. 7, pp. 123-243). London: Hogarth Press. (Original work published 1905)

Freud, S. (1961). Civilization and its discontents. In J. Strachey (Ed. & Trans.), *The standard edition of the complete psychological works of Sigmund Freud* (Vol. 20, pp. 57-145). London: Hogarth Press. (Original work published 1930)

Gay, P. (1985). *Freud for historians.* New York: Oxford University Press.

Gesell, A., & Ilg, F. (1937). *Feeding behavior in infants.* Philadelphia, PA: Lippincott.

Hartocollis, P. (1977). Affects in borderline disorders. In P. Hartocollis (Ed.), *Borderline personality disorders* (pp. 495-510). New York: International University Press.

Hong, K. (1978). The transitional phenomena. *Psychoanalytic Study of the Child, 33,* 47-79.

Isaacs, S. (1948). *Childhood and after.* London: Routledge & Kegan Paul.

Jones, E. (1950). The genesis of the super-ego. In E. Jones (Ed.), *Papers on psycho-analysis* (pp. 145-152). London: Balliere, Tindall & Cox.

Kernberg, O. (1975). *Borderline conditions and pathological narcissism.* New York: Jason Aronson.

Kernberg, O. (1980). Love, the couple, and the group. *Psychoanalytic Quarterly, 49,* 78-108.

Lichtenberg, J. (1975). The development of the sense of self. *Journal of the American Psychoanalytic Association, 23,* 453-484.

Mahler, M. (1974). Symbiosis and individuation. *Psychoanalytic Study of the Child, 29,* 89-106.

Mahler, M., & McDevitt, J. (1982). Thoughts on the emergence of the sense of self. *Journal of the American Psychoanalytic Association, 30,* 827-848.

Meltzoff, A., & Moore, M. (1977). Imitation of facial and manual gestures by human neonates. *Science, 183,* 99-101.

Resch, R. (1979). Hatching in human infants as the beginning of separation–individuation. *Psychoanalytic Study of the Child, 34,* 421-441.

Terhune, C. (1979). The role of hearing in early infant organization. *Psychoanalytic Study of the Child, 34,* 371-383.

Tyson, P., & Tyson, R. (1984). Narcissism and superego development. *Journal of the American Psychoanalytic Association, 32,* 75-98.

Winnicott, D. (1953). Transitional objects and transitional phenomena. *International Journal of Psychoanalysis, 34,* 89-97.

12

Emotion

BACKGROUND

Physiology

Certain patterns of human behavior have been noted to possess a quality termed *emotionality*. It is conceived that this general quality may appear in various forms such as fear, anger, loss, and sadness. Despite the remarkable differences among these patterns of behavior, the commonality of bodily excitation appears to be an element indicative of a common process (Knapp, 1987, p. 210). Thus, most theories of emotion are biological and most definitions are framed in physiological terms (Knapp, 1987, pp. 206–208). Various research findings have been compiled to support the suggestion that there is a similar physiological status for all forms of emotional arousal (Allman & Jaffe, 1987, p. 390; Kimble & Garmezy, 1963, p. 406).

Similar emotional patterns have been reported by many observers of newborn infants (Knapp, 1987, pp. 215, 241). These observations support the assertion that emotional patterns are suggestive of an inborn disposition (Kernberg, 1976, p. 104).

However, careful developmental studies of the emotional patterns of neonates reveal that they are complexly organized behaviors and that the various forms of emotionality are not as sharply defined as previously believed (Emde, 1983). This difference as been alternatively accounted for by the conception that there are primary innate emotions whose observable motor and secretory activities are undifferentiated and that the course of psychic development leads to distinctive secondary emotions (Glover, 1949, p. 43).

Similarly, studies of adults in emotional states have been unable to distinguish reliably between the forms of emotionality according to physiological measures (Bourne & Ekstrand, 1973, p. 199; Kimble & Garmezy, 1963, p. 397). There appears to be the general impression that the various forms of emotional patterns share a hazy physiological core (Knapp, 1987, p. 229).

Cognition

It has long been recognized that the formation of an emotional state necessarily requires considerable representational and synthesizing activity (Dorpat, 1977, p. 10). The preponderant opinion is that cognitive elements provide the only reliable distinctions between emotional forms (Kernberg, 1976, p. 94; Kimble & Garmezy, 1963, p. 405).

There has been a movement away from the conception that emotional patterns are primarily physiological reactions and events, as expressed in the James–Lange and Cannon–Bond theories (Allman & Jaffe, 1978, p. 387). Current opinion is similar to the Krech and Crutchfield theory that the form of emotional experience depends on the person's interpretation of an undifferentiated state of physiological arousal (Kimble & Garmezy, 1963, p. 398). Within psychoanalysis, emotional states are recognized as being a compound of physiological events and associated ideas (Brenner, 1975, p. 10). Many writers today emphasize the understanding that emotional behavior is primarily the result of the cognitive activity of evaluating oneself within an environmental situation (Beck, 1967, p. 261; Lazarus, 1968, p. 258).

Social

In the study of emotional states, it has been recognized that cultural factors play a significant role. Within a particular cultural setting, the forms of emotional patterns are seen to conform to conventional modes (Schafer, 1976, p. 273), and different cultural settings provide other conventional modes. Thus, social factors exert considerable influence on the form of emotion that will be experienced (Bourne & Ekstrand, 1973, p. 199). There has been increasing acknowledgement that the study of the forms of emotional patterns must take into account the role of social norms and expectations (Averill, 1983, p. 1158).

Affect

The recognition that emotional states are notable for both their physiological and psychological aspects has led to the attempt to distinguish between them. Some authors have proposed the term *affect* to refer to the psychological component and the term *emotion* to refer to the physiological (Rapaport, 1950). Other authors show an opposite use of these terms with *affect* connoting an emphasis on biological considerations (Kernberg, 1976, p. 103). However, current opinion holds that this is not a valid distinction and that the terms are synonymous (Knapp, 1987, p. 205).

Summary

The early conception of emotional patterns was to regard them as physiological events that were engendered by particular situations (Schafer, 1976, p. 334), as in the expression "emotional reaction." It was thought that emotional states were physiological reactions and were experienced passively (Schafer, 1976, p. 268). This conception was supported by the frequent perception and report of subjective experience in bodily terms. Observers were misled at that time by their physiological presuppositions and regarded those reports as unmediated perceptions by the subject (Schafer, 1976, p. 288). This objectivist error is no longer made because it is now understood that authenticity is not an inherent property of experience. It is a judgment about experience (Averill, 1983, p. 1158; Schafer, 1976, p. 288). Although an emotional state may subjectively appear unbidden and even uncontrollable by the subject, it is known that unrecognized intentions play a vital part (Knapp, 1967, p. 236) in the phenomenon.

The notion of an emotional reaction is countered by the observation that claims as to the uniformity of emotional patterns are exaggerated. The perceived commonality is better attributed to a similarity of cultural values (Schafer, 1976, pp. 336–339).

Emotional behaviors have been studied from several approaches, and a considerable amount has been learned. However, psychology has neither achieved a singular definition of emotionality (Bourne & Ekstrand, 1973, p. 195) nor a generally accepted theory that explains the phenomenon (Knapp, 1987, p. 205).

RELATIVIST VIEW

It has been noted that the confusion among theories of emotion appears to be due to their different philosophical positions (Schafer, 1976, p. 331). I have identified these philosophies in the classes of objectivist and subjectivist viewpoints. I hold that the realist position in the philosophy of science is more valid and that an examination of this issue by means of relativistic psychology will yield fruitful results.

The phenomena I am singling out for attention are those patterns of behavior commonly identified as fear, anger, love, and so forth. All human behavior is the vector outcome of biological, sociological, and psychological types of transcendent causal power. Those patterns that are identified as indicative of an emotional state take part in the general fabric of human experience. Emotional states are thought to differ in their emphasis on some other hypothesized aspect (Knapp, 1987, p. 241).

Physiology

I assume a priori that a study of various emotional patterns would reveal commonalities indicative of the operation of biological power. The studies I have considered show such a commonality, which I have identified by the term *arousal*. Thus, emotional states are distinguished from nonemotional states according to a significantly heightened, or aroused, level of physiological functioning. This finding is in accord with general experience. For example, the heart is always beating, although it beats considerably faster in emotional states. Therefore, emotional states do not differ from normal states in physiological quality but in quantity. A particular study of the conditions affecting the intensification and abatement of physiological functioning would appear to be of more primary interest for biologists.

Cognition

The studies cited have demonstrated the commonality of physiological arousal among all forms of emotional behavior, and this is indicative of a biological causal power. It has also been demonstrated that emotional states are reliably associated with particular cognitive patterns. The apparent differences among these cognitive patterns have drawn the most attention. Few writers have sought to detect a commonality amid the diversity. Schafer (1976, p. 267) has pointed out that among the cognitive patterns of all emotional states, there is the indication that individuals have a "personal stake in the matter" and that the situation is being evaluated "relative to oneself" (Schafer, 1976, p. 337).

From the relativist position, a self-system is among the group of mental faculties with which all people are born. Because a self is common to all people, emotional states differ from normal states in showing a quantitatively significant increased participation of the self. Recall that the chief motivational characteristic of the self is that of narcissism. Thus, an individual in an emotional state is motivated chiefly by heightened self-interests.

This assertion appears to be contradicted by the form of emotion people call *love*. Many writers have noted that a close study of this apparently selfless behavior reveals the presence of selfishness in the form of romantic illusion. Singer (1987) has supported this conclusion by citing the arguments and agreement of the philosophers Nietzche and Sartre, concluding that the core of a state of love is an egoistic enhancement of the self. The commonality among the cognitive patterns in forms of emotional behavior lies in the significantly greater contribution of self-interest than in normal behavior.

Sociology

My review of emotional behaviors has shown that these states possess both common physiological and mental properties. The data of observation show that these properties also vary regularly in form according to social conditions. This is indicative of the contribution of a sociological causal power.

Relativists assume that biological power is a constant determinant of behavior and is detectable in observations of a regular commonality in all instances. In addition, relativists assume that these commonalities will also vary regularly under the influence of sociological power and that this is detectable in the regular commonality among social instances. These assumptions provide a meaningful ordering of the observations of emotional states.

Psychology

The identification of biological specieswide commonalities among emotional states, and social commonalities among the variations in their forms, provides a foundation for psychological study. From these bases, individual differences can be detected. They serve as a platform from which to make conjectures about an individual's experience in emotional states.

Relativists regard the faculty of experiencing as an inherent mental property of all human beings. Therefore, it is expected that there will be a general commonality of experience in emotional states and a social commonality of experience in emotional states, as well as an individuality of experience in emotional states. It is the latter aspect that is of particular importance for psychology, even though there is a basic interest to learn about biological and sociological experience.

Relativists represent experiencing as taking place in the form of a self-image in regard to an object-image, where the chief motivations of the self are the interests of narcissism, the pleasure principle, and the reality principle. Each of these elements is composed of aspects common to all members of the species, those variations distinguished by groups within the species and those that are individual and personal. Relativist psychologists study these individual variations in order to make conjectures about the particular and relative roles of the motivations of narcissism, the pleasure principle, and the reality principle in the conduct of a person and represent these conjectures in the form of a *self and object constellation*.

The distinction between normal and emotional states has been seen to be quantitative, and it lies within the dimension of motivational importance. The motivational quality particularly emphasized in emotional states is recognized as heightened narcissistic interest. Consequently, an observer may conclude that a person is in an emotional state when judgment sustains that the subject has set aside the normal pleasure and reality principles in favor of narcissistic considerations. Relativists describe a person in an emotional state as possessing a self-image that regards an object-image with unusually heightened narcissistic motivation. I discussed the basic dimensions and vicissitudes of narcissism in chapter 10.

The term *emotional* necessarily implies the judgment that the pattern of behavior being observed is significantly different from a normative standard. To that extent, all emotional states are abnormal by definition. Still, one should be careful to recall that an observation of abnormality is not necessarily indicative of a condition of psychopathology. Each culture has a range within its standards that regards certain abnormalities as being socially acceptable and, quite often, desirable. For example, in American culture the absence of sadness at a funeral is reprehensible. Even though an individual may not "feel" sad, there is considerable social pressure to act that way.

Each culture has its own forms of emotionality that are distinguished by labels such as fear, love, and hate. The form of emotionality called hate (or anger) has been studied, and it has long been known that it is invariably accompanied by the intense conviction of being right (Jones, 1929/1950, p. 306). The individual sees his or her actions as self-justified and has an attitude of righteous indignation. This attitude is recognized as narcissistic. Thus, angry patterns of behavior are indicative of an exacerbated narcissistic state.

The form of emotionality called envy has also been studied. Joffee (1969) reviewed that literature and concluded that the presence of envy was always indicative of a state of disturbed narcissism (Joffe, 1969, p. 540). The study of envy in children confirmed the invariable context of a narcissistic insult (Frankel & Sherick, 1977, p. 258). A study of the form of emotion called shame showed that its essence was a state of disturbed narcissism (Stolorow, 1976, p. 26).

A review of the literature of depressive forms of emotionality indicates that "object-loss" was not a necessary condition either for the particular form or its derivatives (Dorpat, 1977, p. 8). A disturbance in the state of well-being (Dorpat, 1977, p. 7) was found to be a common characteristic distinctive of this pattern of emotionality. Joffee and Sandler (1965) proposed to account for these observations by noting that the patterns of behavior indicated that both the pleasure and the reality principles were being superceded. Relativist psychologists recognize this as indicative of a state of heightened narcissistic motivation. Dorpat also recognized this particular connotation by noting that depressive forms were distinguishable by "an emphasis on the self" (Dorpat, 1977, p. 20) and that they were strongly associated with a condition of narcissistic injury (Dorpat, 1977, p. 23). He supported his contention by pointing out that further studies revealed the presence of screened fantasies of omnipotence. I present this selection of studies of some particular forms of emotional patterns in order to document the contention that all emotional forms are indicative of a state of disturbed narcissistic motivation. Two depressive forms of emotionality that are only pheno-typically similar should be distinguished. Similarities in the patterns of behavior known as *depression* and *sadness* may be observed. Depression is best reserved for that condition in which there is evidence of the presence of a state of narcissistic injury that supercedes motivations of the pleasure and reality principles. Sadness denotes a condition in which the pleasure and reality principles do not supercede narcissistic motivation, despite the presence of narcissistic injury.

Summary

From the point of view of relativist psychology, emotional states are not merely, or even primarily, physiological events. Sociological factors appear to play the major role in determining the form of an emotion state. However, the necessary condition that determines the presence of an emotional state is the heightening of narcissistic motivation. Therefore, emotional states are held to be events of exacerbated narcissism.

Because I regard narcissistic motivation as a normal component of all behavior, the presence of a state of heightened narcissism establishes an abnormal condition by definition. However, one should note that abnormality does not carry with it any necessary implication of psychopathology.

It has long been noted that emotional states contain the strongest motivations (Fenichel, 1945, p. 49). This is so because the strongest of human motivations, narcissism, is exacerbated.

REFERENCES

Allman, L., & Jaffe, D. (1978). *Abnormal psychology in the life cycle*. New York: Harper & Row.
Averill, J. (1983). Studies of anger and aggression: Implications for theories of emotion. *American Psychologist, 38*, 1145-1160.
Beck, A. (1967). *Depression*. New York: Harper & Row.
Bourne, L., & Ekstrand, B. (1973). *Psychology: Its principles and meanings*. Hinsdale, IL: Dryden Press.
Brenner, C. (1975). Affects and psychic conflict. *Psychoanalytic Quarterly, 44*, 5-28.
Dorpat, D. (1977). Depressive affect. *Psychoanalytic Study of the Child, 32*, 3-27.
Emde, R. (1983). The prerepresentational emotional self and its affective core. *Psychoanalytic Study of the Child, 38*, 165-192.
Fenichel, O. (1945). *The psychoanalytic theory of neurosis*. New York: Norton.
Frankel, S., & Sherick, I. (1977). Observations on the development of normal envy. *Psychoanalytic Study of the Child, 32*, 257-281.
Glover, E. (1949). *Psychoanalysis*. New York: Staples.
Joffe, W. (1969). A critical review of the envy concept. *International Journal of Psychoanalysis, 50*, 533-546.
Joffe, W., & Sandler, J. (1965). Notes on pain, depression, and individuation. *Psychoanalytic Study of the Child, 20*, 394-424.
Jones, E. (1950). Fear, guilt, and hate. In E. Jones (Ed.), *Papers on psycho-analysis* (pp. 304-319). London: Bailliere, Tindall & Cox. (Original work published 1929)
Kernberg, O. (1976). *Object relations theory and clinical psychoanalysis*. New York: Jason Aronson.
Kimble, G., & Garmezy, N. (1963). *Principles of general psychology*. New York: Ronald Press.
Knapp, P. (1987). Some contemporary contributions to the study of emotions. *Journal of the American Psychoanalytic Association, 35*, 205-248.

Lazarus, R. (1968). Emotion as coping process. In M. Arnold (Ed.), *The nature of emotion* (pp. 249–260). Baltimore, MD: Penguin Books.
Rapaport, D. (1950). *Emotion and memory.* New York: International University Press.
Schafer, R. (1976). *A new language for psychoanalysis.* New Haven, CT: Yale University Press.
Singer, I. (1987). *The nature of love: Vol. 3. The modern world.* Chicago: University of Chicago Press.
Stolorow, R. (1976). Psychoanalytic relections on client-centered therapy in the light of modern conceptions of narcissism. *Psychotherapy, 13,* 26–29.

III

PSYCHOPATHOLOGY

13

Current Status of Psychopathology

That human beings can be in psychopathological conditions is a tenable assumption supported by common experience. There are the observations of instances of bizarre delusions, obsessions, compulsions, phobias, states of anxiety, and conversion reactions. In each instance there appears to be a particular syndrome that identifies a disorder that is distinguished from other forms of disorder. Each syndrome in its multiple details supports the inference that only a disorder of mental faculties could produce the particular pattern of behavior. It is tenable to assume that mental faculties can be disordered and that the consequences of disorder can be observed in various forms and manifestations.

Although mental faculties, such as that for memory, have not yet been observed directly, there is considerable certainty that such causal entities exist. There is equal certainty that mental faculties can be disturbed. For example, the ingestion of chemicals has a regular and predictable effect on mental functioning. There are also medical conditions in which mental symptoms are regularly observable along with physiological symptoms.

In addition to physical causes of mental dysfunctions, a debate in modern times has been about the possible psychological and sociological causes of mental dysfunctions. There is not yet a consensus and there is no accepted theory of psychopathology (Allman & Jaffe, 1978, p. 65; Bourne & Ekstrand, 1973, p. 348; Coleman, 1972, p. 14; Kimble & Garmezy, 1963, p. 524; Rapaport, 1980, p. 17; Weinshel, 1984, p. 64). One or another theory over the years has been more or less fashionable (Blum, 1978, p. 1030).

Despite the absence of a general scientific foundation, there is a continuing social demand for diagnosis in order to try to make informed administrative, legal, treatment, and research decisions. When confronted by a person in obvious mental distress, psychologists are in the same position as physicians were before the discovery of bacteria. Psychologists cannot deal directly with a person's mental disturbances as long as its essence is unknown. The determination to help brings one to consider the current possibilities of reducing feelings of distress and ameliorating symptoms by recommending what seem to be healthful practices.

Comparative studies of a variety of theories have shown that they all contain assumptions that are true only in delimited instances (Manicas & Secord, 1983, p. 399) and fail to meet the test of generality. Although their basic postulates are undemonstrated, the theories contend with each other in strong disagreement (Fine, 1977, p. 58; Manicas & Secord, 1983, p. 399; Wallerstein, 1978, p. 502; Wallerstein, 1988, p. 7). The philosophical positions of these theories range from logical empiricism to a strict subjectivism. The range of their postulates includes such diversity as adaptation to the environment, immaturity of development, faulty learning, poor patterns of survival, statistical deviation, subjective distress, and intrapsychic conflict. These theories disagree on basic postulates, which are all derived from undemonstrated assumptions.

Despite the lack of certainty as to the essential nature of psychopathology, the pressure of practical needs leads the profession to do its best in as scientific a manner as possible. This is a situation of imperfect tools being used expertly. At the same time, a great deal is known about general psychological functioning and its variation under special conditions. It is this body of knowledge that is consulted by psychologists as a foundation for making inferences regarding psychopathology and its treatment. This situation is similar to that in which various chefs go into the same pantry, each emerging with a selection of different ingredients to cook their favorite dish. Nonetheless, it is this body of knowledge, as well as a fund of relevant experience, that sustains the psychologist in maintaining the conviction that a true and useful path is being pursued. Altogether, this constitutes an expert opinion supportable by consensual validation. However valuable such an opinion might be, within the philosophy of science it has only the rank of an undemonstrated assertion.

VARIOUS POSTULATES

It appears that some aspect of practical necessity leads a particular psychologist to favor one among the variety of theories that seems to be most useful for that purpose. This is almost similar to a physicist choosing either the point or wave theory of light according to the project at hand.

Social Needs

It often occurs that individuals with mental disorder intrude their disturbance into the orderly conduct of social institutions. Therefore, those who are concerned with the operation of facilities for education, the law, marriage, politics, and so on call on psychology for assistance in making informed management decisions.

This concern leads to an evaluation of a mental disorder as to the consequence of discord and collision with society (Loewald, 1981, p. 24). The interest in social results of mental disorder is expressed by the adoption of the criterion that the well-being of the individual depends on the effectiveness of adjustment to the well-being of the group (Coleman, 1972, p. 15). The choice of this criterion assumes that the current forms of grouping are good both for society and the individual, an assumption that is hardly demonstrable. The emphasis on self-modification in order to conform to social custom contains an implied threat as to how society will treat discordant behavior.

Although the maintenance of social institutions is a practical concern, their current forms can hardly be held up as ideals (Loewald, 1981, p. 42). Deviation from a social norm may well turn out to be progressive for social purposes (Loewald, 1981, p. 41) and therefore cannot be taken as a necessary indication of mental disorder. Conversely, behavior that conforms to current social forms cannot be taken as a necessary indication of mental health (Ullman & Krasner, 1969, p. 6).

Education

Individuals with mental disorder are often identified when their behavior is found to be disruptive by educational institutions. These people are regarded as bad and unsocialized. However, especially with young children, sometimes a more sympathetic attitude is taken. They are then often regarded as the passive and innocent victims of unfortunate circumstance. By any humane criterion, one may well agree that their circumstances are indeed unfortunate. However, the question is, does the impact of these circumstances contribute to psychopathology among their unfortunate consequences? The viewpoint that it must have this effect is a necessary corollary of the assumption that the nature of infantile experience is helplessness and hopelessness. Then, children come to be regarded as particularly vulnerable in their mental functioning to the effects of noisome events.

The assumption that noxious events such as "premature and excessive disappointment" (Kernberg, 1975, p. 276; Kohut, 1971, p. 45) are traumatic is a popular one. There is even a considerable following for the extremist position that the mother's mental disorder is the chief agent of psychopathology (Mahler, 1968, p. 37). This assumption is maintained despite the frequent notation that no event necessarily results in mental disorder (Kohut, 1971, p. 190; Slap & Levine, 1978, p. 506).

Although the radical position that there are events that are necessarily traumatic for psychopathology is troublesome to assert openly, the assumption of infantile psychic helplessness often appears in an indirect form. It is maintained that there are events that are traumatic to the normal processes of psychic development. Manifestations of developmental trauma are conceived of as "deficits" (Kohut, 1971, p. 3; Tolpin, 1978, p. 173) and "arrest" or malformation (Eagle, 1986, p. 97). The notion that such developmental "failures" are responsible for mental disorder continues to be maintained despite its contravention by many developmental studies (Holzman, 1978).

Even when it is recognized that psychopathology is not a developmental phenomenon, the assumption of childhood psychic helplessness may be seen in the notion that mental disorder is the persistence of infantile behavior (Reich, 1960, p. 216). However, although some patterns of behavior may be identified as "returning to an earlier mode or object of gratification" (Brenner, 1955, p. 37), it is also noted that these regressions are not necessarily pathological (Brenner, 1955, p. 38). What is identified is a deviation from a norm. However, deviation may sometimes be judged as progressive (Loewald, 1981, p. 41).

Medical

In addition to the call from social institutions to psychology for assistance in the management of persons with mental disorder, it often happens that these people call on medical institutions. Their experience with suffering leads them to seek help for distress where they are accustomed to find it.

In response to the request for physicianlike treatment, psychologists have given their attention to the phenomenon of subjective distress. The examination of many patients has led observers to conclude that suffering is the consequence of conflicted mental functioning (Brenner, 1976, p. 174). It has frequently been detected that patients perform patterns of behavior, the implications of which are strongly in conflict with those of other patterns of behavior (Schafer, 1976, p. 135). It is suggested that the commonality of psychopathological patients is that they act in a self-contradictory manner (Friedman, 1978, p. 364), and this is taken to indicate the presence of contradictory mental functions. This is the usual reference for the term *psychic conflict*.

The view of a person's psychological distress as the outcome of psychic conflict leads to the study of such inferred states. Because psychic activity is not accessible to direct observation, investigators must have recourse to indirect and inferential methods. The most famous of these methods is the procedure proposed by Sigmund Freud, which he called *psychoanalysis*. This specifies the collection of a broad base of observations about an individual, including past and current activities, in considerable detail. These observations are used as a foundation to sustain inferences about the person's mental functioning. Thus, past and present activities are analyzed to cast light on the current psyche.

Various schools of psychoanalysis have developed that differ in their assumptions about which activities and which hypothetical mental faculties are most important. These varying assumptions shape the form in which the inferences are made. These schools are similar in holding the common assumption that disturbed behavior is symptomatic of mental disturbance. This is the usual reference for the term *psychodynamic*.

The philosophical problem with the definition of psychopathology as contradictory patterns of behavior is that these may be observed normally in childhood and that they serve apparent developmental usefulness (Lustman, 1977, p. 122). Therefore, the concept of conflicted mental faculties does not distinguish between normal and pathological states.

Behavior Therapy

Although there is the general impression that psychoanalytic "talking treatment" is usually beneficial to the patient (Coleman, 1972, p. 702), there is also a considerable body of professional opinion that these methods are unimpressive as to therapeutic effectiveness (Bourne & Ekstrand, 1973, p. 414). The lengthy time required by analytic procedure, and its careful gathering of detail, may often be experienced by the patient as an empathic attitude. Being the center of such concentrated attention can often be pleasing, flattering, and generally salubrious. Nonetheless, the length of time may also be experienced with an impatience for specific results.

The existence of nonconscious determinants in the conscious functioning of mental faculties has been an accepted fact in psychology (Allman & Jaffe, 1978, p. 487). However, there has also been, for a long time, a significant sense of frustration in attempts to influence unconscious determinants. Alternatively, Watson (1913) proposed to change the focus of treatment from the patient's experience of distress to the patient's disturbed behaviors. This shift entails the conviction that a change from disturbed behavior to nondisturbed behavior will necessarily be accompanied by a change from the experience of disturbance to an experience of nondisturbance. The assumption of this proposal is that disturbed emotionality is a natural consequence of activity judged to be disturbed.

The most famous implementer of the view that private states can be changed by alterations in the pattern of behavior is B. F. Skinner. He maintained this assumption despite his own observation that private states are almost always poorly correlated with public evidence (Skinner, 1987, p. 783). Nonetheless, recourse to the body of knowledge of learning theory proved to be effective in changing some problematic behavior. Wolpe (1958) reported the successful use of the method of counterconditioning to achieve change of behavior as well as the easing of subjective distress, as did many others (Bourne & Ekstrand, 1973, p. 392).

Many workers employed and reported their use of learning theory to effect changes in behavior by reinforcement and extinction (Kimble & Garmezy, 1963, p. 133). However, such commonsense notions as the belief that praise and success will establish and maintain new patterns of behavior was countered by the results of research (Dweck, 1986, p. 1040). It was found, for instance, that when reinforcers were effective, this was only so when they were regarded by the individual as personally pleasing and socially correct (Powell, 1987, p. 410). These findings have accounted for the observation that behavioral treatments varied greatly in effectiveness (Coleman, 1972, p. 676) and that activities of instigation and contingency had only a transient effect (Eron, 1987, p. 438).

It was R. Lazarus (1968) who pointed out that facilitation or inhibition of behaviors was not an inherent property of environmental conditions but was the consequence of how those conditions were perceived and interpreted by the individual. The general position of current behaviorists is that cognitive factors—such as meanings, beliefs, and expectations—are the chief agents in the establishment and maintenance of behavior patterns (Bandura, 1978, p. 347).

Behavior therapists today are still behaviorists in that they regard phenomena such as obsessive thoughts and uncomfortable feelings as covert behaviors (Allman & Jaffe, 1978, p. 465). Modern behaviorists still consult the same learning mechanisms (Wolpe, 1987, p. 101), but their target to influence is the person's attitudes, standards, and norms (Eron, 1987, p. 439). Problematic behavior is still regarded as maladaptive, in the sense of being socially inappropriate (Bourne & Ekstrand, 1973, p. 414). The concern for understanding sociological causal powers in behavior is expressed in the treatment goals of furthering "maturity, competence, and self-actualization" (Coleman, 1972, p. 663). Thus, the new "social–cognitive" approach of behaviorists (Dweck, 1986, p. 1040) seeks to identify those aspects of social power that maintain behavior patterns. Their prospect is to use learning theory to change those aspects with consequent changes in both behavior and experience. The modern behaviorist is identified as using social learning theory in a cognitive–behavioral program (A. Lazarus, 1987, p. 101).

The study of cognitive factors that determine the interpretation of perceptions has shown that conceptions of oneself and the environment are chiefly determined by considerations of personal welfare and self-esteem (Bandura, 1978, p. 349). The factor of self-concept is found to be more important than either objective measures of behavior or immediate practical consequences (Dweck, 1986, p. 1046). In fact, it has been noted that an active disconfirmation of a person's beliefs is generally ineffective in altering those beliefs (Taylor, 1983, p. 1170). This is consistent with the general wisdom that one will believe what one wants to believe.

It is important to note that those authors' notion of the self-concept is in the context of the assumption that it is determined primarily by social power. Within the realm of behaviorists, this assumption is expressed by the use of the term *operant conditioning* for a type of intervention. The procedure creates a change in the environment that is designed to either encourage or deter a target behavior (Allman & Jaffe, 1978, p. 462). The use of a method of ecological control is supported by the observation that people generally adapt themselves automatically to their surroundings (Kipnis, 1987, p. 31). The alteration of procedure that expresses the assumption of social power is the selection of people in the patient's life as the target objects of the environment. For example, the parents of a child are often selected for training as therapeutic agents (Allman & Jaffe, 1978, p. 43). This activity is based on the assumption that the parents occupy a position of strong influence on the child's self-concept and can be effective in inducing the child to alter his or her behavior.

Any attempt to alter the behavior of an individual through the influence of others may be regarded as being founded on the assumption of social power as a strong determinant of the individual's self-concept. An extension of this assumption is the establishment of token economies in institutions (Allman & Jaffe, 1978, p. 464). The staff is instructed to treat the individual in a manner designed to make it more likely that the behavioral pattern that is desired will occur.

The use of parents as agents effecting changes in the behavior of children has been challenged by the observation that these children are already acting in a manner disapproved of by the parents. It appears that these parents are already ineffective in gaining behavior that they desire. Despite this objection, the behaviorist position is maintained by the claim that the parents must inadvertently be sustaining the very behavior that they dislike. This assertion is an effective rejoinder, but it depends on the tautological use of the assumption of social power as the chief agent in maintaining one's self-concept, and it stands or falls on whether that is true.

Humanistic–Existential

The persistence of the demand for assistance, together with the lack of demonstrated effectiveness of both dynamic and behaviorist treatments, led to the development of a "third force": the humanistic and existential viewpoints (Coleman, 1972, p. 676). This orientation views the phenomena of subjective distress and symptomatic behavior as the outcome of distortions of self-concept occasioned by the problem of individual adaptation to social complexity.

Among the assumptions entailed in this view is the belief in an originally weak self-concept that requires help in dealing with complex social demands. There is then good reason to seek means to shore up the weak self so that it can stand erect in the face of social stress. Treatment is seen as a corrective experience in which education in methods of social adaptation aims at an accommodation to social acceptability with a minimum of stress for the ego (Bourne & Ekstrand, 1973, p. 144).

Because treatment is viewed as a training ground in the means of social adaptation, the formation of therapeutic groups is regarded as a sample introduction to ease the transfer of the application of new social skills to the groups in the individual's life situation (Kimble & Garmezy, 1963, p. 571). The therapeutic groups developed from this view are identified by titles such as growth centers, T-groups, sensitivity training, and encounter groups. A technique commonly used by the therapist of these groups is to direct attention to the notion of personal responsibility for the outcome of either personal distress or growth (Allman & Jaffe, 1978, p. 476). An implication of this technique is that if the person is inadvertently responsible for producing distress, he or she also has the power to change for the better. For one reason or another, it has been observed that the transfer from the insular group to life at large does not regularly take place. Instead, many people cling to their therapeutic groups and become groupies (Allman & Jaffe, 1978, p. 476). The paradox of a person clinging to a group that attempts to foster individuality may be at least partially attributed to something intrinsic to the method. The exercise of these controlling tactics, it has been observed, makes it likely that when one begins with control, one will end with control (Kipnis, 1987, p. 35).

The assumption of an originally weak ego has also led to a sensitization of the view that aspects of the social environment are particularly stressful for an individual's psychological functioning. Those psychologists have focused their interest on the possibilities of effecting social modifications of the environment (Coleman, 1972, p. 676). Out of this concern, one can see the development of the community health movement (Bourne & Ekstrand, 1973, p. 405). Their concern is to attempt to reduce poverty, disease, and injustice because these are conceived to have an impact on a person's psychology as well as physical health.

Summary

There is a large body of professional agreement that the mental health professions have not done an outstanding job in treating disorders (Bourne & Ekstrand, 1973, p. 414; Coleman, 1972, p. 670). After 60 years, the promise of behaviorism appears to be unfulfilled (Pfaus, Blackburn, J., Harpur, T., Mac Donald, M., & Mana, J., 1988, p. 821). It seems that each psychotherapeutic approach has its own package of cherished beliefs that is presented as a dignified body of knowledge (Mahrer, 1988, p. 897). This state of affairs is the inevitable outcome of the lack of a sound philosophic basis for psychology and is accompanied by the maintenance of untenable assumptions. Indeed, it appears that the discipline of psychology is in a most undisciplined condition.

REFERENCES

Allman, J., & Jaffe, D. (1978). *Abnormal psychology in the life cycle*. New York: Harper & Row.
Bandura, A. (1978). The self system in reciprocal determinism. *American Psychologist, 33*, 344–358.
Blum, J. (1978). On changes in psychiatric diagnosis over time. *American Psychologist, 33*, 1017–1031.
Bourne, L., & Ekstrand, B. (1973). *Psychology: Its principles and meanings*. Hinsdale, IL: Dryden Press.
Brenner, C. (1955). *An elementary textbook of psychoanalysis*. New York: International University Press.
Brenner, C. (1976). *Psychoanalytic technique and psychic conflict*. New York: International University Press.
Coleman, J. (1972). *Abnormal psychology and modern life*. Glenview, IL: Scott, Foresman.
Dweck, C. (1986). Motivational processes affecting learning. *American Psychologist, 41*, 1040–1048.
Eagle, M. (1986). Recent developments in psychoanalysis: A critical evaluation. *Psychoanalytic Psychology, 3*, 93–100.
Eron, L. (1987). The development of aggressive behavior from the perspective of a developing behaviorism. *American Psychologist, 42*, 435–442.
Fine, R. (1977). Psychoanalysis as a philosophical system. *Journal of Psychohistory, 5*, 1–66.

Friedman, L. (1978). Trends in the psychoanalytic theory of treatment. *Psychoanalytic Quarterly, 47,* 514-567.

Holzman, P. (1978). What is a borderline patient? In S. Smith (Ed.), *The human mind revisited: Essays in honor of Karl A. Menninger* (pp. 320-332). New York: International University Press.

Kernberg, O. (1975). *Borderline conditions and pathological narcissism.* New York: Ronald Press.

Kimble, G., & Garmezy, N. (1963). *Principles of general psychology.* New York: Ronald Press.

Kipnis, D. (1987). Psychology and behavioral technology. *American Psychologist, 42,* 30-36.

Kohut, H. (1971). *The analysis of the self.* New York: International University Press.

Lazarus, A. (1987). Some significant differences and more significant similarities. *American Psychologist, 42,* 101- .

Lazarus, R. (1968). Emotion as a coping process. In M. Arnold (Ed.), *The nature of emotions* (pp. 249-260). New York: Penguin Books.

Loewald, H. (1981). Regression: Some general considerations. *Psychoanalytic Quarterly, 50,* 22-43.

Lustman, J. (1977). On splitting. *Psychoanalytic Study of the Child, 32,* 119-154.

Mahler, M. (1968). *On human symbiosis and the vicissitudes of individuation.* New York: International University Press.

Mahrer, A. (1988). Discovery-oriented psychotherapy research. *American Psychologist, 43,* 694-702.

Manicas, P., & Secord, P. (1983). Implications for psychology of the new philosophy of science. *American Psychologist, 38,* 399-413.

Pfaus, J., Blackburn, J., Harpur, T., Mac Donald, M., & Mana, J. (1988). Has psychology ever been a science of behavior? *American Psychologist, 43,* 821-822.

Powell, D. (1987). Cognitive and affective components of reinforcement. *American Psychologist, 42,* 409-410.

Rapaport, D. (1960). The structure of psychoanalytic theory: A systematizing attempt. *Psychological Issues, Monograph 6,* New York: International University Press.

Reich, A. (1960). Pathological forms of self-esteem regulation. *Psychoanalytic Study of the Child, 15,* 215-232.

Schafer, R. (1976). *A new language for psychoanalysis.* New York: Basic Books.

Skinner, B. (1987). Whatever happened to psychology as the science of behavior? *American Psychologist, 42,* 780-786.

Slap, J., & Levine, F. (1978). On hybrid concepts in psychoanalysis. *Psychoanalytic Quarterly, 47,* 499-523.

Taylor, S. (1983). Adjustment to threatening events: A theory of cognitive adaptation. *American Psychologist, 38,* 1101-1173.

Tolpin, M. (1978). Self-objects and oedipal objects. *Psychoanalytic Study of the Child, 33,* 167-184.

Ullman, L., & Krasner, L. (1969). *Psychological approaches to abnormal behavior.* Englewood Cliffs, NJ: Prentice-Hall.

Wallerstein, R. (1978). Perspectives on psychoanalytic training around the world. *International Journal of Psychoanalysis, 59,* 477-503.

Wallerstein, R. (1988). Psychoanalysis, psychoanalytic science, and psychoanalytic research. *Journal of the American Psychoanalytic Association, 36,* 3-30.

Watson, J. (1913). Psychology as the behaviorist views it. *Psychological Review, 20,* 158-177.

Weinshel, E. (1984). Some observations on the psychoanalytic process. *Psychoanalytic Quarterly, 53,* 63-92.

Wolpe, J. (1958). *Psychotherapy by reciprocal inhibition.* Stanford, CA: Stanford University Press.

Wolpe, J. (1987). Destigmatization of behavior therapy. *American Psychologist, 42,* 100-101.

14

Relativistic Theory

In the attempt to comprehend the phenomenon of mental disorder, many theories have been proposed that vary widely in their basic assumptions. The patterns of the assumptions of these various theories may be identified as philosophical systems, and these vary from a strict subjectivism to a strict objectivism. I attempt to detail the view of relativism in regarding mental disorder.

Regarding the basic tenets of relativism, recall that psychology is the study of individual personal experience and that the proper entities of observation are individualistic behavior and individualistic subjective experience. Inferences about real structures and their causal powers are expressed in terms of suitable hypothetical entities. Self-images and object-images are the forms of the structure of psychological experience. The causal powers of psychological experience are described in motivational terms as the pleasure principle, reality principle, and narcissism. The inherent biological structures that enable the phenomenon of experience are referred to as mental faculties. I suggest that in the normal operation of mental faculties, personal experience eventuates in a corresponding complexity of self- and object-image constellations.

DISORDERS OF MENTAL FACULTIES

I have noted previously that conditions of medical disease and the ingestion of chemicals are observed to be regularly accompanied by abundant evidence of disordered mental faculties, such as those for memory, motor control, and perception of sensations. In addition, one can note the regular evidence of disordered mental faculties under societal conditions, such as the symptoms of burnout that have been related to stressful work conditions (Farber, 1983, p. 3). Thus, states of disorder of mental faculties due to biological and sociological factors can be identified. I consider the possibility of psychological factors in the production of states of disordered mental faculties later.

A state of disordered mental faculties is regarded as a biological condition regardless of the circumstance within which it comes about. The concern of psychologists is focused on the personal experience of living with this disorder. Thus, psychologists are interested in the individual's experience of social circumstances, such as the family, and the person's experience of biological circumstances, such as injuries.

The individual's experience of social conditions or personal biological conditions may be specified as an attitude of the self-image toward that object-image. Psychology recognizes that an individual experiences all environmental configurations as objects, all other people as objects, one's own body parts as objects, and one's mental faculties as objects.

The mental faculty that allows the voluntary control of mobility enables the individual to exert the possibility of influencing objects. Activity may be organized as an intervention toward the environment, other people, or one's own body. A branch of psychology has recently arisen that studies the possibilities of attitudinal variations in influencing bodily functions and is identified by the term *biofeedback*. The development of devices to refine an individual's ability to control mobility has produced noteworthy increased ability to influence muscular, circulatory, and visceral functioning (Miller, 1985).

One can now see how attitudes may play a significant role in the functioning of mental faculties, both in states of health and disorder. Attitude, either deliberate or inadvertent, may contribute to processes of repair or hamper them.

SYMPTOMS OF DISORDERED MENTAL FACULTIES

Disorders of mental faculties, whether due to biological or sociological causes, are expressed in the disordered functioning of the same biological faculties. Those observations of individual behavior and experience that are indications of a disorder of mental faculties may be termed *mental symptoms*.

It is commonly held that delusions are an unequivocal symptom of disordered mental function. I note that the symptom of delusion occurs in the conditions of both alcoholic psychosis and burnout (Farber, 1983, p. 3). Thus, identical symptoms of mental disorder may arise in states of biological and sociological stress and are not necessarily discriminatory as to the cause of origin.

Psychologists are particularly interested in states of mental disorder that arise from psychological causes. Still, psychological causes that produce disordered mental faculties do not necessarily result in symptoms different from those produced by social and biological causes. Consequently, the use of symptoms of mental disorder in the diagnosis of psychologically produced states—psychopathology—is unreliable for that purpose. This is attested to by the frequent report of uncertainty about diagnosis (Blum, 1983, p. 1028; Bourne & Ekstrand, 1973, p. 414). Mental symptoms occur in states of biologic, sociologic, and psychologic origins.

The phenomenon of mental symptoms may be studied by biologists, sociologists, and psychologists in accord with their particular interest in a type of causal power for human behavior and experience. Those aspects of mental symptoms that are similar among all members of a species would be singled out for observation by biological scientists. Those aspects that are identified with groups would be singled out by social scientists. Those aspects that are distinctive for a particular individual would be singled out by psychologists. This psychological distinction in viewing mental symptoms has been noted by Brenner (1976, p. 153), who noted that although these symptoms have general features, it is the business of the psychologist to search for those that are individual and unique.

I have distinguished states of mental disorder that arise from biological and sociological causes (as well as psychological). It is then clear that a person may suffer a mental disorder that is the consequence of multiple causes.

In any event, the psychologist is interested in studying the experience of the person with a mental disorder. In that regard, aspects of experience will be observable as general (biological), group (sociological), and individual (psychological). The clinical psychologist seeks the personal and unique aspects of experience among the details of the behavior and subjective experience of an individual suffering from mental disorder.

MENTAL DISORDER OF PSYCHOLOGICAL ORIGIN

From my consideration of states of disordered mental faculties, one may understand that they may come about from biological and sociological causes. The relativist notes that from the viewpoint of the individual, the experience in both cases is that the environment has made a significant impact on oneself. However, this statement is not an exact description because one's body is experienced as an object. I have identified mental faculties as inherent equipment and they, too, are experienced as objects. Therefore, one must understand that a state of mental disorder is experienced as an occurrence to one's body-object. In the same way that something happening to my arm is not the same experience as something happening to me, something happening to my memory is not the same as something happening to me. One's arm may well be regarded with considerable personal importance, and one's memory even more so. Nonetheless, one's mental faculties are experienced as objects.

Having clarified the foregoing considerations, I am now in a position to make a statement about psychopathology that is consistent with relativist philosophy and its assumptions. Psychopathology refers to a state in which an individual causes a disorder in his or her own mental faculties.

This conception of psychopathology may appear to be strange, and various objections may come to mind. For example, it is assumed that a state of mental disorder will no doubt be experienced as unpleasant because it appears to violate the pleasure principle. Therefore, it seems that this type of activity would be avoided naturally according to an aspect of human nature. However, I have already shown how one aspect of the pleasure principle can be superceded by another aspect (e.g., by valuation that another course of activity is either considerably more pleasant or unpleasant).

Causing a disorder in one's mental faculties appears to violate the reality principle and to have consequences for adaptation and survival that seemingly must be experienced as undesirable. Although such a course of conduct would ordinarily be avoided, this could be superceded in certain instances. For example, the seeking of a pleasure or the avoidance of an unpleasure may be so highly valued that a particular violation of reality appears worthwhile.

To cause a disorder in one's mental faculties also appears to violate the narcissistic aspect of human nature. Mental faculties are frequently regarded with strong proprietary interest and have implications for self-esteem. However, the three principles of motivation are hypothetical entities and not real singular things. They refer to collections of singular things having common implications for a type of transcendent causal power. Thus, it is reasonable to conceive of a situation in which the individual has valued one narcissistic consideration more highly than another. Behavior may violate a law of motivation in one respect but conform in another.

SUMMARY

The definition of psychopathology as a self-caused disorder of mental faculties may initially appear strange and in violation of the current understanding of human nature. A closer examination of the issues involved clarifies that special conditions can occur in life when such a course of conduct is reasonable. I have shown that this course entails consequences that will be experienced by the individual as undesirable. Therefore, one should recognize that this conduct takes place within the context of something more undesirable, the lesser of two evils.

DEFENSE

The relativist definition of psychopathology as a self-caused disorder of mental faculties may appear strange in its explicit corollaries. The same basic notion, however, was expressed by Freud (1936/1959, p. 65) in his opinion that symptoms are created by the patient in order to avoid a danger. As early as 1928, Fenichel (1928/1953, p. 144) noted that patients used a distortion of the faculty for concentration as a maneuver to reduce the experience of unpleasant sensations. Later, Fenichel (1937/1954, p. 30) detailed the use of self-initiated hypertonus in order to curtail a particular activity.

The same basic notion is implied in the observation that patients alter their attitudes by adopting an exaggerated posture as a defensive stance (Freud, 1936/1959, p. 103). The intent to oppose some psychic tendency be selecting and emphasizing an antithetical attitude is referred to by the term *defense* (Brenner, 1976, pp. 77–78). Brenner (1976, p. 76) pointed out that any faculty may be used defensively.

The usual meaning of the term *defense* refers to activities that are motivated by life preservation. Within psychology there is the additional connotation of protecting oneself from one's own unpleasant thoughts. This understanding is burdened by the unrealistic implication of two "inner people" in an adversarial relationship. The relativist definition of defense is different, and I use the word with that definition in mind. Thus, *defense* refers to the observation that an individual has caused and maintains a disorder of mental faculties and that this activity is highly motivated. A defense is often maintained despite the considerable suffering entailed in violations of the pleasure and reality principles. Despite this consequent suffering, defense is maintained for its countering usefulness. This was recognized by Hartmann (1950/1964, p. 293) in his conclusion that observations of defense do not carry the necessary implication of an observation of psychopathology.

DIAGNOSIS AND TREATMENT

Defense attitudes are initiated and maintained in the effort to avoid an experience of major distress. The adoption of a defense attitude entails a distortion of mental faculties and inevitable consequences that are experienced unpleasantly in a variety of qualities and quantities. When these unpleasant consequences become perceived as burdensome, the individual may seek relief.

From the vantage point of relativism, I distinguish two different issues in the patient's presentation of a complaint. First, there is the outcome of disturbed mental faculties. Second, there is the situation that led to the adoption of a defensive attitude.

The distortion of a mental faculty need not be experienced unpleasantly. For example, the phenomenon of forgetting may arise under many conditions, such as senility and narcosis. In the context of psychopathology, it is a refusal to remember and serves the individual's purpose of defense. This has the connotation of a pleasant evaluation in the sense of relief or, at least, acceptance. Generally, purposive forgetting tends to spread. Those events that are closely associated by that person also become the target for motivated forgetting because their recognition would tend to recall that which the person is determined to avoid. One can easily imagine a situation in which a new line of activity is undertaken that requires access to an interdicted memory. In that case, the refusal to remember something in Context A, which is an acceptable position, also has consequences in Context B, which is experienced as not acceptable and frustrating. The patient is not presenting a complaint about forgetting in Context A but is complaining about his or her memory in Context B. From the psychologist's view, the patient's Context B complaint is legitimate. The person does suffer the natural consequences of a disturbed memory in Context B. At the same time, note that there is also a disturbed memory in Context A, even though the patient may not complain about the natural consequences of that disorder. In addition, the psychologist may evaluate the associative causal connection between Context A and Context B.

Thus, two different plans of intervention may evolve from the complexity of the situation. The disturbed memory in Context B may be targeted with the goal of enabling the desired activity to proceed. Also, the disturbed memory in Context A may be targeted with the goal of obviating the patient's need to maintain a defensive distortion of memory. The techniques, skill, and experience proper to the first treatment plan may be designed as *counseling psychotherapy*. The techniques, skills, and experience proper to the second treatment plan may be designated as *psychoanalytic psychotherapy*.

When a patient applies for assistance, it seems necessary for the psychologist to determine if there is a psychopathological state. One seeks evidence indicating that the patient, probably inadvertently, is maintaining a distortion of mental faculties that is related to his or her complaint of disturbance. In that case, with the diagnosis of psychopathology, the psychologist might well make the professional judgment about which treatment plan is the most suitable for that individual.

INTRAPSYCHIC CONFLICT

The relativist conception of psychopathology appreciates the inevitable complexity of the psychology of the person who applies for treatment of his or her presenting complaint. On the one hand, the patient has the wish for relief from some of the unpleasant consequences of his or her self-caused disorder of mental faculties. On the other hand, the patient does not ordinarily wish to be relieved from some other unpleasant consequences. In this latter aspect, the patient is willing to suffer an unpleasantness that appears to him or her as considerably less than an alternative unpleasantness. The patient's attitude toward the distorted mental faculties may be described as a complex experience.

The conflicted experience of psychological patients was recognized by Freud as an essential component of their condition. He attempted to grasp the essence of this intrapsychic conflict first by theorizing that the difference was in the qualities of consciousness and unconsciousness (Freud, 1900/1953, pp. 536–537). However, he later observed that the conflicting elements can be observed in all states of consciousness (Freud, 1920/1955, p. 19; 1923/1961, p. 27). He then theorized that the essence of this conflict was to be found among different functional groups of mental faculties: the id, ego, and superego (Freud, 1923/1961, p. 38).

The terms used in Freud's *structural theory* of the phenomenon of intrapsychic conflict refer to differences among groups of functional classes of mental faculties (Brenner, 1955, p. 45), not to a hypothetical causal agency. Although one often comes across the usage of "the ego" as "an integrator," and so on, this is a fundamental error (Hartmann, 1950/1964, p. 139). A recent attempt to correct this error is Schafer's (1976, p. 218) reminder that id, ego, and superego do not refer to mental agencies but to a quality of how the person operates those agencies.

Making use of Waelder's (1936) concept that all psychic activity is the consequence of multiple functions, Brenner (1976, p. 4) conceived that intrapsychic conflict is a compromise formation among id, ego, and superego types of functions. This theoretical view implies that a state of psychic conflict is a natural consequence of the competing interests among the varieties of mental endowment. The compromise formation is defined as an inevitable conflict, and it is assumed that this must be experienced as conflict. It has been noted (Rangell, 1988, p. 328) that compromise formations are not the only possible outcomes in conflict situations; there is always the possibility of decisions of choice.

However, the assumptions of structural theory are questionable and explanations built on them will prove to be unsatisfactory in explicating experience. It seems that Brenner (1976) recognized this theoretical deficiency by proposing an alternative explanation. He regarded wish, anxiety, guilt, and defense as the elements of psychic conflict that are present in all such states (Brenner, 1976, p. 10). Although this alternative conception may be clinically useful, especially in such expert hands, it is deficient at the theoretical level. The terms used lack definition in accord with a singular philosophy of science, a body of demonstrated basic assumptions, and a commonality of meaning. Despite stipulated qualifications, I find that the terms used by both Freud and Brenner refer to hypothesized causative agencies inferred to reside within the individual. Therefore, the basic conception of conflict in this view is of an internal event that has an impact on the individual. This is in contrast to the relativist view that conflict is initiated and maintained by the individual.

Another effort to understand better the occurrence of the phenomenon of intrapsychic conflict in psychopathological states was presented by Kris (1985). He noted that the conflicts usually reported are of a convergent type appearing to the person as obstacles (Kris, 1985, p. 540) or in the form of competing interests (Kris, 1985, p. 542). This is conceived to require the person to develop a compromise formation in an effort to adapt. He indicated that there is also a divergent type of conflict that appears to the person as a painful choice with the necessity to give up an important interest (Kris, 1985, p. 540). This requires the person to undertake a process akin to mourning in the effort to adapt (Kris, 1985, p. 553). Kris acknowledged that his presentation is a refinement of Rangell's (1963, p. 104) observation of oppositional and dilemma types of conflict.

Relativism regards Kris's (1985) work as a refinement in the making of observations arising from skillful clinical work. However, these observations are described from a theoretical position having assumptions that I hold as untenable. The different conflicts are viewed as having an impact on the individual rather than my view of being initiated and maintained by the individual.

The phenomenon referred to as intrapsychic conflict has been addressed by Freud, Brenner, and Kris from different angles. Nonetheless, they have in common the same philosophical position that I identify as objectivistic. Causative agencies outside of the person are seen as having an impact on the "psyche" (to borrow a term from among Jung's prolific coinage) and producing a distorting experience of conflict. The philosophical position is parallel to the medical biological model of such causes resulting in injury to a person. It is certain that such unfortunate situations do occur and that they cause distortion of mental faculties. However, I have pointed out that the same patterns of distorted faculties may arise in psychopathological situations in which they have a significantly different meaning. Although objectivists may be sharp observers, relativists view these same data with different interpretations of meaning and understanding.

CONCLUSION

I have considered various data of observation relevant to the study of psychopathological states. I have also considered a relativist interpretation of those data and contrasted it with other views. I have attempted to demonstrate my conviction that the relativist view is better in that it is founded on tenable basic assumptions. Although some relativist conclusions may appear unfamiliar, and some may contradict long-cherished beliefs, I hold that they are "more real" and of more scientific usefulness.

Relativism defines psychopathology as a state consequent to a self-caused distortion of mental faculties. The suffering entailed by this distortion is tolerated because of its defensive usefulness in mitigating a greater suffering.

REFERENCES

Blum, H. (1983). Splitting of the ego and its relation to parent loss. *Journal of the American Psychoanalytic Association, 31*, 301–324.

Bourne, L., & Ekstrand, B. (1973). *Psychology: Its principles and meanings.* Hinsdale, IL: Dryden Press.

Brenner, C. (1955). *An elementary textbook of psychoanalysis.* New York: International University Press.

Brenner, C. (1976). *Psychoanalytic technique and psychic conflict.* New York: International University Press.

Farber, B. (1983). Introduction: A critical perspective on burnout. In B. Farber (Ed.), *Stress and burnout in the human service professions* (pp. 1–22). New York: Pergamon Press.

Fenichel, O. (1953). Organ libidinization accompanying the defense against drives. In H. Fenichel (Ed.), *Collected papers* (Vol. 1, pp. 128–146). New York: Norton. (Original work published 1928)

Fenichel, O. (1954). Early stages of ego development. In H. Fenichel (Ed.), *Collected papers* (Vol. 2, pp. 25–48). New York: Norton. (Original work published 1937)

Freud, S. (1953). The interpretation of dreams, Pt. 2. In J. Strachey (Ed. & Trans.), *The standard edition of the complete psychological works of Sigmund Freud* (Vol. 5, pp. 339–627). London: Hogarth Press. (Original work published 1900)

Freud, S. (1955). Beyond the pleasure principle. In J. Strachey (Ed. & Trans.), *The standard edition of the complete psychological works of Sigmund Freud* (Vol. 18, pp. 1–64). London: Hogarth Press. (Original work published 1920)

Freud, S. (1959). The problem of anxiety. In J. Strachey (Ed. & Trans.), *The standard edition of the complete psychological works of Sigmund Freud* (Vol. 20, pp. 77-175). London: Hogarth Press. (Original work published 1936)

Freud, S. (1961). The ego and the id. In J. Strachey (Ed. & Trans.), *The standard edition of the complete psychological works of Sigmund Freud* (Vol. 19, pp. 3-66). London: Hogarth Press. (Original work published 1923)

Hartmann, H. (1964). Comments on the psychoanalytic theory of the ego. In H. Hartmann (Ed.), *Essays on ego psychology* (pp. 113-141). New York: International University Press. (Original work published 1950)

Kris, A. (1985). Resistance in convergent and divergent conflicts. *Psychoanalytic Quarterly, 44*, 537-568.

Miller, L. (1985). Some comments on cerebral hemispheric models of consciousness. *Psychoanalytic Review, 73*, 129-144.

Rangell, L. (1963). Structural problems in intrapsychic conflict. *Psychoanalytic Study of the Child, 18*, 103-138.

Rangell, L. (1988). The future of psychoanalysis: The scientific crossroads. *Psychoanalytic Quarterly, 3*, 313-340.

Schafer, R. (1976). *A new language for psychoanalysis.* New Haven, CT: Yale University Press.

Waelder, R. (1936). The principle of multiple function. *Psychoanalytic Quarterly, 15*, 45-62.

15

Resistance

BACKGROUND

The relativist view of individuals suffering from psychopathological states sees them as having adopted a defensive posture through both the initiation and maintenance of distorted mental faculties. Such people defend themselves from experiencing some major distress, compared with the relatively minor distress associated with distorted mental faculties. Consequently, it is predictable that they will resist any effort to dissuade them from their defensive position. The defense represents a compromise formation that expresses the probable minimum distortion and distress that the people are able to live with. They do so unhappily, as if choosing the lesser of two evils. As long as this compromise is able to be experienced as livable, these people probably will not seek treatment for the distress that accompanies distortion of faculties.

Nonetheless, the self-distortion of mental faculties establishes the presence of a condition of psychopathology. Thus, there are probably many people who are "sick" but who do not seek treatment. They elect to live with their condition. The same state of affairs is often found and remarked on by the medical profession.

When a person presents himself or herself for treatment, this may occur in significantly different contexts. For example, social pressure from family, friends, and coworkers may bring the person to the office. Also, it is not rare for loneliness to be the significant motivation. Putting these considerations aside, I focus attention on the person who primarily is seeking relief from distress associated with living with distorted mental faculties.

Probably most psychologists of all types would gather information from the person in order to make an informed conjecture about the source of the person's complaints. Despite differences in theoretical background, the conjecture would likely assume some form of distorted mental faculties. Even though a person's actions may be undertaken with good intention and possibly good result, these actions would also be understood as being responsible for the person's sense of distress. Action undertaken with a particular aim may have unforeseen consequences. With a background of special knowledge and experience, the psychologist may present to the patient expert information and advice. This procedure makes the reasonable assumption that if the person follows the expert's recommendations, he or she will experience relief from the distress. This advice may be received with thanks and used by the person to reshape his or her life in a more satisfactory manner. This type of psychological intervention is termed *guidance*. If the body of knowledge used by the psychologist is psychoanalysis, then this type of intervention is termed *psychoanalytic guidance*.

However, there are many instances when expert guidance meets with strong resistance from the person. It is then clear that the person is either unable or unwilling to accept or implement the recommendations. A popular presentation of such stalemate situations is in the report of Carl Roger's (1961) work with college students. He found that giving expert information was often of no use to the students (Rogers, 1961, p. 32) and that the psychologist must create a special experience in the office in order to enable change (Rogers, 1961, p. 33). This type of intervention is called *counseling*. If the body of knowledge used by the psychologist is psychoanalysis, then this intervention is termed *psychoanalytic counseling*. I have already discussed the theoretical basis of psychoanalytic counseling; the techniques appropriate to that activity are detailed elsewhere (e.g., Fischer, 1971).

PSYCHOANALYTIC PSYCHOTHERAPY

Resistance phenomena are frequently encountered in the practice of counseling when intervention seeks to change defensive behaviors in order to enable the performance of a desirable activity. Thus, counseling aims to confront only partially a patient's basic defensive position so that there are limited resistant consequences. Psychotherapy aims toward a full confrontation with the person's defensive position so that resistant consequences will appear more sharply. This stronger presentation enables a better study of and dealing with resistance.

CONSCIOUS RESISTANCE

Freud (1914/1957, p. 16) remarked that he frequently observed phenomena of resistance when attempting to provide the help that the person requested. The patient may be observed to act in ways that indicate reservations and a mistrust of the method, of the person of the therapist, or of the moral judgment of the therapist (Schafer, 1983, p. 73). These motivations are referred to as *conscious resistances* (Kernberg, 1975, p. 142), and it is possible to address them and achieve a resolution satisfying to the patient.

Even when conscious resistances are acknowledged and cleared away, Freud found that patients continued to behave with patterns that betrayed a resistant attitude (Freud, 1926/1959, p. 159). The therapist's attempts to deal with unconsciously maintained resistant attitudes are referred to both as "working through" (Freud, 1926/1959, p. 159) and much of what is implied by "analysis of the ego" (Freud, 1937/1964, p. 213; Schafer, 1983, p. 166).

REPRESSION RESISTANCE

The first form of unconscious resistance identified by Freud was the plea of failure of memory (Freud, 1914/1957, p. 16). Although the patient's memory of an event was sufficient to provide many details, the patient claimed that other details were not recoverable. Because it was known that the faculty for memory did not operate in that way, it appeared that the patient resisted the recollection of those absent details through a defensive distortion of memory by omission. These observations were understood at that time according to Freud's drive theory as an instance of "repression" (Freud, 1914/1957, p. 16) in which a "natural" impulse to remember was "pressed down" by a greater counterforce.

At that time treatment was understood as the overcoming of repression-type resistance by uncovering unconscious material and making it conscious (Freud, 1916/1963, p. 438). The hermeneutic method of psychoanalytic investigation provided the means for the discovery of unconscious material, and the method of reconstruction provided the means for confrontation. The perception of the resistance of the patient to attempts to make conscious what is being held unconsciously was the observational foundation for Freud's (1933/1964, p. 68) theorizing.

However, Freud observed that the insights gained by the patient through the undoing of repression were often insufficient in bringing about changes in manifestly disturbed behaviors (Freud, 1916/1963, p. 445). Although manifestations of repression resistance were undone and were no longer an impediment, other patterns of resistance continued to be observed (Freud, 1926/1959, pp. 159–160).

SECONDARY GAIN

Malingering

Patients present a disability and, despite claims of suffering and requests for help, they often resist efforts at assistance. This contradiction raises the possibility of *malingering*: that the presented disability and suffering are pretended and motivated by secret advantage. Such instances range from playing sick to avoid a school test to feigning an injury to collect insurance.

Malingering may be regarded as a self-caused distortion of faculties, both mental and otherwise, that is motivated by an effort to adapt to a perceived situation (Katz, 1963, p. 26). The psychologist may regard the malingering person as bad, making a moral evaluation that this way of dealing with the situation is socially reprehensible. The malingerer may also be judged bad according to a "health value" (Hartmann, 1960, p. 55), when the manner of dealing with the situation violates a medical view of a healthy way of life.

A diagnosis of malingering implies the establishment of evidence that a self-caused distortion of faculties is consciously undertaken. Many faculties may be subject to this intention, and this is enabled by the faculty for control of mobility. This same phenomenon may be viewed from biological, sociological, and psychological positions because there are these particular interests.

Psychology's interest in malingering is focused when the evidence establishes that the person has caused a distortion specifically of mental faculties. In that case, malingering is a type of psychopathology.

Attempts to intervene in a condition of malingering are bound to be met with the patient's resistance, and I distinguish two components of that opposition. A conscious component centers about the person's attempt to deal with some perceived aspect of the environment. The person's concerns in this regard are expressed in the form of *conscious resistance* and may be reduced by expert knowledge and advice. It may be presumed that the expert can find alternative advantageous adaptations other than the use of a distortion of mental faculties and that these are accessible to the person. However, it may also occur that the symptoms of mental distortion persist despite following the advice and changing behavior. It may also occur that the person experiences an inability to implement the advice. In either case, the attempt to examine further the psychology of the patient is met by patterns of resistance that are termed *unconscious resistance*, and the person then experiences no conscious justification for continuing those behaviors.

Primary Gain

In many cases the "secondary," or adaptive, gains of an illness are apparent to an observer. The failure to distinguish conscious from unconscious self-causations in the distortion of mental faculties leads to regarding all such persons as malingerers (Freud, 1920/1955, p. 213). An increased appreciation of the concepts *gain from illness* and *flight into illness* was furthered by the study of war neuroses (Freud, 1925/1959, p. 54). However, this view was limited by a consideration only of the external advantages of that illness (Freud, 1916/1963, p. 391) and its sociological consequences.

Freud was generally interested mainly in the psychological aspects of illness. He understood that an illness may be used as an interpersonal weapon, for protection or revenge, and to elicit caring (Freud, 1916/1963, p. 391). He was more concerned with the personal suffering entailed in living with distorted faculties, whether acknowledged or not. Both sensitivity to a person's suffering and the study of psychopathology are eroded by the diversion of interest to the sociological consequences of illness (Brenner, 1955, p. 207).

Freud attempted to counter unpsychoanalytic "external" interpretations of the term *secondary gain* by using the term *primary gain*. He meant to emphasize that something more primary and "internal" was going on in psychopathological states that involved an egoistic protective necessity (Freud, 1916/1963, p. 390). This idea is known by the term *defense*, a basic concept in understanding psychopathology. Thus, primary gain is a reference to the defensive utilization of a distortion of faculties. However, the term *gain* has misleading connotations in referring to a state of suffering (Katz, 1963, p. 47) that accompanies handicapped faculties.

The notion that primary gain is an important concept of psychoanalysis (Eissler, 1951, p. 227) is mistaken. What is primary is the understanding that whatever the discomfort of self-caused distortion of mental faculties, it is experienced as being less than another alternative. This understanding is expressed in psychoanalysis by the term *defense*.

WORKING THROUGH

My inquiry into the patterns of resistance encountered by psychoanalytic psychologists has led to distinguishing the forms of conscious from unconscious resistance. In the latter category, there is the pattern of repression resistance. Freud had found that after reducing conscious and repression resistance, there still remained evidence of a continuing unconscious resistance (Freud, 1926/1959, p. 159). The therapist recognizes that there is more analytic work to be done.

Despite changes in the patient's insight and behavior that may be judged positively, there remains an apparent need to work through and analyze further resistance (Greenson, 1965, p. 282; A. Kris, 1985, p. 542; Loewald, 1980, p. 39).

It has been noted that working through unconscious resistance often results in the patient's experiencing a process similar to mourning (A. Kris, 1985, p. 550; Stewart, 1963, p. 484).

I now discuss the various forms of unconscious resistance as they are met in working through.

REPETITION COMPULSION

After reducing conscious and repression resistance, Freud observed that patients maintained a resistant attitude against further examination of their distorted mental faculties (Freud, 1920/1955, p. 18). Because those behaviors were performed by the patient in the face of the unpleasure of that experience, it appeared as though the person was being compelled to act that way by an agency outside consciousness (Freud, 1926/1959, p. 160).

He noted that patterns actively repeating unpleasant experiences could also be seen in cases of traumatic neurosis and in certain frequent aspects of children's play (Freud, 1920/1955, p. 23). The observation of self-initiated unpleasant experiences was taken by Freud to be an indication of a psychological causal power that superceded both the pleasure and reality principles as they described human nature. He termed the manifestation of this power the *repetition compulsion* (Freud, 1920/1955, p. 19).

His investigations of these patterns of resistance could not localize the context of psychological motivation as described by either the pleasure or reality principles. It was clear to him that some other fundamental condition of motivation was in effect (Freud, 1937/1964, p. 241). These phenomena are comprehended by the third principle of motivation: narcissism. However, as I have discussed, Freud had abandoned the notion of narcissistic ego instincts when it had conflicted with his assumption of *infantile psychic helplessness.*

It is only by a fault in theoretical position that Freud came to attribute these phenomena, "perhaps not quite correctly" (Freud, 1937/1964, p. 242), to speculations about other fundamental id conditions such as the repetition compulsion. He developed these speculations, together with those about an instinct for destruction and aggression, in the hypothesis of a death instinct (Freud, 1937/1964, p. 243).

Glover expressed the opinion that controversial hypothetical entities such as unconscious resistance are attempts to cloak both a lack of understanding and the failure to identify the true source of a "fugitive resistance" (Glover, 1955, pp. 298–299). However, there is still the unfounded assertion that "the compulsion to repeat is clinically evident" (Sedler, 1983, p. 91).

What is clinically evident is that patterns of self-caused distortion of mental faculties are deliberately maintained in the face of evident suffering. The conclusion that this phenomenon indicates a new causal power is an outcome of the assumption of an initial experiential state of infantile psychic helplessness. Other observers of this same phenomenon hold different assumptions and come to different conclusions. For example, Menaker (1942) and Menaker and Menaker (1953) assumed that the normal infantile state includes an instinct for survival. The phenomena referred to by repetition compulsion are better seen to indicate the presence of extraordinary conditions for the indirect pursuit of survival. Eisenbud (1967) combined this notion with White's (1960) proposition that the infantile state includes a need for competence and effectance. She concluded that these same phenomena were an indication of conflicts about that need (White, 1960, p. 25).

Those writers disagreed with the assumption that the initial infantile state is characterized by psychic helplessness. However, their omission of the recognition of narcissism as the strong force of human motivation led them to seek understanding by hypothesizing new forms of transcendent causal power.

Despite the confusion in understanding due to the insufficiencies of Freud's philosophical position, I may credit his intuition in retaining both the concept that defense against a dangerous perception is common to all psychopathology (Freud, 1926/1959, p. 159) and the precept that the analysis of defense is the crux of psychoanalytic psychotherapy. The patterns that are interpreted as evidence of a repetition compulsion are better seen as defensive formations within the context of narcissistic motivation. These patterns are termed by relativist psychology as *repetition resistance*.

CLINGING TO ILLNESS

After reducing conscious and repression resistances, Freud noted that the pattern of resistance sometimes appeared similar to that observed in normal states of mourning (Freud, 1917/1957, p. 245), except that neither the patient nor the therapist could identify the lost object. There was a similar "loss of interest in the outside world": being unattracted by previously attractive possibilities for happiness or relief offered by treatment (Freud, 1917/1957, p. 244). The use of mental faculties in dealing with the world now seemed burdened by a general inhibition (Freud, 1917/1957, p. 244).

The resistance appeared to be in the form of "clinging to an illness" (Freud, 1923/1961, p. 71), similar to clinging to an object that is recognized as dead (Freud, 1917/1957, pp. 244–245). Society appears to accept a person's clinging to a dead object as normal, with the assumption that the person holds onto pleasant memories and struggles against the implication of never again having these enjoyments. Relativists take issue with the correctness of this common understanding. The taking of pleasure from memories, such as leafing through an album of photographs, is not jeopardized by the current death of an object. These memories continue to be accessible. A current death is no barrier to current remembering. It is true that the current and future availability of the object for pleasure is negated by the object's death. However, in accord with the pleasure principle, the object's reevaluation on death may be changed from pleasant to unpleasant. An unpleasant object will tend to be avoided. Thus, clinging to a dead object violates both the pleasure and reality principles.

Relativists understand that narcissistic motivation has the power to supercede both pleasure and reality considerations. Clinging to a dead object is a self-caused distortion of mental faculties that serves a defensive purpose in conditions of narcissistic injury. One may speculate that it is narcissistically painful to accept the delimitation that one cannot have what one wants, when one wants it, and in the way one wants it. This understanding of the clinging to illness patterns of resistance is presented as an alternative to the proposition that they represent the retention of a "love-object" (Freud, 1937/1964, p. 241).

Because mourning involves a self-caused distortion of mental faculties, it should be recognized as a kind of psychopathology. Note that in many cases there soon seems to be a spontaneous remission. It then appears to be an illness whose usual course is not serious, perhaps similar to the advent of a pimple. However, it also may persist unduly or worsen and then become an occasion for professional intervention.

A clinging pattern of resistance implies the observation of a person's efforts to retain his or her illness and to resist passively and indirectly any attempts to change his or her position. Thus, one can observe manifestations of an attitude such as "leave me alone," often understood as withdrawal of interest from the world (Freud, 1917/1957, p. 244). At the same time, such people show a flattened affect with an apparent inhibition of previous enjoyments and enthusiasms. Relativistic psychologists term these patterns *clinging resistance*.

MORAL MASOCHISM

Resistant patterns often appear similar to those seen in states of masochism. These are unlike the pattern of clinging that is described as an attitude of resignation toward living with disability (Freud, 1940/1964, p. 180) and "psychic inertia" (Freud, 1940/1964, p. 181). Masochistic persons are active and persistent in performing patterns that they recognize as being contrary to their own interests. These patterns are troublesome in expediency and ruinous of self-beneficial future prospects (Freud, 1924/1961, p. 169). It was noted that their symptoms of self-caused distortions of mental faculties frequently vanished with the advent of an external occasion for misery, such as a financial disaster or a serious disease (Freud, 1924/1961, p. 166). It appeared that these people were determined to maintain a degree of suffering in every and any circumstance.

The steadfast pursuit of activities, even though they were recognized to be necessarily accompanied by unpleasant experience, suggested a simile with the pathological condition of masochism. In both states there was the same conscious resolution to bring about an unpleasant experience, in apparent violation of the pleasure principle.

In masochism this takes place in a sexual context. The person is unable to achieve genital orgasmic satisfaction within a normal pleasurable context but is able to do so within an unpleasant context of being bound, beaten, or debased (Freud, 1924/1961, p. 162). This condition is regarded as one of a variety of activities used to overcome a disability in normal sexual functioning, and it is the context of the technical term *perversion*. Thus, masochism is a type of perversion (Grossman, 1986, p. 386).

The perversion of masochism was understood to accord with the pleasure principle because it could be demonstrated that a degree of self-caused unpleasure was endured in the interest of achieving a degree of otherwise unavailable sexual pleasure. The simile to masochistic patterns is applied to other patterns of self-caused unpleasure, with the assumption that there is a context of undetected pleasure. However, the manifest pleasure of masochistic patterns is absent in these compared states. Those states are not characterized as pleasure seeking but as seeking the maintenance of suffering (Freud, 1924/1961, p. 165). Thus, the simile between these two states is based on a component that is observable in one and only hypothesized in the other. These two states fail to qualify as analogous because they are dissimilar in their chief elements.

Freud was aware that the patterns of resistance he found similar to masochism were lacking indications of any manifest accompanying pleasure. However, he was burdened by the theoretical delimitations of his drive theory, that the pleasure and reality principles described human motivation. This form of resistance was both directly and indirectly contrary to the reality principle. Although this resistance was directly contrary to the pleasure principle, there was a possibility that it was indirectly and unconsciously a pleasure, if not in the sense of gratification, then in the sense of relief (Freud, 1924/1961, p. 162).

His theoretical position led him to assume that some sort of relief pleasure must be the secret motivation sustaining this pattern (Freud, 1924/1961, p. 165). In this regard, he recognized another simile in comparison with states of conscious guilt. The unpleasant experience of guilt is observed to be relieved by acts of expiation (Freud, 1924/1961, p. 162). He assumed that the pattern of resistance in question was accompanied by an "unconscious sense of guilt" or, "more correctly, a need for punishment" (Freud, 1924/1961, p. 166). He referred to matters of conscience as functions of a superego, a hypothetical entity with causal powers. Thus, he identified the pattern as a superego-type of resistance, or moral masochism (Freud, 1924/1961, p. 161; Freud, 1937/1964, p. 242).

I have shown the failure of the attempt to identify the form of this pattern of resistance as an analogy to masochism. It has been noted that the evocation of this term is imprecise and misleading both theoretically and clinically (Grossman, 1986, p. 381). The phenotype of a person's seeking and maintaining painful experience has been observed in a variety of pathological states (Grossman, 1986, p. 381). The manifest pattern may appear in conditions of realistically endured suffering, deliberate self-injury, and poor judgment (Grossman, 1986, pp. 382–383). Behaviors that are judged to be self-injurious by an observer may be organized self-regulations that serve variety of purposes not apparent to the observer (Grossman, 1986, p. 408).

Activities of self-regulation are enabled by the mental faculty for the control of mobility. When self-regulation is applied to cause a distortion of other mental faculties, there is a defined state of psychopathology. Whatever may be the evaluation of a person's unfortunate situation, there must be alternatives of dealing with the situation other than the institution of a self-distortion of mental faculties.

For example, one may pretend to have distorted mental faculties. One may pretend to be ill to avoid a test at school where there is the probability of failure and significant consequences. Although these behaviors may be judged to be morally reprehensible and indicative of a social problem, they are not psychopathological.

At the same time, self-distortion of mental faculties is frequently observed in childhood and appears to be a normal developmental part of learning how to deal with the world (Grossman, 1986, p. 403). Nonetheless, relativists regard these as psychopathological states. However, one may well judge that they are not serious conditions that call for professional intervention because they may be temporary and not interfere significantly in the person's conduct of life. A pimple is pathology but need not necessarily require treatment.

When conscious and repression resistances have been reduced, a pattern of seeking and maintaining unpleasurable experience may be observed. I have examined several propositions of understanding this observation that have proved to be untenable. Relativists recognize that the manifest pattern violates both the pleasure and reality principles and that analytic investigation has failed to detect evidence of their unconscious operation. Differing from drive theory, which must seek understanding in the identification of a new aspect of psychological causal power, relativism is familiar with this situation. Narcissistic motivation is often recognized to supercede the pleasure and reality principles. In addition, the defensive use of distortions and an endurance of their accompanying unpleasant consequences are familiar psychopathological patterns of coping with experiences of narcissistic injury. Consequently, those patterns identified as moral masochism are regarded as better comprehended by the understanding that they indicate the presence of a defensive state within a narcissistic context. Relativist psychologists refer to these patterns as *narcissistic resistance*.

REGRESSION

It has been noted that certain patterns of people's behavior have a quality judged to be regressive. Invariably, the judgment is made according to a temporal standard. This assumes that the standard has a developmental sequence that is distinguishable quantitatively or qualitatively.

This concept proved to be a useful tool in Freud's (1891) biological explorations, especially in neurology. He also used it to good effect in understanding human psychosexual development (Freud, 1905/1960), the development of mental ego faculties (Freud, 1913/1955), and the development of social conscience (Freud, 1917/1957). However, when used in individual psychological studies, Freud and others have used the term and the concept with a wide variety of meanings and significations (Arlow & Brenner, 1964, p. 56).

Standards

One source of the variation in meaning of regression may be attributed to the use of different standards in judging the observations. The most frequent standard used by psychologists is that of ego functions (Arlow & Brenner, 1964, p. 78). These are understood to play an essential role in everyday activities ranging from artistic to sexual contexts. Another reason why psychologists are interested in ego functions is that they are understood to play an essential role in psychopathology (Arlow & Brenner, 1964, p. 74).

The term *ego functions* is a theoretical translation of what is otherwise referred to as "hereditary, inborn, psychic apparatus" with "primary autonomous functions" (Hartmann, 1939/1958). These qualities are regarded as characteristics of a hypothetical entity called ego (Hartmann, 1939/1958). For philosophical reasons, relativism regards these qualities as being characteristic of all mental faculties. Mental faculties, such as sense perception and memory, are biological endowments that normally undergo maturational and developmental processing.

The scientific study of the commonalities within human behavior has identified patterns that are proven to be valid and reliable indicators of types of mental faculties. Further study of these patterns has shown that these faculties regularly show significant changes in their functional capabilities during the normal course of life. The common understanding of observations of regular significant functional changes is expressed by the terms *phases*, or *stages*, of development. The review of these stages in chapter 11 demonstrates the quantum increases in functional capacity of these biological mental faculties.

Biological and Sociological Norms

Study of the regular changes in the functional capacity of mental faculties has led to their codification in the form of schedules of development that correlate these stages with age. One such popular schedule is that proposed by Anna Freud (1965) and her coworkers.

The establishment of developmental schedules allows the detection of departures from those norms. However, the meaning of any such departure is far from unequivocal. The data of observation refer to functional changes of biological faculties, whether these faculties are directly perceptible or validly inferred. In either case, one understands philosophically that the functioning of any biological faculty is the vector outcome of biological, sociological, and psychological causal powers.

The differential diagnosis of which type of causal power is most responsible for an observed variation in a particular instance depends on the accumulation of evidence to substantiate that judgment. Evidence supporting the conclusion that the functional variation from the norm is individualistic may be cited to support the contention that the phenomenon is a matter particularly for psychological interests.

I have shown how departures from biological developmental norms may be caused by biological, sociological, and psychological powers. These departures are maintained as the vector outcome of those powers. In any case, the identification of departures as individualistic establishes the significant contribution of psychological powers. Thus, psychologists have an interest in studying biological and sociological developmental norms in order to have a basis for the detection of individual variations.

Psychological Norms

The term *psychological norm* refers to the observation of a person performing regular patterns of behavior that deviate significantly from the biological and sociological schedules of normal functioning. Within the generality of individual functional variation, only those that have been established as indicative of mental faculties are of primary importance for psychology. Psychologists seek to identify individualistic patterns of functional variations, especially in the performance of mental faculties. They seek to identify patterns that are characteristic of an individual. These individual patterns are recognized by terms such as mannerism, oddity, peculiarity, eccentricity, personality, and genius. The choice of adjective reflects a personal evaluation by the observer.

The identification by psychologists of individualistic patterns in the performance of mental faculties constitutes a basis for the study of the regular changes in those patterns over the course of time. The detailing of these patterns and the identification of stages in their variation is referred to by relativist psychology by the term *psychological norm*. These considerations provide a theoretical justification for the use by psychologists of the methods of individualistic longitudinal case studies.

PSYCHOPATHOLOGY

Departures from biological, sociological, and psychological norms may be due to the major contribution of a psychological cause. When the details of observation indicate that the functional departure is of a self-caused distortion of mental faculties, there is a state of psychopathology. This labeling recognizes the inevitable distress accompanying any distortion. A germ is a germ. However, having a germ does not necessarily mean having a disease. The diagnosis of disease depends on an informed and experienced evaluation of the person's total experience within which this distress is one element. The decision may be mitigated by the presence of significant biological, sociological, or other psychological factors. These may be judged to be exceeding in degree of contribution that which is indicated by the original observation.

When a state of distorted mental faculties cannot be justified by the person, an evaluation of causal powers is required. The finding of self-causation is distinguished by the term *defense*. Any defense is psychopathological but not necessarily indicative of disease. The judgment of regression according to a psychological norm identifies a state of defense and psychopathology. Therefore, it is necessary to evaluate a condition of regression as constituting only a germ or a significant disease.

The identification of regressive phenomena that are judged to be benign can be recognized in the literature under the label "regression in the service of the ego" (E. Kris, 1934/1952, pp. 175–177). E. Kris reported that some regressions were eminently useful as adaptations to environmental conditions that were experienced as undesirable but unalterable (E. Kris, 1934/1952, p. 177). It was also noted that regressions may be useful in maintaining a sense of security (Fenichel, 1944/1954, p. 279). These findings would mitigate judgment about the severity of a psychopathological state.

It has been noted that innate mental faculties generally show increased functional utility during the regular course of development. This sense is implied in descriptions of these patterns as "primary and autonomous" (Hartmann, 1939/1958). The increased utility to the person of the development of functional variations of faculties is recognized in the description of them as "resistant to regression" (Hartmann, 1964, p. xi). Although later developed methods of employment are generally of greater usefulness, this does not mean that earlier patterns may not be employed usefully for particular circumstances, such as play.

The interpretation of regression refers to a judgment that the person is performing a functional pattern that has been generally superceded by a different pattern. A new pattern that has become characteristic for the person and a part of his or her current psychological norm is replaced by an earlier pattern. Although behavior patterns can be identified as part of a person's earlier norm, even that of an infantile period, this observation carries no necessary implication of psychopathology (Arlow & Brenner, 1964, p. 71; Brenner, 1968, p. 428; Loewald, 1981, p. 24). In fact, the person's use of both old and new functional patterns has been likened to the process of trial and error and may be regarded as contributing to a favorable course of development (A. Freud, 1965, p. 99).

When such qualifications as "reversal of developmental progression" (A. Kris, 1985, p. 547) are added to regression, it is an attempt to convey the impression that the particular regression takes place in a context of psychopathology. In that

142

THE SCIENCE OF PSYCHOTHERAPY

case, regression is not regarded as in the service of the ego but is being used defensively. Then, it is not the specific aim of psychotherapy to "undo the regression" (Beres, 1971, p. 23) but to undo the defensive use of the regression.

Regression Resistance

After the reduction of conscious and repression resistance, a patient's continuing resistant attitude against further examination of his or her self-caused distortion of mental faculties may appear in patterns described as regressive. These may be detected by comparison with biological, sociological, or personal psychological norms. In the event of a psychological context, the pattern of regression resistance is maintained as a defense in conflicts involving the pleasure and reality principles or narcissism.

REFERENCES

Arlow, J., & Brenner, C. (1964). *Psychoanalytic concepts and the structural theory.* New York: International University Press.

Beres, D. (1971). Ego autonomy and ego pathology. *Psychoanalytic Study of the Child, 26*, 3–24.

Brenner, C. (1955). *An elementary textbook of psychoanalysis.* New York: International University Press.

Brenner, C. (1968). Archaic features of ego functioning. *International Journal of Psychoanalysis, 49*, 426–429.

Eisenbud, R.-J. (1967). Masochism revisited. *Psychoanalytic Review, 54*, 5–26.

Eissler, K. (1951). Malingering. In G. Wilbur & W. Muensterberger (Eds.), *Psychoanalysis and culture* (pp. 218–253). New York: International University Press.

Fenichel, O. (1954). Remarks on the common phobias. In H. Fenichel (Ed.), *Collected papers* (Vol. 2, pp. 278–287). New York: Norton. (Original work published 1944)

Fischer, H. (1971). Psychoanalytic counseling. *Psychotherapy Bulletin, 4*, 11–13.

Freud, A. (1965). *Normality and pathology in childhood.* New York: International University Press.

Freud, S. (1953). *On aphasia.* (E. Stengel, Trans.). New York: International University Press. (Original work published 1891)

Freud, S. (1955). Animism, magic, and the omnipotence of thoughts. In J. Strachey (Ed. & Trans.), *The standard edition of the complete psychological works of Sigmund Freud* (Vol. 13, pp. 75–99). London: Hogarth Press. (Original work published 1913)

Freud, S. (1955). Beyond the pleasure principle. In J. Strachey (Ed. & Trans.), *The standard edition of the complete psychological works of Sigmund Freud* (Vol. 18, pp. 1–64). London: Hogarth Press. (Original work published 1920)

Freud, S. (1957). Mourning and melancholia. In J. Strachey (Ed. & Trans.), *The standard edition of the complete psychological works of Sigmund Freud* (Vol. 14, pp. 237–258). London: Hogarth Press. (Original work published 1917)

Freud, S. (1958). On the history of the psychoanalytic movement. In J. Strachey (Ed. & Trans.), *The standard edition of the complete psychological works of Sigmund Freud* (Vol. 14, pp. 7–66). London: Hogarth Press. (Original work published 1914)

Freud, S. (1959). An autobiographical study. In J. Strachey (Ed. & Trans.), *The standard edition of the complete psychological works of Sigmund Freud* (Vol. 20, pp. 7–70). London: Hogarth Press. (Original work published 1925)

Freud, S. (1959). Inhibitions, symptoms and anxiety. In J. Strachey (Ed. & Trans.), *The standard edition of the complete psychological works of Sigmund Freud* (Vol. 20, pp. 77–176). London: Hogarth Press. (Original work published 1926)

Freud, S. (1960). Three essays on the theory of sexuality. In J. Strachey (Ed. & Trans.), *The standard edition of the complete psychological works of Sigmund Freud* (Vol. 7, pp. 123–243). London: Hogarth Press. (Original work published in 1905)

Freud, S. (1961). The economic problem of masochism. In J. Strachey (Ed. & Trans.), *The standard edition of the complete psychological works of Sigmund Freud* (Vol. 19, pp. 159–172). London: Hogarth Press. (Original work published 1924)

Freud, S. (1961). The ego and the id. In J. Strachey (Ed. & Trans.), *The standard edition of the complete psychological works of Sigmund Freud* (Vol. 19, pp. 3–66). London: Hogarth Press. (Original work published 1923)

Freud, S. (196?). Introductory lectures on psycho-analysis. In J. Strachey (Ed. & Trans.), *The standard edition of the complete psychological works of Sigmund Freud* (Vols. 15, 16; pp. 9–496). London: Hogarth Press. (Original work published 1916/1917)

Freud, S. (1964). Analysis terminable and interminable. In J. Strachey (Ed. & Trans.), *The standard edition of the complete psychological works of Sigmund Freud* (Vol. 23, pp. 216–253). London: Hogarth Press. (Original work published 1937)

Freud, S. (1964). An outline of psycho-analysis. In J. Strachey (Ed. & Trans.), *The standard edition of the complete psychological works of Sigmund Freud* (Vol. 23, pp. 137–207). London: Hogarth Press. (Original work published 1940)

Freud, S. (1964). New introductory lectures on psycho-analysis. In J. Strachey (Ed. & Trans.), *The standard edition of the complete psychological works of Sigmund Freud* (Vol. 22, pp. 1–175). London: Hogarth Press. (Original work published 1933)

Glover, E. (1955). *The technique of psycho-analysis*. New York: International University Press.

Greenson, R. (1965). The problem of working through. In M. Schur (Ed.), *Drives, affects, behavior: Vol. 2. Essays in honor of Marie Bonaparte* (pp. 277–314). New York: International University Press.

Grossman, W. (1986). Notes on masochism: A discussion of the history and development of a psychoanalytic concept. *Psychoanalytic Quarterly, 55,* 379–413.

Hartmann, H. (1958). *Ego psychology and the problem of adaptation* (D. Rapaport, Trans.). New York: International University Press. (Original work published 1939)

Hartmann, H. (1960). *Psychoanalysis and moral values*. New York: International University Press.

Hartmann, H. (1964). Introduction. In H. Hartmann (Ed.), *Essays in ego psychology* (pp. ix–xv). New York: International University Press.

Katz, J. (1963). On primary gain and secondary gain. *Psychoanalytic Study of the Child, 18,* 9–50.

Kernberg, O. (1975). *Borderline conditions and pathological narcissism*. New York: Jason Aronson.

Kris, A. (1985). Resistance in convergent and divergent conflicts. *Psychoanalytic Quarterly, 44,* 537–568.

Kris, E. (1952). The psychology of caricature. In E. Kris (Ed.), *Psychoanalytic explorations in art* (pp. 173–178). New York: International University Press. (Original work published 1934)

Loewald, H. (1980). Hypnoid state, repression, abreaction, and recollection. In *Papers on psychoanalysis* (pp. 32–42). New Haven, CT: Yale University Press. (Original work published 1955)

Loewald, H. (1981). Regression: Some general consideration. *Psychoanalytic Quarterly, 50,* 22–43.

Menaker, E. (1942). The masochistic factor in the psychoanalytic situation. *Psychoanalytic Quarterly, 11,* 171–186.

Menaker, E., & Menaker, W. (1965). Ego in evolution. New York: Grove Press.

Rogers, C. (1961). *On becoming a person*. Boston: Houghton Mifflin.

Schafer, R. (1983). *The analytic attitude*. New York: Basic Books.

Sedler, M. (1983). Freud's concept of working through. *Psychoanalytic Quarterly, 52,* 73–98.

Stewart, W. (1963). An inquiry into the concept of working through. *Journal of the American Psychoanalytic Association, 11,* 474–499.

White, R. (1960). Competence and the psychosexual stages of development. In M. Jones (Ed.), *Nebraska Symposium on Motivation* (pp. 84–102). Lincoln: University of Nebraska Press.

16

Transference

BACKGROUND

In many situations in which there were no obvious manifestations of conscious or repressive resistance, Freud noted that the patient's attitude of resisting further analytic examination took a form in which the therapist was not only regarded as an authority but as an "authority figure" (Freud, 1938/1964, pp. 174–175). Instead of complying with the therapist's request to report subjective experience and biographical information, the patient acted as though an authority figure had made the request (Freud, 1938/1964, p. 176). Two observations led him to conclude that this form of resistance was particularly important: (a) It emerged regularly in the course of the treatment of a wide variety of psychopathological states, and (b) the reduction of this form of resistance was a potent experience and resulted in the most significant gains (Freud, 1938/1964, p. 177).

Freud was struck by the simile to the attitude of children toward their parents, in that children often treat their parents with excesses of adulation as well as derogation. In accord with his theoretical assumptions, he interpreted these observations as indicating that the patient transferred emotions appropriate to a past authority figure onto the person of the present authority figure of the therapist. Thus, the concept of *transference* has reference to the patient's experiences both in the past and the present.

Theory

The importance of the phenomenon of transference is documented by its citation in almost any publication of psychoanalytic theory or practice. However, not only did Freud use the term in a variety of meanings, many authors have since then (Sandler, 1983, p. 10). There is a general sense that transference refers to an element of importance in every human relationship (Brenner, 1955, p. 112) and that it is crucial to psychoanalytic theory and practice (Cooper, 1987, p. 97). From the beginning of Freud's work with Breuer from 1893 to 1905 (detailed in Cooper, 1987, p. 77) to the last of his work (Freud, 1940/1964, p. 177), Freud maintained that the phenomenon of transference indicated the presence of factors essential to a study of psychology. Nonetheless, there has not been any generally accepted definition of the phenomenon (Cooper, 1987, p. 77).

The difficulty in arriving at a singular definition of transference has been attributed to the fact that the phenomenon has been viewed from a variety of theoretical positions (Cooper, 1987, p. 78; Laplanche & Pontalis, 1973, p. 456; Rangell, 1988, p. 319). The maintenance of such multiple and conflicting theories within psychoanalysis gives it the appearance of a fragmented science (Rangell, 1988, p. 333). There has been a recent movement to elevate the undefined phenomenon of transference to a position that nearly excludes any other consideration (Rangell, 1988, p. 322). Perhaps it is the difficulty in comprehending the complexity of a transcendent reality that motivates the search to find some single theory on which to grasp hold.

Historical Theories

As a science using hermeneutic methodology, psychoanalytic psychology seeks to establish inferences of demonstrable reliability and validity. Therefore, it depends on a base of observations that are reliable and valid. Because this science studies individual experience, the data base is composed of observations of the individual. One class of such observations concerns the personal historical facts of the individual. These facts place a limit on and serve as a guide for inferences and reasonable interpretation (Cooper, 1987, p. 84).

The usefulness of personal historical facts in making inferences about an individual's current status is reflected in the fact that obtaining an anemnesis has become a standard part of psychological examination. The use of established developmental schedules of mental faculties is routine in the selection of historical facts. In the same manner, psychologists often use biological (Cooper, 1987, p. 84) and sociological developmental schedules. Psychoanalysts often use developmental schedules of psychosexual stages and stages of object relations.

The usefulness of personal historical facts in making inferences about an individual's current status has been judged to be of varying importance. Freud's theoretical position viewed transference as a "reincarnation" of historical fact (Freud, 1938/1964, p. 175), and its reconstruction was regarded as essential. His theoretical position was consonant with the philosophy of science held at that time. This philosophy assumed that current observed reality was knowable by learning its history (Kermode, 1985, p. 3). This ontogenetic theory of reality makes untenable objectivist assumptions about the nature of observation. Today, historical facts are no longer taken as being literally related to current events but are used in making inferences about current events (Cooper, 1987, p. 83).

RECONSTRUCTION

Historical Facts

The data of observation relevant in the effort to learn historical facts may be distinguished in two classes. There is the testimony of the individual, which may be called "subjective." There is the testimony of other people in the form of reports and records, which may be called "objective."

Objective Data

I put the term "objective" in quotes as a warning against the tendency to accept uncritically the testimony of witnesses, even in written form. All testimony is subject to error and falsification and must be evaluated before its use as a basis for inference.

Within the category of written reports, school records may be relevant. These may include the notation of special events both at school and at home. In addition, patterns of performance at school may be identified as indications of important personal problems (Jarvis, 1969, p. 297).

Among "objective" data there is a category in which the therapist is an "eyewitness" to the patient's behavior. The person's postures and gestures are familiarly viewed as body language. However, a scientific approach requires that only behaviors that are demonstrated to be conspicuously repetitive and idiosyncratic qualify as a basis for psychological inference (McLaughlin, 1987, p. 558). There is considerable literature on the usefulness of these observations in making conjectures about the person's current status (e.g., McLaughlin, 1987). These same patterns may be studied as to the circumstances of their adoption and their relation to important historical facts.

These observations are functional. Relativists understand that functions are the vector outcome of biological, sociological, and psychological causal powers on biological capacities. Therefore, any observation of functioning is equivocal toward those elements and requires evaluation. Changes in functioning are not necessarily indicative of the arrival of new faculties or causal powers. In the absence of specific data that demonstrate such an arrival, changes in functioning are assumed to reflect an increase in the utility of existing faculties during development.

The therapist is also an eyewitness to the patient's verbal behavior. Apart from the content of what is being said, there is the form in which it is said. In patterns of speech, those constituents of an "individual signature" can be identified (McLaughlin, 1987, p. 573). For example, the detection of a marked accent is a strong indication of birthplace.

Attention to the person's form of language may indicate the frequent and idiosyncratic use of particular words and phrases, so-called "pet terms." These terms may be used in a metaphoric manner, as the conveyance of an unusual connotation that marks a personal insistence. The study of a person's metaphors has proven useful in the identification of historical facts of psychological significance (Sharpe, 1940/1950). For example, the marked use of "I can't control," "making a mess," "reeking," "squeezing," and "making a fuss" were indications of problems about toilet training.

The observation that the use of these terms was accompanied by particular emotional expressions suggested to Sharpe (1940/1950) that the person's experience included a strong element of sensory impressions. The metaphoric usage appeared as a conveyance of the sensory impressions related to the experience of a historical event (Sharpe, 1940/1950, p. 156).

A theoretical understanding of this phenomenon was proposed by Ferenczi (1911/1950a). He studied the usage of obscene words among many people and observed that they were often accompanied by evidence that the person was experiencing motor and perceptual qualities of unusual intensity. He theorized that in the acquisition of language, words have strong motoric and sensory associations that are gradually weakened in the course of socialization. Obscene words are usually excluded from that development and retain those qualities in large measure (Ferenczi, 1911/1950a).

Although such an ontogenetic speculation appears difficult to verify, it seems to be reasonable and is heuristically useful. Jones (1920/1951) found it valuable in understanding a peculiarity of the English language, with its history of Saxon, Norman–French, and Latin words. The Saxon words appeared to be most vividly

associated with motoric and sensory qualities that are more shadowed in the equiv-
alent words of Norman–French. These appear even more adumbrated in the use of
Latin words. The progression is illustrated among the synonyms "gut," "bowel,"
and "intestine" (Jones, 1920/1951, pp. 93–94). This knowledge may be useful in
making inferences about a person's current status. Regarded as metaphor, it may
be indicative of important historical facts.

In American usage, "gut" is also regarded as an indelicate reference, whereas
"bowel" is the word ordinarily used. "Intestine" is generally reserved for its
emotionally aseptic medical connotation. Because the history of the American
language is different from that of English, a similar study would prove useful in
the detection of metaphoric usage and as an indication of important personal his-
toric facts.

Subjective Data

The other source of personal historical facts is the "subjective" one of the
person's report of memory. This source has problems of validity and needs evaluation. I have discussed the method of evaluation called *clarification*. In addition, the
clarification of reports from memory are furthered by the psychoanalytic methods
for the reduction of conscious and repression resistances. Note that the reduction
of other forms of resistance often results in a further clarification of historical
facts, both as experience and as witness. Also note that the reconstruction of
historical facts is continuously refined and that their probability is continually
increased by extending the data base used to draw an inference. The evaluation of
historical facts drawn from memory is assisted by knowledge of the functioning of
the mental faculty of memory.

Clarification

The hermeneutic method involves the gathering of a variety of data of observation about the version of reality as it appears to the subject. Guided by the principles of relativist psychology, those data are clarified and evaluated. These new
data of understanding are then used to draw inferences about a new version of
reality. The new version may not be perceptible to the subject and is a construction
of the understanding of the subject's reality. Consequently, one arrives at a constructed view of reality that is held to be more realistic than the subject's subjective
view of reality. I refer to these constructed views as *constructs*. When the hermeneutic method is applied to constructing personal historical facts, I refer to that
activity as *reconstruction*. This is different from the construction of current personal facts, which I refer to as an activity of construction.

Summary

Methods for the determination of personal historical facts were first developed
under the assumption that current patterns of resistance, in which the therapist was
treated as an authority figure, were the continuing enactment of an earlier relationship with a parent. This assumption is now seen to be untenable. Nonetheless,
occasionally transference is referred to as a repetition of a childhood conflict

(Brenner, 1955, p. 119), although with some qualification. This assumption is an objectivist error. Relativists regard the determination of personal historical facts as one important guide for drawing reasonable inferences about current status. The method of reconstruction guides the construction of current reality.

CONSTRUCTION

The modern view of transference phenomena was presented by Strachey (1934). He regarded the current conflicted phenomenon as a new edition of impossible conflicts, so that they were resolvable in the present (Strachey, 1934, p. 132). However repetitive those patterns may be, they are a current experience for the patient (Schafer, 1976, p. 57). Therefore, transference refers to observations of a person's experience, particularly when the form is an attitude toward an authority figure.

There are therapeutic systems that hold it as unnecessary to know personal historical facts in order to understand and treat the person's present difficulty. Such systems hold that the past does not currently exist and that the term is a euphemism for remembering, which is something the person does in the present (Cooper, 1987, p. 83). With my philosophy of science, one can demonstrate that a construction of current reality will be less true with the omission of historical facts.

At the same time, it has been noted that demonstrably untrue constructions may be used with considerable effectiveness and good result (Emde, 1981, pp. 217–218). However, the finding of a good result is not proof that the method constitutes a treatment. A method is not demonstrated to be a treatment even if it can be shown that it regularly induces changes in function. For example, the prescription of aspirin in cases of bacterial infection will regularly induce changes in achiness and temperature but will not affect the bacteria. In order to test a method as a treatment, the essence of the disease must be defined and detectable. This is described as the *structure* of the disease, and only methods that induce changes in the structure of disease qualify as treatments.

Reconstruction of personal historical facts may be used in the reconstruction of a prior state of disease. A reconstructed state of disease may have ontogenetic implication in understanding a currently constructed state of disease, although not necessarily. A study of the similarities and differences between the reconstructed state and the constructed state would have bearing in judgments on that issue.

AUTHORITY FIGURES

Freud observed that in the course of treatment the patient related to the therapist, not only as an authority but as an authority figure (Freud, 1937/1964, p. 239). Regarding people as authority figures is the usual attitude of children in relation with their parents. The specification of the elements in this phenomenon, together with their variations in the course of development, was described by Ferenczi (1913/1950b).

Psychologists are accustomed to noticing the continuation of this phenomenon in the child's dealing with teachers and police officers. Psychologists are even accustomed to referring to people in such positions as authority figures, assuming that their status will inevitably elicit this particular attitude. Of course, that elicitation is not inevitable. Still, it is so frequent that the term *authority figure* has general merit as a social term. The generality also holds for adults and is documented by the fact that the question, "How does the person deal with authority figures?" is a standard part of psychological examinations.

The term *authority figure* refers to the observation that people perceive an individual in authority with qualities that are both "objectively" merited as well as "unrealistic." This phenomenon also refers to the difference between two observers in regarding the same subject matter, a principle of transcendental realism. Relativism, being concerned with matters of psychological interest and the construction of individual experience, recognizes that a child experiences his or her parent as an authority. This is sufficiently explanatory for understanding why the child does what he or she does. That this perception differs from that of other people, even to the extent of marked abnormality, has no relevance for the question of psychopathology. However, this notion may be of greater importance in sociological considerations.

There is a general tendency for children to perceive parents as authority figures. This refers to the observer's conclusion that the image of the parent is endowed by the child with an additional quality termed *authority*. For the purpose of relativist psychology, I single out the implication that the parent is perceived to be superior to oneself. The term *superior* refers to an evaluation in accord with a standard and is meaningful only when the standard is specified.

Among the standards known to be frequently used by children, standards that have the possibility of accounting for the observation of a general and similar evaluation of quality, is that of size. In this example, one can understand that people are endowed with mental faculties enabling the perception of size and the perception of differences of size. It is reasonable to assume that all infants will perceive that their parents are of larger size than themselves. Infants will perceive that their parents are larger than themselves in a biologically determined way. "Bigger," then, is a perceptual fact in the experience of children that is determined primarily by biological causal power.

The experience that someone else is bigger is different from the experience that someone else is superior. The latter experience requires that the perceived "bigness" has also been evaluated according to a standard other than size. There is a general understanding that bigger is not necessarily better. Consequently, it is an error to think that the observed generality of observation—that children regard their parents as superior—is an inevitable consequence of the perception that they are bigger. The evaluation of bigger as superior implies the influence of different causal powers.

In other previous discussions, I showed that all perceptual experiences are evaluated by the person according to the innate motivations represented by the pleasure principle, reality principle, and narcissism. I represented my estimation of the contribution of these motivations in the mathematical categories of plus, zero, and minus. Using these conceptual technical tools of relativist psychology, I can now describe the understanding of the observed phenomenon. The perceived bigness of parents is regularly and generally evaluated as being positive to a child's interests. The generality of this finding indicates the additional contribution of sociological causal power.

The vector outcome of a positive evaluation of parental bigness is understood in these component contexts. The positive evaluation of parents was recognized by

Freud (1914/1957) as the general outcome of the fact that usual childcare activities were experienced as satisfying both the pleasure and reality principles (Freud, 1914/1957, p. 87). He thought that the positive evaluation was so inevitable that he referred to it as "anaclitic" (Freud, 1914/1957, p. 87). At the same time, he recognized that parenting activities were experienced as gratifying to narcissistic motivations (Freud, 1914/1957, p. 88). A modern study of how parenting is experienced as narcissistically gratifying is presented in the work of Kohut (1971, pp. 123–125).

Applying these relativist understandings to the example of the child's perception of parents as bigger, one sees that the evaluation of authority is the vector of evaluations according to pleasure, reality, and narcissism. Thus, under varying conditions, one of these motivations will be found to make a more significant contribution than the others. The three classes of condition will correspond to different behavioral patterns and may be distinguished by these different terms. The term *authority* is a general reference to these three significantly different conditions.

The generality of authority refers to an individual's adoption of an attitude involving a degree of delimitation of self-government and free will. This implies a commitment to accept the opinions and decisions of another person in the exercise of the faculty of control of mobility. The term *authority* describes one form in which one can detect the increasing role of sociological causal power during the course of human development. This is indicated by the regularity and generality of authority patterns that do not have the biological connotation of inevitability. The study of the introduction and evolution of authority patterns is an important dimension in the study of human development.

Authority patterns are distinguishable in three forms. When the delimitation is accepted in the pursuit of pleasure principle motivations, I describe this as a condition in which the object-image is perceived as a *pleasure authority*. The other conditions may be distinguished as *reality authority* and *narcissistic authority*. These terms refer to the construction of a person's experience in the form of authority patterns that is based on the observation of patterns of behavior. Relativists recognize the fact that investing people with authority is a normal sociological aspect in the development of human experience. This particular understanding of the phenomenon called transference can be found among the various understandings of transference. It is given particular notice in remarks about the generality of its appearance (Rangell, 1988, p. 325) in every human relationship (Brenner, 1955, p. 119).

SUMMARY

The term *transference*, with its connotation of carrying something from one place to another, appears to be a suitable description for the details found in my examination of the phenomenon. However, there are important differences in signification from that derived from the point of view of traditional drive theory. That view assumes that the confluence of causal powers (traditionally described as sexual and aggressive) both initiates the phenomenon and determines its form. In contrast, relativists assume that the phenomenon is initiated by sociological causal powers and that its form is shaped by the individual according to pleasure principle, reality principle, and narcissistic motivations. Drive theory implies that the objectivist distortion of parent figures into authority figures is initiated and formed by a biological causal power and is automatically transferred into the relationship with other people. Relativists hold that the objective distortion is initiated by sociological powers and may be motivationally transferred into a relationship with other people. A person's experience in the performance of any faculty is represented in relativism by a construction. Experiences in performing a sociological faculty are represented by a transference construction.

As I noted originally, after reducing conscious resistance and repression resistance, the continuation of an attitude resistant to further psychological examination often takes the form of a transference pattern. This means that evidence has been detected of a significant departure from the patient's personal norm of regarding the therapist as a *transferential authority figure*. That personal norm might have been constructed by the therapist in a particular form that describes the element of the transference phenomenon accounting best for the characteristic pattern. Common constructs of transference include the therapist as a *reality authority*, with subtypes of *survival authority* and *adaptation authority*. The data of observation should support the contention that these constructions of inference have probabilistic validity and reliability.

The establishment of an individual's personal transference norm is useful for the detection of departures. Relativists recognize that departures from a personal norm may be due to biological and sociological causal powers, as well as psychological. The identification of the departures as a matter of psychological interest depends on evidence that the departure is self-caused.

The identification of a departure in transference patterns as self-caused establishes the phenomenon as psychological. The departure is used defensively in the context of conflicts. On examination, those conflicts may be seen as biological, sociological, or both. People do encounter problems of situational and interpersonal stress, and psychologists are concerned to study their experience of those problems.

However, the specific interest of clinical psychology is aroused when the defensive departures from a personal norm are in the context of a conflict of motivation among the pleasure principle, reality principle, and narcissism. This is the relativist definition of a state of psychopathology and "internal conflict."

One can observe a self-caused distortion of the social faculty of transference. Because it is a social faculty that is distorted by the person, it may well be experienced as a sensible and satisfactory solution to either situational or interpersonal problems. In the event that it is experienced as unsatisfactory, the situation may be accessible to improvement by guidance or counseling. This state is different from that of a self-caused distortion of mental faculties that necessarily implies some degree of suffering by the person. Distortion of social faculties may often be experienced as worth that price in the resolution of conflicts. Distortion of mental faculties in dealing with conflicts must always be experienced as not worth that price; they are unreasonable to the judgment of the person who performs them.

Therefore, defensive departures from a personal transference norm in a state of psychopathology will be identified by the person's experience of that behavior as unreasonable, except as the lesser of two evils. One can anticipate that the therapist might often experience difficulties in obtaining data of that kind. Obtaining psychological data requires the cooperation of the person. That is problematic when the subject matter is regarded by the patient as being unpleasant, distasteful, or even frightening. I discuss the therapist's dealing with this problem in chapters 19 and 20. In any event, note that constructions from observations of defensive transference in psychopathology will include the person's experience that the behavior pattern is unreasonable and the lesser of two evils.

Because transference departures in psychopathological states serve to reduce the unpleasant experience of fully confronting the greater evil, the therapist's at-tempts to examine this area are expected to meet with resistance. Various forms of resistant attitude have been identified and distinguished. I now identify another form of resistance called *transference resistance*. Transference resistance occurs when the patient causes a distortion in the form of his or her usual transference pattern and uses this to resist the therapist's examination. This description coordi-nates with the relativist understanding of all forms of resistance. Despite the addi-tional distress entailed in maintaining the transference resistance, the person re-gards it as a lesser evil than confronting the motivational conflict.

The therapist may construct the patient's personal norm of transference in the general conduct of life. The therapist may construct departures from that general norm that are instituted only in particular situations, including that of the therapy situation. An attempt to examine either the general transference or the specific transference pattern may meet with resistance in a variety of forms, one of which is transference resistance.

The therapist's examination of areas of the patient's experience other than trans-ference phenomena may meet with a variety of resistances, including transference resistance.

Even though people seek professional help, they regularly present patterns of behavior indicative of a resistant attitude toward the psychologist's efforts at exam-ination. Some patterns indicate conscious reasons for resistance, and I label these forms *conscious resistance*.

After the reduction of conscious resistance, the persistence of a resistant atti-tude is observed to be maintained unconsciously. One form, that of *repression resistance*, is well known and familiar to psychoanalytic psychologists. Note that after the reduction of repression resistance, the resistant attitude is frequently still maintained. Then, it is crucial to the purpose of psychotherapy to be able to detect the subtler forms of resistance (Weinshel, 1984, p. 89).

I have identified several other forms of resistance that are frequently encoun-tered and have distinguished them with descriptive labels. These include repeti-tion, clinging, and narcissistic resistances. The forms of resistance are understood as forms of defense and are maintained as efforts by the person to cope with conflicts involving the motivations described by the pleasure principle, reality principle, and narcissism.

REFERENCES

Brenner, C. (1955). *An elementary textbook of psychoanalysis.* New York: International University Press.

Cooper, A. (1987). Changes in psychoanalytic ideas: Transference interpretation. *Journal of the Ameri-can Psychoanalytic Association, 35,* 77–98.

Emde, R. (1981). Changing models of infancy and the nature of early development: Remodeling the foundation. *Journal of the American Psychoanalytic Association, 29,* 179–220.

Ferenczi, S. (1950a). On obscene words. In E. Jones (Ed.), *Sex in psychoanalysis* (pp. 132–153). New York: Basic Books. (Original work published 1911)

Ferenczi, S. (1950b). Stages in the development of the sense of reality. In E. Jones (Ed.), *Sex in psychoanalysis* (pp. 213–239). New York: Basic Books. (Original work published 1913)

Freud, S. (1958). On narcissism. In J. Strachey (Ed. & Trans.), *The standard edition of the complete psychological works of Sigmund Freud* (Vol. 14, pp. 67–104). London: Hogarth Press. (Original work published 1914)

Freud, S. (1964). Analysis terminable and interminable. In J. Strachey (Ed. & Trans.), *The standard edition of the complete psychological works of Sigmund Freud* (Vol. 23, pp. 216–253). London: Hogarth Press. (Original work published 1937)

Freud, S. (1964). An outline of psychoanalysis. In J. Strachey (Ed. & Trans.), *The standard edition of the complete psychological works of Sigmund Freud* (Vol. 23, pp. 141–208). London: Hogarth Press. (Original work published 1938)

Freud, S. (1964). Splitting of the ego in the process of defense. In J. Strachey (Ed. & Trans.), *The standard edition of the complete psychological works of Sigmund Freud* (Vol. 23, pp. 273–278). London: Hogarth Press. (Original work published 1940)

Jarvis, V. (1969). Learning disability and its relation to normal fantasy formation. *Psychoanalytic Review, 56,* 288–298.

Jones, E. (1951). A linguistic factor in English characterology. In E. Jones (Ed.), *Essays in applied psychoanalysis* (pp. 88–94). London: Hogarth Press. (Original work published 1920)

Kermode, F. (1985). Freud and interpretation. *International Review of Psychoanalysis, 12,* 3–12.

Kohut, H. (1971). *The analysis of the self.* New York: International University Press.

Laplanche, J., & Pontalis, J.-B. (1973). *The language of psychoanalysis.* New York: Norton.

McLaughlin, J. (1987). The play of transference. *Journal of the American Psychoanalytic Association, 35,* 557–582.

Rangell, L. (1988). The future of psychoanalysis: The scientific crossroads. *Psychoanalytic Quarterly, 57,* 313–340.

Sandler, J. (1983). Reflections on some relations between psychoanalytic concept and psychoanalytic practice. *International Journal of Psychoanalysis, 64,* 1–11.

Schafer, R. (1976). *A new language for psychoanalysis.* New York: Basic Books.

Sharpe, E. (1950). An examination of metaphor. In E. Brierly (Ed.), *Collected papers* (pp. 155–169). London: Hogarth Press. (Original work published 1940)

Strachey, J. (1934). The nature of the therapeutic action of psychoanalysis. *International Journal of Psychoanalysis, 15,* 127–159.

Weinshel, E. (1984). Some observations on the psychoanalytic process. *Psychoanalytic Quarterly, 53,* 63–92.

IV

PSYCHOTHERAPY

17

Relativist Theory

Practitioners generally understand that the disease and the suffering that bring the patient to seek treatment are also brought into the office. Practitioners also understand that the disease results in patterns of distorted functioning in all life situations, including the office. The successful treatment of disease in the office is successful treatment of the disease in everyday life. This is the chief clinical meaning of the term *transference*.

Patients are aware of only some consequences of their disease that are perceived as unpleasant. Some patients are also troubled by the implications of having a psychological disease, the nature of which is beyond their awareness. The psychoanalytic therapist knows that the essence of the disease entails matters of greater unpleasure for patients but that this experience is blunted by the unconscious adoption of antithetical attitudes. This is the chief clinical meaning of the term *defense*.

Because the unconscious disease is understood to be the patient's sorest spot, the therapist anticipates that ministrations toward that direction are likely to exacerbate that soreness. Therefore, those means used defensively are expected to be automatically heightened in an effort to soften any increased soreness. This is the chief clinical meaning of the term *resistance*.

Clinical wisdom is summated in the understanding that the effort to treat psychopathological disease will have to deal with transference, defense, and resistance. Knowledge of the details of these aspects of treatment can guide efforts to apply and to improve both the form and the effectiveness of methods of treatment.

My examination of the phenomenon of transference shows that its manifestation in the treatment situation is in the form of resistance. Consequently, for the purposes of treatment, it is not necessary to study details of the entire phenomenon but only that of its manifestation as transference resistance.

Detailing the forms of resistance in treatment is important because these are used as guides toward the patient's sorest spot and the locus of the disease. Successful efforts in reducing resistance enable a closer approach to the disease itself. The continuing process of reducing resistance is an important principle defining psychoanalytic treatment.

The process of reducing resistance also affords the therapist a progressively clearer conception of the patient's disease. Therefore, the psychoanalytic diagnosis of psychopathology is a continuing process of refinement that achieves its maximum accuracy when treatment is successfully completed.

THEORY OF THE CONSTRUCTION
OF RESISTANCE

General Considerations

A conclusion that the patient is performing patterns of resistance is "objectively" sustainable by appropriate data of observation. However, it is the particular interest of relativist psychology to study the "subjective" experience of the patient in performing resistance.

The principles of relativism are guides for making inferences about an individual's experience in the form of constructions. One principle holds that experience occurs in the form of a coordinated set of self- and object-images. I may liken this to drawing a picture. Each image can be drawn in varieties of biological dimensions, such as big and fat, and sitting and eating. Each image can also be drawn in varieties of sociological dimensions, such as uniformed and naked, and talking or fighting. The forms of both biological and sociological elements may be combined in many ways. The particular form chosen to characterize an image in an event can be specified by a descriptive term, such as bigger.

Another principle holds that individual experience occurs in the form of a motivated attitude. Attitudes are the vector outcome of basic human motivations, described by the terms *pleasure principle*, *reality principle*, and *narcissism*. I may liken the specification of attitude in an event to the addition of color to a drawing. The three "basic colors" of motivation may be combined in many ways. The particular hue chosen to characterize an image can be specified by a descriptive term, such as sad or happy.

Therefore, the task of "detailing" resistance requires the construction of a patient's experience by specifying the particularities of a self-image, a coordinated object-image, and an attitude of that self-image. A construction in these three dimensions is an unequivocal representation of the therapist's understanding of observing a patient's pattern of resistance.

Specific Considerations

The raw data of observation relevant for the therapist's attention are the patient's verbal reports and the patient's behavior. These may be supplemented by written and oral reports of other observers. Relativists hold that these data do not possess any intrinsic quality of validity or reliability. Each raw datum must be examined by the process of clarification in order to arrive at a scientific fact that has a demonstrated probability of truthfulness and accuracy. In subsequent discussions I assume that the raw data of observation have been processed by the therapist into scientific facts that merit confidence.

Consequently, the therapist's examination of the patient will result in the accumulation of a large body of scientific facts about the patient. The theory of relativism provides a guide for the organization of these facts in order to make meaningful inferences about the psychology of the individual.

Knowledge of biological and sociological norms allows the detection of individualistic variations. Thus, the facts can be organized to form personal norms of the individual's biological and sociological activities. The particular conglomerations of characteristics can distinguish one individual from another.

This organization of facts in terms of individual characteristics can be considered to be scientifically and objectively established. Although this organization may be sufficient for the interests of various biological and sociological sciences, it is not useful enough for psychological science.

Because psychologists study individual experience, these personal norms have to be translated into another form useful for that purpose. The form proper for relativism is that of a construction in terms of self- and object-images, and the attitude of the self-image. For convenience, I refer to this specification as a *self-object-attitude construction* (S–O–A construction). Note that this term is similar to one used by Kernberg (1976, p. 26), "S–O–A units," but there are important differences. Consequently, the relativist psychotherapist will organize facts into patterns normative for the patient. The experience of the patient in performing these patterns will be represented by S–O–A constructions.

Intrapsychic Conflict and Defense

I have said that the state of psychopathology is constituted by the person's adoption of a distortion of mental faculties in the interests of moderating a nontolerable experience. The notion that experience is intolerable means that the person cannot maintain his or her usual patterns of the performance of mental faculties but institutes a distortion of them. The usual patterns might have been objectively distorted but not experientially distorted. The term *nontolerable* distinguishes experiential distortion. I regard a nontolerable experience as the essence of psychological disease and the mental distortions as efforts of living with the disease. Thus, psychopathological states are composed of two elements: the experience of the disease and the experience of efforts to cope with the disease. The experience of coping with the disease is referred to by the term *defense*. The experience of the disease may be referred to by the term *anxiety*, which I consider in detail later.

The experience of coping with a disease is represented as an S–O–A construction referring to particular patterns of behavior. Because of their defensive utility, these patterns are performed with a preponderant positive evaluation as a comparative relief from anxiety. Despite whatever the negative evaluation of the consequences of distorted mental faculties, the relief from anxiety will ensure a general experience of positiveness. Thus, construction of defense must be understood as always being essentially positive from the patient's viewpoint.

The experience of the disease is represented as an S–O–A construction referring to particular patterns of behavior. Because they are related to anxiety about a nontolerable experience, these patterns are performed with a preponderant negative evaluation. Thus, construction of anxiety must be understood as always being essentially negative from the patient's viewpoint.

This organization of facts serves to identify defensive and anxiety constructions. What they have in common is that the patterns indicate a normative characteristic self-caused distortion of mental faculties. These constructions differ in that defense constructions are ultimately experienced positively in the sense of relief, whereas anxiety constructions are ultimately experienced negatively in the sense of the greatest disease.

Because defense constructions are positively experienced and anxiety constructions are negatively experienced, they are antithetical within experience. The maintenance of antithetical experiences is one use of the term *intrapsychic conflict*.

Both defense and anxiety are describable as S–O–A constructions. Their antithetical relationship can be detected in a comparison of their self-images, object-images, and attitudes. The maintenance of antithetical hypothetical entities is another use of the term *intrapsychic conflict*.

Treatment

My considerations thus far are proposed for understanding the experience of persons in a state of psychopathology during the course of life in general. Those persons who seek assistance and receive psychoanalytic treatment will evidence these same considerations within the context of resistance.

The therapist accumulates facts and organizes them as defense and anxiety constructions, noting their antithetical relationship. These constitute a personal norm for the patient, and a psychological examination clarifies this understanding further. The examination may meet with resistance in one or the other of its recognizable forms: conscious, repression, clinging, narcissism, and transference. A study of these new patterns can also be organized as defense and anxiety constructions. Therefore, the therapist has one normative set of constructions and another set of resistance constructions.

Comparisons between the normative and resistance constructions will identify those that are antithetical, and their polarity can be specified in terms of the following elements: self-image, object-image, and attitude. This polarity between normal and resistive hypothetical entities, both in general and in the specifics of their elements, is a third use of the term *intrapsychic conflict*.

The change of patterns of behavior, indicative of a polar departure from normative defense and anxiety constructions to those of resistance defense and anxiety constructions, is of special concern to the therapist. It is not of special concern for the analytic psychotherapist to note the difference between normative constructions and the healthy constructions of a nondistorted use of mental faculties. This would only identify the general state of psychopathology. Nor is it important for the therapist to note the fact of difference between normative "sick" and resistance "sick" constructions. This would only identify that the state of psychopathology is manifested in the office and can, on occasion, be exacerbated. The crucial issue for treatment is the disease and its presence in the office in the form of defense and anxiety constructions of resistance.

The analytic therapist seeks to arrive at constructions of resistance. These are then refined to defense and anxiety constructions. These are then further refined to antithetical S–O–A constructions. This refinement constitutes a specification of the locus of resistance. The reduction of resistance constitutes the psychoanalytic treatment of psychopathology. Identification of the locus of resistance allows refinement in the application of methods for its reduction by sharpening the conception of the target.

Dissociation

Over the years of working with people in various states of psychopathology, therapists have accumulated considerable observational information. Analytical therapists have also accumulated inferred information. Out of this experience, one conclusion has stood the test of time as to its rank of first importance: that antithetical attitudes toward the same subject matter are characteristic of patients with psychopathology and that an alteration of these attitudes is the most effective treatment.

The term *attitude*, in the sense used here, refers to a characterization of a pattern of behavior in any one of several dimensions. Study of these characterizations can identify those with antithetical implications. For example, one pattern may be characterized as a caring attitude toward a person. Another pattern may indicate a careless attitude toward the same person.

The maintenance by the patient of contradictory attitudes has the manifest implication of confusion both in subjective experience and the consequences of behavior. The therapist has the distinct conviction that the maintenance of contradictory attitudes is the cause of the observed maladaptive behavior and that reducing the contradiction is the essence of psychoanalytic treatment.

History

Study of contradictory attitudes led Freud to notice that his patients were unaware of one of those attitudes; that one attitude was in an unconscious condition. He referred to this antithesis in consciousness as "repression" because it was as if one attitude were being automatically "pushed down" below the "level of consciousness" (Freud, 1910/1957b, p. 24).

The conclusion that the attitudes were antithetical as to consciousness led to the development of methods of reducing this discrepancy. The first of these aimed at making the unconscious conscious. Under hypnosis, the patient could be induced toward an awareness of that attitude, together with the recollection of a background of emotional experiences that made this sensible (Freud, 1910/1957b, p. 13), called a "complex" (Freud, 1910/1957b, p. 32). In cases of hysteria, this procedure often resulted in marked improvement.

However, hypnosis was abandoned because not all subjects could be hypnotized and, even then, areas of exploration proved refractory (Freud, 1910/1957b, p. 26). He set about to work with the normal conscious state and aimed at increasing tolerance toward recognizing the unconscious attitude (Freud, 1910/1957b, p. 22). Recalling an experience with Bernheim, Freud used an insistent technique in directing the patient's attitudes (Freud, 1910/1957b, p. 23).

Although insistence was helpful in expanding recognition of the problematic behaviors and their implications, it often met with resistance by the patient in the forms of hesitations and silence. It was revealed that the patient was withholding thoughts that were regarded problematically in accord with ethical and other standards (Freud, 1910/1957b, p. 24). He then asked the patient to agree not to withhold thoughts that seemed irrelevant, incorrect, or disagreeable (Freud, 1910/

1957b, p. 32). The request for the patient's agreement to "free associate" was an effort directed at increasing the patient's conscious acceptance of the disagreeable implications of the unconscious attitudes. Relativists regard these considerations under the heading of the reduction of conscious resistance.

With the achievement of confidence that conscious resistance had been reduced, the patient's departures from reasonable associations to the subject matter being explored by the therapist could be regarded as indirectly related to the patient's complex (Freud, 1910/1957b, p. 32). The indirection was understood as necessitated because the exploration brought the patient's attention closer to the "sore spot of the mind" (Freud, 1910/1957b, p. 52). At the same time, because there was an indirect relationship, this allowed the construction of an inference about the patient's "unconscious complex" (Freud, 1910/1957b, p. 32). I regard the presentation of a construction to the patient as an intervention, which I discuss later.

In summary, I have discussed how the reduction of conscious resistance clarifies the conscious–unconscious antithesis between contrary attitudes. Intervention by the presentation of constructions about an unconscious attitude are termed confrontations. Confronting the patient's conscious attitude with constructions about the unconscious attitude are regarded as the method of reducing repression resistance. This is the psychoanalytic method of making the unconscious conscious.

Splitting

The construction of attitudes has revealed that all individuals maintain a multiple complexity of varying attitudes and that this is a normal state that characterizes the richness of the human condition (E. Kris, 1950). There appears to be a mental faculty for integration and synthesis that enables the maintenance of this complexity with relative coherence and harmony (Hartmann, 1950/1964, p. 139; Searles, 1977, p. 441).

Among an individual's various attitudes, there may be those whose relationship is precisely contradictory. It is only that pairing of attitudes identified and demonstrated as inappropriate and antithetical that are correctly describable as indicative of intrapsychic conflict. Only in the condition that the attitudes are contradictory is it a necessary conclusion that the person must sustain unfortunate consequences (Friedman, 1982, p. 364).

When the antithetical attitudes were also contrary as to consciousness, Freud (1910/1957b, pp. 19, 22) referred to the attitudes as "split" and "dissociated"; they were split as to consciousness. However, Freud noted that even after the split was healed by the reduction of repression resistance, the patient was often still in a disturbed condition and continued to maintain consciously antithetical attitudes (Freud, 1920/1955, p. 19). He concluded that it was not sufficient to make unconscious matters conscious.

This understanding led Freud to abandon the topographic theory and to arrive at the structural theory, with its new definition of psychoanalytic treatment as the analysis of defenses (Freud, 1926/1959). From then on, the term splitting referred to antithetical attitudes independent of their state of consciousness. He noted that one attitude of the antithesis served as a disavowal of the other (Freud, 1927/1961, p. 156). Despite the suffering entailed in the maintenance of discordant attitudes, the patient appeared more unwilling to accept some other painful reality (Freud,

1938/1964a, p. 161). Freud (1938/1964b, p. 275) summarized his experience in stating that splitting, the stable coexistence of contrary attitudes, may be the general condition of all psychopathological states.

Differentiation

The recognition of the importance of split attitudes in pathological states led to several efforts to comprehend the difference between them. Freud (1917/1957, p. 156) noted that each attitude used different ego functions (mental faculties). Sterba (1934) noted that the different faculties were those of reasoning and experiencing. Greenson (1967, p. 47) noticed the usual pairing of rational observation versus an irrational experiencing, as when people think one way but feel quite another. Fliess (1961, p. 83) noticed that these differences followed from the person's adopting different attitudes, characterized as "I" and "myself". Because people can adopt a variety of points of view in regarding a singular subject matter, with the consequence of maintaining multiple but different attitudes, Fliess recognized that this process must be similar in normal and pathological states. He proposed the term *division* for normal multiple attitudes and reserved *split* for the abnormal (Fliess, 1961, p. 92).

Splitting, in the sense of division, has come to be seen as part of normal development (A. Freud, 1946, pp. 132–133; Kernberg, 1976, p. 44; Klein, 1946/1952, p. 300). Even when the difference of attitudes can be identified as that between a "true self" and a "false self" (Winnicott, 1965, p. 121) or differing "object-images" (Fairbairn, 1952), it is found that the differences can coexist without tension (Greenacre, 1958, p. 11; Kris, 1950; Winnicott, 1953, p. 39).

Sterba's (1934) choice of "division" to refer to the multiplicity of attitudes during development is equivocal because it also bears connotations of disagreement and opposition that are characteristics of a pathological state. Normal development has connotations of growth, elaboration, and maturity. I propose the term *differentiation* as bearing the connotation of increased functional efficiency. In the course of development, one can observe that attitudes become differentiated into multiple attitudes (Freud, 1927/1961, p. 136). These are now more consonant with the complexity of reality and are more useful for adaptation. Differentiation of attitudes has also been described as "multiple consciousness" (Natsoulos, 1978, p. 913) where they coexist in a supplementary, complimentary, and mutually harmonious relationship within the experience of the individual.

Conflict

The word *split* has connotations of damage, breakage, and disintegration. It is suitable as a reference to those differentiated attitudes that are in opposition, dissonant, and contentious. The term also reflects the understanding that states of psychopathology are experienced as states of intrapsychic conflict.

Among a patient's differentiated attitudes, there can be some that are identified as being split. Split attitudes can be demonstrated as antithetical, polar, opposed, and contrary. This carries the necessary implication of an experience of disorder, unease, illness, and disability.

The classic conception of split attitudes views them as the consequence of the maintenance of conflicting wishes (Brenner, 1976, p. 174). The term *wish*, as frequently used in psychology, does not have a standard definition. In the classical sense, it is called the mental representation of an impulse. This mental phenomenon is conceived of as the automatic consequence of a biological phenomenon, an instinct. From that view, the impulses happen to be pursuing aims with conflicting consequences.

Differing impulses have been identified as "divergent conflicts" (A. Kris, 1985, p. 540) involving painful choices. The painfulness in such a condition can be considerable and is one of "the ills that flesh is heir to." Although this condition can be described as intrapsychic, it is not intrapsychic conflict. Differing wishes or impulses are not necessarily in conflict. The pain in such a condition is contingent on the person's failure to find a personally suitable resolution. The failure may be due to biological, sociological, or psychological problems. Therefore, the presence of divergent conflict is not necessarily an indication of psychological disorder but one of its possible consequences.

Differing impulses may or may not lead to painful experience. When the experience is painful and due to a psychological cause, this must occur in the context of split attitudes. Only in splitting is pain an inevitable consequence. Then, the identification of splitting and its necessary pain requires something other than the identification of differing impulses and their differentiated attitudes. It requires a necessary factor.

The polarity and pain in a split cannot be in accord with innate faculties. The same individual is performing both attitudes and doing so with the same faculties (Lustman, 1977, p. 138). The concepts of wish and impulse refer to a universal endowment of capacity with a differentiation of application.

Anna Freud (1946, p. 123) noticed that one attitude accepted a wish, whereas the other repudiated the same wish. The impulse and the wish were the same for both attitudes (Kernberg, 1977, p. 278). In one attitude the wish was accepted, whereas in the other it was disclaimed (Schafer, 1976, p. 132). She tried to understand this repudiation in terms of a divergent conflict among id, ego, and superego interests. However, her father had cautioned not to take the difference between ego and id too hard and fast (Freud, 1923/1961, p. 34). Van der Waals (1952) demonstrated that patterns interpreted as indications of id were analyzable as attitudes of the entire personality. Schafer (1976, pp. 283–284) demonstrated that patterns interpreted as indicative of superego were analyzable as disclaiming attitudes of the entire personality.

The wise conclusion reached by Hartmann after his study of antithetical attitudes seems to be unnoticed in the literature, perhaps because of the exotic and tendentious nature of his English prose. He concluded that "the opposite of object-cathexis is not ego-cathexis, but cathexis of one's own person, i.e., self-cathexis" (1950/1964, p. 127). Among the implications of this finding is that id, ego, and superego refer to classes of innate faculties and their functional differences. Therefore, they are inevitable components of all attitudes held by a person and cannot serve as a distinction among them. Thus, all attitudes have their id, ego, and superego aspects.

The observation that split could be comprehended as the simultaneous acceptance and repudiation of the same wish was recognized as having opposite implications for the patient's sense of self. It was noted that the attitudes were antithetical for the sense of identity (Mahler, 1968, p. 11) and necessitated the consequence of tension (Segal, 1962, p. 214). Kernberg (1977, p. 104) reported that the behavioral patterns of these attitudes in cases of severe pathology had implications for the patient's sense of self as extremely oppositional, to the extremes of self-idealization and self-debasement.

Rangell (1985, p. 324) summarized the range of studies as showing that the opposition in splits could be found in both "systemic" dimensions of self- and object-images and in the "intrasystemic" dimensions of id, ego, and superego. I understand this to mean that split attitudes are found to be antithetical according to any component of attitudes and that this is a characteristic of the general condition of psychopathology. The contribution of the concept of splitting is the provision of a sensible context within which psychologists can appreciate the inevitable experience of suffering of persons in a state of psychopathology. Because attitudes characterize important components of the sense of self, split attitudes imply a split sense of self that can occur along many dimensions. The splitting of the sense of self is the necessary causal factor for the inevitable experience of pain in states that maintain antithetical attitudes.

Dissociation

I have discussed how the search for the essence of the contradiction between split attitudes sought to identify a difference in the presence or absence among the constructed components of attitudes. Research brought this to a negative conclusion. Instead, the findings indicated that each attitude represented a differentiated sense of self and that these were antithetical.

I have also discussed how the search for the essence of the contradiction between two senses of self sought to identify a difference in the presence or absence according to polar qualities of a person. These qualities included openness and reluctance, conscious and unconscious, rational and irrational, reasonable and impulsive, and truth and falsity. Research brought this to a negative conclusion.

Note that the search to understand the opposition of split attitudes sought a correlation with polar qualities. This search entails a mistaken assumption. The existence of the split is real according to relativism because that inference is supported by a range of data of observation. Splits are real entities. Qualities are not entities but judgments about entities. Black and white do not exist; there is always a blacker-black and a whiter-white. What may be held to exist is gray, and this occurs in many gradations. Black and white refer to a judgment of a gradation of grays and are polarities of that judgment. Black–white and rational–irrational have an antithetical meaning only as comparisons (Freud, 1910/1957b, p. 157) of entities of observation to some standard.

Relativism draws attention to the fact that the identification of split attitudes as distinguished by polar qualities is an objective conclusion by the observer. This does not address the issue of psychology about the patient's experience in performing both attitudes.

One may observe that a singular patient is performing two sets of activities that are each indicative of a type of personality. This is the observer's concept of differentiation, with implications of developmental enrichment. Among these I have identified those pairs of patterns that are antithetical and split, with implications of pathology. The observer notes that this is a case in which "the collar and the cuffs don't match." Something is going on that is not "kosher." The person has red hair but black eyebrows. The observation of behaviors that establish self-contradiction sustains the conclusion that the patient is lying. Of course, this may be performed unconsciously.

The manifestation of split attitudes is not indicative of a split sense of self in the case in which the person is lying. However reprehensible that may be judged socially, it is not indicative of psychopathology. Split attitudes are not symptoms of psychopathology when the person is lying consciously. Psychological examination is required to obtain a data base to sustain a conclusion about whether the person is consciously lying.

For discussion, assume that the person is lying unconsciously. In that event, attention is drawn to the polar qualities used to establish the presence of split attitudes. As I have discussed, the psychological observer may interpret the observation with the mistaken assumption of polar entities. Therefore, one attitude is viewed as adaptive, rational, truthful, and reasonable. The other is seen as maladaptive, irrational, false, and impulsive. Relativists understand that one attitude is seen as having more or less of that quality compared with a judgment about the other attitude.

This relativistic interpretation coordinates with the theoretical conclusion that the patient is unconsciously lying in the maintenance of both attitudes, not only in one. In conscious lying, either the red hair or the black eyebrows indicate the person's real hair color. In lying unconsciously, neither is indicative of the real color. In unconsciously performed split attitudes, both will be found to be defensively exaggerated even though one may not appear that way at the moment to the observer. However, I have already discussed the point of manifest normality being accompanied by latent abnormality. This mistake occurs when observation is taken as manifest fact without examination for substantiation.

Recall the fundamental relativistic distinction between a person's subjective experience and the scientific construction of experience. Therefore, one arrives at the understanding that the patient does not experience lying in the performance of both split attitudes. Nonetheless, one has confidence in the construction that the patient experiences lying. Split attitudes represent derivative senses of self, with the person conducting herself or himself from both points of view. The person may use one or another derivative self on many occasions. These variations contribute to the richness of human personality that is described as the *self-system tenet of psychology*.

However useful for biological maintenance or social adaptation the consequences of split attitudes may be judged by an observer, they cannot be suitable for the patient. First, because the attitudes are antithetical, whatever is suitable for one sense of self must be experienced as unsatisfactory by the other sense of self. Second, because the senses of self are derivatives of a latent sense of self, neither attitude can be experienced as satisfactory. Third, the concealment of the latent sense of self by the adoption of manifest multiple senses of self requires a self-caused distortion of mental faculties that must be experienced as unpleasant.

Description of various senses of self that may be constructed in cases of split attitudes has become cumbersome. For purposes of brevity, I refer to the general multifaceted latent sense of self as the person's *real self*. I refer to the derivative, circumscribed senses of self as *defensive selves*.

Construction of a person's real self will consist of a totality of partial selves inferred from patterns of behavior. Split patterns are excluded because the detection of their antithesis establishes them as not authentic for this purpose because they are defensively distorted. When the defensive distortion is reduced, the subsequent pattern of behavior may be used to identify a new self-aspect contributing to an enriched understanding of the person's real self.

Summary

In psychoanalytic treatment the therapist attempts to examine the patient's split. Because the split is maintained defensively, resistance will be encountered by the therapist in exploring both attitudes. The same familiar varieties of resistance may be presented by the patient toward the examination of both attitudes.

From an objectivist view, the therapist may note how each of the split attitudes depart from each other and how the defensive selves depart from the real self. However, the relativist therapist views the defensive selves as the personal norm of the patient and specifies them with separate S–O–A constructions. They are distinguished further as being defensive or anxiety constructions according to whether they are experienced positively or negatively.

The concern to sharpen treatment interventions by sharpening the determination of the locus of resistance has led to the understanding that resistance is met attempting to examine both of the split attitudes regardless of whether they may be characterized as defense or anxiety constructions.

COMPLEXITY OF SPLIT ATTITUDES

General

The analytic therapist attempts to clarify not only both split attitudes as presented by the patient but also the presentation of variations of each attitude of the split. The therapist's attention is specially drawn when variations have implications antithetical to those of the corresponding split attitude. One may conceive of this phenomenon as a splitting of the split attitude, resulting, in the most complicated case, in four pairs of split attitudes. Each of the pairs represents a stable pattern of behavior.

An individual situation may turn out to be even more complicated. Other original split attitudes may be identified, and these may also have stable and antithetical variations. Thus, the therapist's effort to comprehend the variety of behaviors symptomatic of split attitudes will lead to an impression of complexity and layering. The therapist's attempt to examine any of these attitudes will meet with resistance. This complexity was recognized by Freud when he noted that ''the patient presents a mind torn and divided by resistances'' (Freud, 1938/1964a, p. 161). In relativistic terms, Freud means that the patient's mind is torn and divided by split attitudes.

Defense Mechanisms

The objectivist understanding of psychopathology leads to a vision of the patient's maintenance of a complexity of antithetical attitudes and the therapeutic aim of attempting to influence those attitudes. The nature of the antithesis in splits has been identified by the term *defense mechanisms* and include repression, regression, reaction formation, isolation, undoing, projection, introjection, turning against the self, reversal, and displacement (A. Freud, 1946, p. 47). However, it has been noted that after successful treatment, the mechanisms are still perceptible, although they appear diminished (Brenner, 1976, p. 72). Therefore, *defense* does not specify the nature of the antithesis but only its form as perceived by the therapist.

Consequently, the psychoanalyst is advised to use several precepts that include, besides defense, those of drive, anxiety, and compromise formation (Brenner, 1976, p. 64). The psychotherapist has a multiplicity of concepts of psychotherapy to apply in the attempt to deal with a multiplicity of split attitudes. This is a formidable array that justifies the usefulness in training of years of supervision by someone more experienced in handling this complexity.

Object-Relations Theory

As a consequence of the objectivist view of the patient, there have been studies aimed at specifying both split attitudes and their components. Toward that goal, object-relations theory has been used. I have discussed the development of that theory and the relativist conclusion that psychological experience is best described in terms of constellations of self-image, object-image, and attitude of the self-image. Therefore, those authors have studied splits to comprehend their antithesis in terms of the S–O–A components of attitude.

I have noted reports that splits can be identified in the form of polar self-images (Winnicott, 1965, p. 121) and in the form of polar object-images (Fairbairn, 1952). There have been studies of the development of self- and object-images, such as Mahler's (1968) work.

Kohut (1971, p. 185) emphasized that splits may vary in consciousness ("horizontal split") or not ("vertical split"). Kohut (1977, p. 115) also noted that the polarity of self-images was characterizable in terms of the development of abnormal narcissism.

The application of object-relations theory to splits from an objectivist viewpoint has shown other important characterizations of the polarity between split attitudes. These include idealization (Kohut, 1971, p. 75) and good–bad (Kernberg, 1975, p. 61).

Summary

These findings are a contribution to the multiplicity of concepts of psychopathology and make apparent further varieties in the forms of split attitudes. However, the distinction as to the forms in which splitting can be recognized is a functional difference. The essence of splitting, as I have discussed, is a self-caused distortion of mental faculties as defense of the real self.

The patterns of distorted mental faculties coordinate with patterns of behavior identifiable as split attitudes. These splits are recognizable in forms described as defense mechanisms, internal object-relations, and differences in normal or abnormal narcissism. Other forms may be discovered that are useful to recognize the polarity between split attitudes.

RELATIVIST CONSIDERATIONS

General

The main theme in the foregoing discussion is the state of psychopathology brought into the office by the patient. The patient's real disease is transcendent to both the patient and the therapist. However, the therapist has special conceptual tools to bring to bear on the data of observation that can provide valid and reliable inferences about the disease. The therapist's primary data of observation are those behaviors of the patient showing patterns of resistance to psychological examination. The therapist's primary conceptual tools are the precepts of relativism.

Relativists hold that resistance in all of its forms is a manifestation of the painfulness of the disease as it is exacerbated by the therapist's attempts at examination. They also hold that the reduction of resistance has implications for the reduction of the state of the disease. It is recognized that resistance is a symptom and that reduction of a symptom does not necessarily indicate the reduction of a disease.

That the disease itself is reduced is made more probable by two other considerations. First, that only psychological methods are used reduces the probability of biological and sociological factors. Second, and more important, the methods of analytical psychotherapy allow a progressively clearer picture of the fons et origio of the disease. An appreciation of the essence of the patient's disease permits an assessment of its reduction. Consequently, relativists hold it as reasonable that methods for the reduction of resistance constitute a treatment by psychotherapy.

Relativists hold that all efforts at objective constructions of resistance are essentially irrelevant to the purpose of the discipline of psychology and to the practice of analytic psychotherapy. That interest is better expressed in constructions of the patient's experience in performing resistance.

Transference Resistance

My discussions of the literature so far have mainly dealt with objectivist constructions of resistance. As a group they represent a range of concepts about psychopathology that attempt to detail the therapist's experience of the patient's resistance patterns. This may prove more useful for considerations that come under the heading of countertransference.

The relativist concern to construct the patient's experience of resistance has more to do with the concept of transference and its interpersonal connotations. I have discussed how the term is used with reference both to an attitude toward all persons and to only authority figures. It is also used to refer to a special form of resistance in which the therapist is regarded as authoritarian.

As a special form of resistance, it is distinguished from others objectivistically. However, from the relativist view, these other forms have the clear implication that the patient experiences the therapist as an authority. Therefore, it is meaningful to state that all forms of resistance in psychotherapy are forms of transference.

Relativists regard the two terms as referring to the same phenomenon. Resistance refers to the therapist's experience of the phenomenon, whereas transference refers to the patient's experience of it. The compound term *transference resistance* refers to the patient's experience of performing behaviors resistant to the person of the therapist.

Construction

My theoretical search for the locus of resistance has led me to identify it as transference resistance. Relativism requires that the patient's experience be specified in the theoretical terms of S–O–A constellations. Some object-relations therapists have applied this concept toward understanding the patient's experience.

Idealization–Devaluation

I have mentioned the work of Kohut (1971, p. 75) and his specification of the attitude of "idealization." In this transference pattern, the attitude of the patient toward the therapist is that of *idealization*. In the transference pattern of the grandiose self, this attitude is more important than any experience of the therapist as an object (Kohut, 1971, p. 123). Both attitudes describe a distortion of the therapist's real activities and are forms of resistance (Kohut, 1971, p. 9) in transference. Because this concept only specifies a self-image, I regard this as insufficient to establish an unequivocal construction of the patient's experience.

A review of Kohut's data of observation sustains the conclusion that the polarity of the split attitude is identified in the dimension described as *idealization–devaluation*. The self-image may be constructed as either idealized, neutral, or devalued. The object-image may also be constructed in those dimensions, in accord with observed patterns of behavior. Then, nine different split attitudes are distinguishable, each with their own distinctive pattern of behavior.

An experienced idealized self-image may be coordinated with an object-image that is experienced as idealized, neutral, or devalued. Each pairing refers to distinctive patterns of behavior. Similar coordinations of a neutral or devalued self-image would refer to distinctive behavior patterns and distinctive experiences of transference resistance.

An attitude is constructed by specifying S–O–A constellations of idealization-devaluation in terms of plus, minus, or zero evaluations. Kohut has brought attention to the idea that resistance may also appear in the form of idealization-devaluation and that this is recognizable in several patterns.

Good–Bad

I have mentioned the work of Kernberg (1976) and the specification of split attitudes in the dimension *good–bad* (Kernberg, 1976, p. 36). He identified this dimension in observations of patterns of behavior during treatment and was particularly interested in using it for constructions about the development of psychopathology (Kernberg, 1976, p. 79) and its identification. He regarded this dimension as unimportant for the patient's experience of resistance (Kernberg, 1976, p. 79). However, he recognized the usefulness of the concept in comprehending certain clinical problems.

Kernberg (1976, p. 66) mentioned that the specifications of good and bad self-representations, together with good and bad object-representations, do capture the essence of certain patterns of behavior as various manifestations of this dimension. With the theoretical guide of relativism, one can recognize the usefulness of this dimension for constructions of the patient's experience of transference resistance.

The polarity of split attitudes in the dimension of good–bad can occur in nine different variations. This emotional dimension may be specified as a good, bad, or neutral self-image in coordination with a good, bad, or neutral object-image. Each of these specified constellations refers to a distinctive pattern of behavior, together with a distinctive experience of transference resistance. Kernberg (1976) has brought attention to the idea that resistance may also appear in the form of good-bad splits and that this is recognizable in several patterns.

Resistance and Transference Resistance

Relativism makes it clear that the same data of observation that are identified as patterns of resistance may be used as a base for making inferences concerning differing interests. One category of psychological interest is the exploration of the general state of psychopathology. To that purpose, the person's self-caused distortion of mental faculties is seen as being manifested in the maintenance of split attitudes. The specification of maintenance indicates the understanding that the patient who experiences challenges to those patterns will resist them. This is detectable in the person's everyday life and contributes to the understanding of the particular patterns of behavior performed by the person in specific situations. Thus, resistance has a general meaning that refers to one consequence of conducting life with any state of psychopathology.

The study of general resistance has distinguished resistant patterns that, although bearing a similarity, occur in distinctive forms of behavior. Inference is then made from the assumption that distinctive forms of behavior are indicative of distinctive forms of causal power. Inferences of causal power are expressed as hypothetical entities, or psychic structure. The general causal power for these patterns is termed *resistance*, and its functional variations are indicated by terms such as conscious, repression, regressive, and so on. Each of these entities may be specified further in terms of S–O–A constellations. Knowledge of the dimension of general resistance in states of psychopathology is helpful in the management of those people according to various social concerns.

In this book I am particularly interested in exploring the management of people who seek assistance from analytic psychotherapists. Therefore, I limit my study to exploring the patient's experience of resistance in the context of a treatment situation. In exploring general resistance, situations that are perceived to be challenging the maintenance of split attitudes are specified as object-images. In the treatment situation, the object-image is always the person of the therapist. The form of general resistance that includes the therapist is termed *transference resistance*. Transference resistance refers to the generality of a patient's experience in performing resistant behaviors, and it includes the object-image of the therapist.

S-O-A Constellations

The general concept of transference resistance expresses the understanding that the experience of the patient always includes the object-image of the therapist. This generality is necessary but insufficient to explain the specific pattern of resistance encountered in a specific instance by the therapist in the office.

The therapist's chief concern is to understand the patient's immediate experience in performing resistance. This understanding will be in the form of a construction of the patient's experience. Relativism requires that all constructions of experience be framed in terms of S-O-A constellations. These are the minimal dimensions to represent experience in a singular and unequivocal fashion.

Especially at the beginning of treatment, there may be insufficient data of observation to substantiate a valid and reliable conclusion specifying any of these dimensions. If the occasion seems to demand some intervention before this is achieved, the therapist must make an educated guess from the information at hand.

I assume that in the course of treatment (perhaps this period should be called *diagnostic study*), the therapist will take special pains to obtain those particular data that are appropriate to establish constellations. When the constellation of transference resistance is established, the therapist is in a position to consider what means are effective in reducing the specific resistance that is presented in the office. Therefore, I have refined my search for the locus of resistance to the specific constellation encountered by the therapist at any one particular moment.

REFERENCES

Brenner, C. (1976). *Psychoanalytic technique and psychic conflict*. New York: International University Press.

Fairbairn, W. (1952). *An object-relations theory of the personality*. New York: Basic Books.

Fliess, R. (1961). *Ego and body ego*. New York: International University Press.

Freud, A. (1946). *The ego and the mechanisms of defense*. New York: International University Press.

Freud, S. (1955). Beyond the pleasure principle. In J. Strachey (Ed. & Trans.), *The standard edition of the complete psychological works of Sigmund Freud* (Vol. 18, pp. 1–64). London: Hogarth Press. (Original work published 1920)

Freud, S. (1957a). The antithetical meaning of primal words. In J. Strachey (Ed. & Trans.), *The standard edition of the complete psychological works of Sigmund Freud* (Vol. 11, pp. 153–161). London: Hogarth Press. (Original work published 1910)

Freud, S. (1957b). Five lectures on psychoanalysis. In J. Strachey (Ed. & Trans.), *The standard edition of the complete psychological works of Sigmund Freud* (Vol. 11, pp. 9–55). London: Hogarth Press. (Original work published 1910)

Freud, S. (1957c). Mourning and melancholia. In J. Strachey (Ed. & Trans.), *The standard edition of the complete psychological works of Sigmund Freud* (Vol. 14, pp. 237–258). London: Hogarth Press. (Original work published 1917)

Freud, S. (1959). Inhibitions, symptoms and anxiety. In J. Strachey (Ed. & Trans.), *The standard edition of the complete psychological works of Sigmund Freud* (Vol. 20, pp. 77–176). London: Hogarth Press. (Original work published 1926)

Freud, S. (1961). Fetishism. In J. Strachey (Ed. & Trans.), *The standard edition of the complete psychological works of Sigmund Freud* (Vol. 21, pp. 142–158). London: Hogarth Press. (Original work published 1927)

Freud, S. (1961). The ego and the id. In J. Strachey (Ed. & Trans.), *The standard edition of the complete psychological works of Sigmund Freud* (Vol. 19, pp. 3–66). London: Hogarth Press. (Original work published 1923)

Freud, S. (1964a). An outline of psychoanalysis. In J. Strachey (Ed. & Trans.), *The standard edition of the complete psychological works of Sigmund Freud* (Vol. 23, pp. 141–208). London: Hogarth Press. (Original work published 1938)

Freud, S. (1964b). Splitting of the ego in the process of defense. In J. Strachey (Ed. & Trans.), *The standard edition of the complete psychological works of Sigmund Freud* (Vol. 23, pp. 273–278). London: Hogarth Press. (Original work published 1938)

Friedman, L. (1982). The humanistic trend in recent psychoanalytic theory. *Psychoanalytic Quarterly, 51*, 353–371.

Greenacre, P. (1958). Toward an understanding of the physical nucleus of some defense reactions. *International Journal of Psychoanalysis, 39*, 69–76.

Greenson, R. (1967). *The technique and practice of psychotherapy*. New York: International University Press.

Hartmann, H. (1964). Comments on the psychoanalytic theory of the ego. In H. Hartmann (Ed.), *Essays on ego psychology* (pp. 113–141). International University Press. (Original work published 1950)

Kernberg, O. (1975). *Borderline conditions and pathological narcissism*. New York: Jason Aronson.

Kernberg, O. (1976). *Object relations theory and clinical psychoanalysis*. New York: Jason Aronson.

Kernberg, O. (1977). The structural diagnosis of borderline personality. In P. Hartocollis (Ed.), *Borderline personality disorders* (pp. 87–122). New York: International University Press.

Klein, M. (1952). Notes on some schizoid mechanisms. In M. Klein (Ed.), *Developments in psychoanalysis* (pp. 292–320). London: Hogarth Press. (Original work published 1946)

Kohut, H. (1971). *The analysis of the self*. New York: International University Press.

Kohut, H. (1977). *The restoration of the self*. New York: International University Press.

Kris, A. (1985). Resistance in convergent and divergent conflicts. *Psychoanalytic Quarterly, 44*, 537–568.

Kris, E. (1950). Notes on the development and on some current problems of psychoanalytic child psychology. *Psychoanalytic Study of the Child, 5*, 24–46.

Lustman, J. (1977). On splitting. *Psychoanalytic Study of the Child, 32*, 119–154.

Mahler, M. (1968). *On human symbiosis and the vicissitudes of individuation*. New York: International University Press.

Natsoulos, T. (1978). Consciousness. *American Psychologist, 33*, 906–914.

Rangell, L. (1985). The object in psychoanalytic theory. *Journal of the American Psychoanalytic Association, 33*, 301–334.

Schafer, R. (1976). *A new language for psychoanalysis*. New York: Basic Books.

Searles, H. (1977). Dual- and multiple-identity processes in borderline ego functioning. In P. Hartocollis (Ed.), *Borderline personality disorders* (pp. 39–40). New York: International University Press.

Segal, H. (1962). The curative factors in psycho-analysis. *International Journal of Psychoanalysis, 43*, 212–217.

Sterba, R. (1934). The fate of the ego in analytic therapy. *International Journal of Psychoanalysis, 15*, 117–126.

Van der Waals, H. (1952). Discussion of the mutual influences in the development of ego and id. *Psychoanalytic Study of the Child, 7*, 66–68.

Winnicott, D. (1955). The depressive position in normal emotional development. *British Journal of Medical Psychology, 28*, 89–100.

Winnicott, D. (1965). *The maturational processes and the facilitating environment*. New York: International University Press.

18

Psychological Pain

ANXIETY AND UNPLEASURE

Thus far I have stated that the patient's psychopathology is brought into the office. The pathology appears as the consequences of having a disease and trying to protect the sore spots of the disease. The therapist's effort to examine either of these aspects may produce a significant departure from the patient's personal norms. These departures are understood as the patient's resistance to being touched on his or her sore spot or being disturbed in the maintenance of his or her protective attitudes.

Consequently, one can distinguish theoretically two different contexts of transference resistance with different specifications of S–O–A constellations that will represent similar but different experiences of the patient. Touching the sore spot will be experienced as painful, whereas touching the protective devices will be experienced as an anticipation of pain.

Unpleasure

It is recognized in common experience that unpleasure is distinguishable in various qualities such as fear, depression, guilt, sadness, and so forth, all of which may be experienced with painful intensity. Reference to this generality is found in the literature under the terms *unpleasure* and *dysphoric affect*. In the discussion of emotion, I suggested that these attitudes may come about through biological, sociological, and psychological causal powers. Where dysphoric affect is a component of psychopathology, I am concerned only with the aspect of unpleasure that is self-caused. The term *affect* has a biological causal connotation and is unsuitable for psychological purposes. The term *unpleasure* has a personal evaluative connotation that is suitable for my purpose.

Anxiety

Among the variety of experiences identified as unpleasure, that quality distinguished as anxiety has received considerable attention. Analytic therapists have frequently had the impression that the experience of anxiety is categorically different from the experience of other qualities of unpleasure.

When Freud (1936/1959) studied the problem of anxiety, he felt he could demonstrate that anxiety was not a type of unpleasure per se but a danger signal that unpleasure was about to be experienced (Freud, 1936/1959, p. 167). Brenner refined this distinction by pointing out that anxiety refers to the perception of danger (Brenner, 1975, p. 5) that is imminent (Brenner, 1975, p. 11).

With these considerations, relativists define anxiety as the experience of anticipating an experience of unpleasure. One then understands that constructions of a
patient's patterns of transference resistance to the examination of any split attitude
must include anxiety. I refer to these as *constructions of anxiety resistance*.

Because I have conceived that defense refers to the institution and maintenance
of split attitudes as a protective device against the experience of unpleasure, it is
not precise to also refer to the function of defense as an avoidance of anxiety
(Brenner, 1976, p. 9). The function of defense is to avoid unpleasure. The difference referred to is better comprehended by the understanding that resistance may
occur in the contexts of anxiety and unpleasure.

Unpleasure Experience

I have distinguished anxiety as the anticipation of an experience of unpleasure.
In considering the nature of unpleasure, Freud thought that it had to do with a
sense of loss (Freud, 1936/1959, p. 167) experienced by the self (Freud, 1938/
1964, p. 199). Brenner pointed out that anxiety is found in the contexts of physical
injury and illness (Brenner, 1974, p. 553), as well as in those of real or fantasized
loss (Brenner, 1975, p. 24). He concluded that the nature of unpleasure was a
more personal "something bad" and that this general experience may be referred
to as "depressive affect" (Brenner, 1975, p. 24).

Brenner noted that one way that therapists attempt to distinguish among states
of unpleasure is quantitatively (Brenner, 1974, p. 543). I use the term *worry* to
denote a slight experience of fearfulness and the term *panic* for one of intensity.

On distinguishing qualities of unpleasure such as fear and sadness, Brenner held
that this can be done only by reference to the ideational content of the experience
of unpleasure (Brenner, 1974, p. 543). Although he recognized that cultural variations of unpleasure could be identified (Brenner, 1974, p. 545), the experience was
essentially unique for each individual. He concluded that distinguishing categories
of unpleasure was undesirable because of the imprecision of that process and its
resulting confusion (Brenner, 1974, p. 544).

Despite the imprecision of categorizing unpleasure, Brenner and other clini-
cians have found it useful to distinguish constructions such as shame, guilt, and
depression (Greenson, 1967, p. 107). A theory should provide a rational basis for
defining and distinguishing (Brenner, 1974, p. 542) categories of unpleasure. The
current status of psychoanalytic theory is insufficient for that task.

Relativistic theory sees that the problem of categorizing experiences of unpleasure is parallel to the problem of categorizing experiences of pleasure and that
these constitute the general problem of categorizing emotional experiences (Brenner, 1974, p. 536). I previously stated that the dimensions of emotional experience
are the vector outcome of three classes of psychological causal power. The vector
represents a compromise formation of the individual's evaluation of an event as
plus, zero, or minus according to each class of motivation.

Experiences of pleasure are represented as the plus vector summation of all of
these motivational factors. This accords with the common experience that although
a situation is evaluated as definitely negative in some respect, one may nonetheless
regard it as a pleasant experience. This also accords with the common experience
that although an individual may report experiencing an event indifferently, close

examination may reveal strong indications of considerable seething beneath the surface.

My particular concern at the moment is the application of relativistic theory to the categorization of experiences summated negatively. In that regard one can appreciate that there are a delimited range of possibilities in which the chief contributor to a negative summation may arise from an overriding negative evaluation as to one or another class of motivation.

Sadness

When an experience of unpleasure may be attributed to a negative evaluation according to the pleasure principle, I refer to that category of experience as *sadness*. When I use the term, I distinguish it from the same term used to represent a person's understanding of subjective experience. Sadness is a technical term here and represents a professional conclusion based on scientifically established facts.

My choice of the term *sadness* to represent negative evaluations according to the pleasure principle has to do with the psychological tenet of the antithetical sense in terms of comparison that I discussed previously. Sadness, indifference, and happiness refer to categories of evaluation according to the pleasure principle. Sadness has the necessary implication of the loss of happiness. Sadness is invariably an unpleasure experience and may vary in intensity up to pain. The degree of sadness is the reciprocal of the degree of happiness, a pleasure experience perceived as possible in the situation.

Fear

When the experience of unpleasure may be attributed to a negative evaluation according to the reality principle, the situation is more complicated. The reality principle refers to the individual's experience of the world as objects, and these are evaluated according to self-interest. This type of evaluation is often referred to with the terms *adaptation* and *reality testing*. However, I have found it necessary to take into account a categorical distinction made by the self in its perception of the world of objects. The self regards its own body as an object distinct from all others and treats it with a special attitude and patterns of behavior. Therefore, the self evaluates the body-object independently and in accord with the reality principle.

When an experience of unpleasure may be attributed to a negative evaluation of the body-object according to the reality principle, I refer to this categorically as *fear*. My choice of the term *fear* to represent negative evaluations about the body-image according to the reality principle refers to the antithesis between life and death. "Salubrious," "indifferent," and "noxious" refer to categories of this evaluation. Fear has the necessary implication of the dread of death. Fear is invariably an unpleasure experience and may vary in intensity up to pain. The degree of fear is the reciprocal of the degree of healthfulness perceived as possible in the situation. This understanding accords with the common experience that although death may be perceived as imminent, an attitude of hopelessness precludes the experience of fear.

Guilt

When the experience of unpleasure may be attributed to the negative evaluation of any other person as an object according to the reality principle, problems of adaptation to those people are problems of social relationships. I refer to this category of experience as *guilt*. My choice of the term *guilt* to represent negative evaluations of other people as objects according to the reality principle refers to the antithesis between acceptance and rejection. The categories of "accepted," "indifferent," and "rejected" refer to evaluations regarding other people according to the reality principle. Guilt has the implication of possibly incurring antagonism and necessarily increasing the loss of acceptance. Guilt is invariably an unpleasure experience and may vary in intensity up to pain. The degree of guilt may be seen as the reciprocal of the degree of virtuousness perceived as possible in the situation.

This understanding accords with the common experience that the attempt to influence people aversely may be accomplished by both the introduction of unpleasure and the taking away of pleasure. To that end, the social technique of exiling may be quite effective.

Depression

When the experience of unpleasure may be attributed to a negative evaluation according to narcissism, I refer to this category as *depression*. My choice of the term *depression* to represent negative evaluations according to narcissism refers to the antithesis between experiences of grandiosity and humiliation, between prideful display and shameful concealment. "Pride," "indifference," and "depression" refer to categories of this evaluation.

Depression has the implication of low self-esteem that is invariably experienced as unpleasure and may be of an intensity that is painful. The degree of depression is the reciprocal of the degree of specialness perceived as possible in the situation.

The variety of terms I have used in describing an experience of narcissistic evaluation as positive or negative is an attempt to give a flavor of the changing constructs of narcissistic experience during the course of development. Since the original work of Ferenczi (1913/1950), little attention has been devoted to detailing these changes. I have discussed the main theoretical issues of such a project in chapter 9.

This understanding and definition of depression accords with the distinction between states of melancholia and depression as delineated by Freud (1917/1957a) and Abraham (1908/1953). However, note that the essential difference put forth by them no longer appears among the modern list of criteria for the diagnosis of psychotic depression (American Psychiatric Association, 1980, p. 214).

Excitement

The relativist definition of anxiety experience as the anticipation of an unpleasure experience provides a basis for inferring a mental faculty for anticipation to account for the phenomenon. My theoretical system allows the prediction that this faculty may also be applied to the anticipation of a pleasure experience. I refer to this category of experience as *excitement*. My choice of the term *excitement* to refer to the experience of anticipating an experience of pleasure has to do with its antithetical relationship to the experience of anxiety.

AREAS OF IMPRECISION

Pleasure Principle

The terms *pleasure experience* and *unpleasure experience* refer to the person's summary of simultaneous evaluations according to the pleasure principle, reality principle, and narcissism. Note that it is a confusing artifact to choose the term *pleasure* to refer to both a summation and one component of that summation. Different terms that are reflective of the contextual difference are required.

Pleasure Principle Experiences

Pleasure experience appears to be a suitable term to refer to the summation of such evaluations, because "to please" has connotations both of individuality and personal taste. What is evaluated as pleasing on one occasion may be evaluated otherwise on another occasion. What is pleasing for one person may be evaluated as otherwise by other persons. Consequently, the terms *pleasure* and *unpleasure* and the term *pleasure principle* are insufficient to take into account these distinctions and should be replaced.

As I have done with experiences of unpleasure, I distinguish, categorize, and define experiences of pleasure according to motivational causal powers. My study of what is called the pleasure principle has identified that the self evaluates physical sensations of the body-object. The detailing of the positive and reciprocally negative evaluations of bodily sensations will provide a range of scientifically established facts and inferences. These facts will allow reasonable constructions to represent both the positive and negative evaluations. The terms chosen for these constructions would constitute a more reasonable basis to select a general term to refer to this factor of human motivation. Because I limit this book to the elaboration of relativistic theory in order to provide a foundation for the understanding and treatment of psychopathological states, I do not address that.

Pleasure Experiences

Even though I recognize that my detailed explanation of the pleasure principle is imprecise, it may be sufficient to sustain valid and reliable judgments, especially when supplemented by the wisdom of professional experience. Therefore, it is feasible to undertake a categorization of pleasure experience according to the chief contribution of positive evaluations according to the pleasure principle, the reality principle, or narcissism, but I do not do that in this book.

Pain

I have identified categories of unpleasure experience as sadness, fear, guilt, and depression. I have noted that these may be experienced with mild, moderate, and painful intensity. In regard to the conception of a patient's sore spot, these categories represent qualities of a person's experience of a sense of soreness. Therapists assume that mild and moderate degrees of soreness may be tolerated by a person in various manners. Relativists hold that one distinction is most important in the context of psychopathology, that the soreness arises from a self-caused distortion of mental faculties. For that purpose, a mild experience of unpleasure can be defined as the toleration of that condition with no evidence of such distortion. A moderate experience can be defined as a toleration of that condition with evidence of the distortion of mental faculties. A painful experience of unpleasure can be defined as an intolerance of that condition with the institution and maintenance of split attitudes. I define *psychological pain* as an intense summation of sadness, fear, guilt, and depression. In any one instance, the painful intensity may be attributed to any one or combination of components.

The identification and specification of varieties of psychological pain suggest that the same identification and specification of biological and sociological pain can be fruitful for the purpose of those disciplines. Again, such a study is outside the purpose of this book.

TRANSFERENCE RESISTANCE TO PAIN

Pain in Current Theory

It seems a commonsense expectation to find the experience of psychological pain in theoretical propositions of psychopathology. However, a survey of psychoanalytic, behaviorist, humanistic, existential, object-relations, and interpersonal theories (Coleman, 1972, p. 17) fails to reveal any mention of pain. The closest inclusion in a theoretical formulation is found in psychoanalysis. Psychopathology is referred to as "intrapsychic conflict" that includes a component of "anticipated danger" (Brenner, 1976, p. 9). Anticipated danger is recognized as anticipation of an unpleasure experience of psychological pain.

The clinical wisdom of psychoanalysis includes a reference to the centrality of pain in describing the goal of treatment as increasing the patient's awareness of "unpleasure affect" (Brenner, 1974, p. 552). Another clinical reference to the centrality of pain is contained in the advice to analytic therapists to focus on the patient's symptoms (Brenner, 1976, p. 134). Pain is also implied in the statement that patients (not "clients") come to treatment (not "assistance") for relief of suffering from pain (Brenner, 1976, p. 134). Anna Freud pointed out that defenses are descriptions of the patient's struggle with painful or unendurable "affects" (A. Freud, 1946, p. 45). S. Fraiberg (1980, p. 165) pointed out that access to childhood pain is a powerful deterrent against the repetition of poor parenting patterns.

Using "a new language for psychoanalysis," Schafer (1976, p. 263) did not include "pain" in his lexicon while discussing resistance. A recent bit of clinical wisdom advises the diversion of a patient's attention from symptoms (Weinshel, 1984, p. 75). In general, the concept of psychological pain occupies only diluted references within the concept of intrapsychic conflict.

Constructions of Fact and Experience

In Anna Freud's discussion of defense mechanisms, her notion of painful affect is derived from the assumption of infantile helplessness. The "little ego" dreads the strength of its impulses (A. Freud, 1946, p. 181) and the punishment of the "outside world" (A. Freud, 1946, pp. 58, 61). Consequently, her observations of patterns of resistance, both in and out of the office, are described in those terms. Whatever the merit of such a procedure, it follows an interest different from that of the relativist conception of psychopathology.

Relativists regard the patient in the office as possessing a sore spot that is guarded by the maintenance of protective attitudes. A therapist's examination is noted on particular occasions to provoke a noticeable intensification of the patient's protective attitudes. This is taken to indicate that the patient is experiencing an exacerbation of unpleasure. The pattern of the protective attitude is a pattern of transference resistance, a construction of scientific fact. The presence of an exacerbated state of unpleasure is also a scientific fact.

Relativists require that scientific facts about the patient be translated into constructions of the patient's experience. What is the patient's experience in the performance of transference resistance? What is the patient's experience of a state of exacerbated unpleasure?

Acknowledgement of Pain

The tenets of the relativistic theory of psychopathology hold that the patient, at best, can only partially experience the essence of his or her particular psychological pain. This partial awareness may be experienced in two forms: the acknowledgement of pain in a nonpsychological context and the acknowledgement of psychological pain in a tangential manner.

The acknowledgment of nonpsychological pain appears in two forms: the attribution to either biological or sociological causal powers. Biological attribution appears in two classes: either one's own body or environmental stress. These may be manifest, for example, as "I didn't get much sleep" or "The weather is nasty today." Sociological attribution also appears in two classes: significant persons and other persons. These may be manifest, for example, as "My spouse is unsympathetic" or "My boss makes unreasonable demands" and "People are cruel" or "People only care about themselves."

The acknowledgement of nonpsychological pain in transference resistance includes the therapist. This may be manifest, for example, as "Your chair is no good for my back problem," "You have the office too warm," "You are overly professional," and "You psychologists are all chauvinists."

The acknowledgement of psychological pain appears in two forms: either misattribution to a state of fear, sadness, guilt, or depression or the attribution to a mixture of these with one exclusion. In the first form, despite a variety of circumstances, "upsetness" is invariably attributed to either fear, sadness, guilt, or depression. This may be manifest, for example, as "I'm afraid of crowds," "I'm afraid of being laughed at," "I'm afraid I might cry," and "I'm afraid to ask for a raise." In the second form, despite a variety of circumstances, upsetness is never attributed to either fear, sadness, guilt, or depression. These are manifest, for example, in people never acknowledging experiencing apprehension, crying, being sorry, or being blue.

The acknowledgement of psychological pain in transference resistance may be manifest, for example, as "I'm always afraid of what you might say," "That makes me feel sad," "I'm sorry if that offends you," and "I can't understand what you mean," or the appearance of all these forms except one.

One can see that the commonality of all of these acknowledgements of painful experience is their incompleteness. The resistance takes the form of an incomplete and therefore false representation of experience. From the data of observation in the transference, construction of the true quality of the pain being resisted can be established.

Disavowal

In summary, there are many forms of the acknowledgement and avowal of psychological pain. Constructions of pain from these claims are antithetical to the construction of pain from general data of observation. They constitute defensive attitudes that resist the acknowledgement and admission of other truly painful aspects of the person's experience. These other aspects are concealed and sealed in privacy. The meaning of these disavowals is antithetical to that of avowal, which has connotations of an open and full acknowledgement. Therefore, I choose the term *disavowal* to represent the general condition of a partial acknowledgement of psychological pain. For example, Brenner noted that the acknowledgement of unpleasant remorse has served to disavow a more painful state of jealousy (Brenner, 1974, p. 551). Another reason for the choice of this term is to coordinate with Freud's opinion that disavowal would be found to be the general condition of psychopathology (Freud, 1938/1964, p. 204).

Discussion

The data of observation referred to by the term *defense mechanisms* are constructed differently by relativism. The "displacement" of Little Hans's anxiety from his father toward an animal (A. Freud, 1946, p. 75) is now seen as a disavowal of guilt by attribution to an object. The "regression" of his fear of castration into a fear of being bitten (A. Freud, 1946, p. 75) is now seen as a disavowal of pain regarding the body-object by the attribution of fearfulness to an object.

Observations of the patient's partial acknowledgement of unpleasure experience during transference resistance can be constructed as disavowal. The specification of disavowal in S–O–A terms allows a detailed comparison with the specification of the patient's experience of unpleasure as it is constructed from the data of observation. Consequently, the location of splits can be identified as being between self-images, object-images, or self-attitudes. This locus becomes the specific target for the therapist's application of methods of reducing transference resistance.

WORKING THROUGH

Current Conception

Of constant concern to analytic therapists has been the fact that although they are primarily satisfied with their ability to understand the psychopathology of their patients, treatment appears to be a slow process. This issue is addressed in the literature with the term *working through* (Brenner, 1967, p. 94). Freud (1914/1957b, p. 155) used that term to refer to the general overcoming of resistance. Greenson (1965) viewed this as a resistance to change whose slow reduction is accomplished by the therapist's efforts at reconstruction, repetition, and elaboration. Although the nature of resistance is disputed, there is general agreement that working through is required to reduce it (Brenner, 1987, p. 95) and that working though constitutes an operational definition of analytic psychotherapy (Brenner, 1967, p. 103). Successful working through is found to usually result in psychic changes of significant value to the patient (Brenner, 1967, p. 107). The psychoanalytic theory of psychopathology suggests that working through must involve an analysis of all of the components of conflict in order to be successful (Brenner, 1967, p. 103).

Relativistic Conception

Relativist psychopathology holds that the cause of mental disorder is attributable to a locus of psychological pain. Although current theory offers no explanation for the slowness of treatment (Brenner, 1967, p. 101), I suggest that it is the consequence of attempting to deal with the patient's source of intense pain.

Sedler's (1983) review of Freud's use of the concept of working through contains no mention of pain. However, current clinical theory of psychoanalysis does include the working through of resistances associated with the patient's anxiety regarding impulses, defenses, and superego (Brenner, 1967, p. 88). Brodsky (1967) mentioned that working through enables the patient's increased tolerance of anxiety or severe narcissistic motivations. Glenn (1978, p. 44) pointed out that working through helps the patient in mourning for lost objects.

The relativist conception of psychological pain is both more specific and comprehensive than those other notions. I recognize distinctions of pain by the qualities of fear, sadness, guilt, and depression. Methods of psychotherapeutic treatment are aimed at increasing the patient's ability to tolerate psychological pain and to reduce the experience of its intensity from painful to moderate or mild.

The centrality of psychological pain in the relativist theory of psychopathology raises another important distinction. Therapists understand that in pathology, an event is perceived painfully. Therapists also understand that any perception is a function of attitude. People adopt a variety of attitudes in perception so that the same event has a simultaneous variety of meanings for the individual. This understanding can be applied to observation of the person's perception of painful experience. Psychological pain is always a compound of the qualities of fear, sadness, guilt, and depression. Painful experience is always a compound of experiences of fear, sadness, guilt, and depression. Consequently, a theoretically successful treatment requires that the patient is helped to achieve a tolerance for all of the painful aspects of an unpleasant event. Thus, working through is defined as the work of reducing transference resistance to all four aspects of painful experience. The goal of accomplishing this multiple task explains why analytic therapy is slow. However, the specifications of relativistic psychology may sharpen the therapist's perception of the work to be done and how to do it with greater efficiency and speed.

Discussion

I have defined analytic psychotherapy as the application of methods for the reduction of transference resistance. The methods that increase the patient's tolerance of psychological pain are effective by a reduction of resistance.

Anna Freud (1946, p. 69) mentioned that children must learn in the course of development to tolerate pain without recourse to defense and that this is the business of education, not treatment. Relativist theory understands this to mean that educational philosophy should include a curriculum to assist the child in the development of tolerance for biological and sociological unpleasures of mild and moderate intensity. I suggest that the management of pleasure in each of these regards would also be a useful part of the curriculum. However, the relativist definition of a state of severe intensity of unpleasure experience, psychological pain, also defines a state of psychopathology. This is not particularly the business of education but that of psychology and its treatment of psychopathology.

DENIAL OF PSYCHOLOGICAL PAIN

In working with a patient, the relativist theory of psychopathology requires the detection, construction, and specification of patterns of behavior as split attitudes. The patient's institution and maintenance of the psychic structure of split attitudes is understood as the person's attempt to cope with psychological pain. The particular pattern of S–O–A specifications of the split will indicate both the quality of pain being dealt with and the type of disavowal being used defensively. These evaluations are scientific facts whose assertion is supported by both the theoretical foundation and the data of observation.

I have stated that the therapist's attempts to examine the splits meet with resistance. I have considered that form of transference resistance classed as disavowal. The commonality in the class of disavowal is the patient's partial acknowledgement of psychological pain. Relativist theory recognizes this acknowledgement as a negative summation in evaluating motivational experience. The theory predicts that any experience can also be summated as positive or zero. Applied to psychopathology, therapists predict that the patient's experience of transference resistance may appear in the forms of negative, zero, or positive summation.

Positive Transference Resistance

I have considered the negative form of the experience of transference resistance that I have classed as disavowal. There are cases in which the data of observation support the therapist's conclusion that the patient is experiencing psychological pain and, instead of being partially avowed, the patient claims a pleasant subjective experience (A. Freud, 1946, p. 79). The patient's claim is sometimes referred to as a pleasant "fantasy" (A. Freud, 1946, p. 79) or a "hallucinatory gratification" (A. Freud, 1946, p. 87). Although the use of these terms bears unacceptable assumptions, relativists can agree with the description that pain is being "denied" (A. Freud, 1946, p. 79) by the claim of pleasure. This positive form of transference resistance is classed as *denial of painful experience*.

It has been noted that people tend to institute and maintain pleasant fantasies (unsustained beliefs) in the conduct of everyday activities. These may be used in constructive thinking and actions despite their inefficiency for learning and adaptation (Taylor, 1983, p. 71), as well as in psychopathological states for their defensive value. In normal states, when confronted by disconfirmation, the patient will shift easily to another pleasant fantasy. However, in states of pathology, the person meets disconfirmation with resistance. Consequently, therapists do not regard the pleasant fantasies of a patient as gratifying (Brenner, 1975, p. 21) but as maintained defensively despite their essentially ungratifying nature.

Denial attitudes may be shaped to deny biological, sociological, or psychological pain. In cases of the denial of biological pain, the apprehension of physical disorder (both in the sense of noticing as well as that of anxious expectation) appears as an exaggeration of healthfulness together with a dismissal of the importance of any physical disorder. This is often called a "flight into health." In cases of sociological pain, denial appears as the exaggeration of one social quality and the dismissal of the importance of another. For example, one patient regarded himself as being socially desirable even though he was systematically excluded from parties. Although he was proud of not imposing his troubles on other people, he was oblivious to presenting a displeasing manner.

Denial attitudes may also be shaped to deny the particular qualities of painful psychological experience. A commonly noted denial of fearful experience is the adoption of a "counterphobic" attitude (Brenner, 1975, p. 21), such as, "It's not something I dread and wish to avoid, it is challenging and I seek it." Denial of sadness may be expressed in the "Mary Poppins syndrome," in which there is the taking of delight in the most routine of tasks. Denial of guilt may appear in the form identified as "altruistic surrender" (A. Freud, 1946, p. 138). The unpleasure of surrendering a wish is denied by the claim of sufficient vicarious enjoyment in the satisfaction of that wish by another person. The denial of depression is observable in the paradoxical attitude described as "pride in modesty."

The commonality among these forms of denial is in the attribution to one's self of an attitude that is antithetical to an experience of pain, claiming an experience of pleasure. In addition to direct forms of denial, there are corresponding indirect forms that are also frequently observable.

The indirect forms follow a generality noted by Jones (1950, p. 306), that anger is always accompanied by the conviction of being right. The adoption of any angry attitude is always in the form of an opposition to some quality selected about an object-image. The person maintains an attitude that exaggerates the negative evaluation of a quality of the object. Angry attitudes are indirectly oppositional by the attribution to one's self of an exaggeration of the antithesis of the evaluation. Thus, the direct forms of positive denial all exaggerate a positive attitude of the self, whereas the indirect forms of positive denial all exaggerate a negative attribute of the object. The intensity of angry denials may be distinguished in their range from annoyance to hostility.

The angry indirect form of the denial of fear may appear in the commonly recognized pattern of "identification with the aggressor" (A. Freud, 1946, p. 129). The object is a sissy and deserves it. The angry denial of sadness may appear in regarding the object as a wet blanket or a sad sack. The angry denial of guilt may appear in an insistence to impute qualities of badness or wrongness to the object. The angry denial of depression may appear in ridicule of the object (A. Freud, 1946, p. 94) or the attribution of inferiority to the object (Grinberg, 1977, p. 131). Both the direct and indirect forms of denial of psychological pain may also be recognized in the office when they appear in the context of transference resistance.

Passive Transference Resistance

I have discussed the varieties of defense attitudes that are summated as negative and positive. Attitudes that maintain a zero summation of experience in regard to pain are classed as the *passive form of denial.*

The maintenance of an indifferent attitude requires the maintenance of the passive form of activity. The usual connotation of passivity is an absence of activity. In the view of relativism, the only situation in which passivity can be regarded as descriptive of reality is in the case of death. Only a dead person can be truly described as passive. The reality of a live person is perceivable only in manifestations of activity. Therefore, *passivity* must refer to a distinguishable form of activity.

My interest is directed to an understanding of the passive forms of maintaining defense attitudes. It has been noted that a person may avoid and refuse to encounter an occasion for the experience of pain (A. Freud, 1946, p. 100). However, in psychopathological states, the experience of pain is already a fact. In that instance, what is avoided and refused is the acknowledgement of the experience of pain.

The adoption of a defensive attitude with a negative summation is a partial acknowledgement of painful experience. When the attitude is a positive summation, there is an avoidance of any acknowledgement of pain. Zero attitudes are defensively maintained to avoid the acknowledgement of pain.

The presence of painful experience is established by observations of the state of a significant reduction in the person's ability to use his or her faculties. The perception of self-handicapped functioning is indicative of unpleasant experience that may be painful. Consequently, the avoidance of the acknowledgement of pain requires refraining from the performance of those activities in which the handicap is perceivable. The avoidance of performing handicapped activities may serve the avoidance of the acknowledgement of pain. Therefore, passive forms of activity may be used to refrain from performing in a handicapped manner. I term this condition the passive form of denial of pain when it is used defensively.

The passive form of denial may be used in the presence of biological, sociological, and psychological pain. In the passive denial of biological pain, patterns that avoid occasions for the exercise of physiological faculties are observable. Constructions of the person's experience of avoidance will be in the form of a zero summation or an attitude of indifference. This may appear as "I no longer wish to play golf" or "I don't do anything about that because it no longer bothers me." In the passive denial of sociological pain, this may appear as "I no longer enjoy the company of those people" or "Their company is not as bad as I used to think."

Passive denial may be used in the presence of psychological pain. Particular patterns of passive denial have not yet been identified that correlate with particular patterns of psychological pain. Instead, two forms have been noted to occur with a variety of qualities of pain. In one form, an "intellectual awareness" is acknowledged while its emotional relevance is denied (Kernberg, 1975, p. 31). This may appear as "I see what you mean, but it's of no concern to me" or "It's a good idea, but I don't feel like it." Another form of passive denial is identified as maintaining an attitude of "idling" (A. Freud, 1946, p. 103) or "boredom" (Greenson, 1953, p. 10). This may appear as "I have no wish to do anything" or "I'd rather just watch." Both forms of the passive denial of psychological pain may be recognized when they appear in the office in the context of transference resistance.

DISCUSSION

Negative Descriptions

In the discussion of passivity, I noted that an absence of activity cannot be a real description of data of observation except in the case of death. "Lacks," "absences," and "nonexistence" cannot be observed in the activities of living people. These terms express the judgment by an observer about the data being observed in the form of a construction of "absence." In the philosophy of science of transcendental realism, it is an error to construct an "absence" as an inference of causal power for an existing activity. Constructions of cause for an activity must be in a positive and declarative form.

Relativists require that constructions of psychological experience be in a declarative form. Negative forms, such as "lack," are not acceptable. "Absences" cannot be experienced by either the patient or the therapist. Kernberg studied patterns that were described as instances of a lack of control and found them to be specific, selective, and defensive (Kernberg, 1976, p. 47). He also examined patterns described as ego weakness and found them to be solid defensive structures (Kernberg, 1975, p. 170).

Hostility and Anger

The observation of the prevalence of hostile behaviors has been taken as an indication of an innate aggressive impulse. I have shown that this inference is untrue. The term *hostile* refers to an observer's judgment that uses social criteria and represents a social classification of those behavior patterns.

The relativist position recognizes that any socially hostile behavior may be performed with a variety of personal experiences. For example, hostility may be undertaken for political and economic motives. It is untenable to assume that hostility is always performed with a personal experience of anger.

When a person perceives himself or herself to be the target of hostile behavior, it is untenable to assume that this will be experienced angrily. Even if a person concludes that his or her life is in jeopardy and that protective action should be taken, this may be performed with a variety of attitudes. The person's evaluations of the pleasure principle, reality principle, and narcissism may be summated in positive, negative, or zero attitudes. In situations in which a person's life is seen to be in imminent danger, the decision to kill may be executed with an attitude of regretful necessity. This may particularly represent a psychological ideal. Regardless of the situation, relativists hold that an experience of anger is never natural or justified. Angry attitudes are held always to be defensive structures and recognized as indirect denials of psychological pain.

Defense Against Painful Experience

I have shown that split attitudes have been identified where the data of observation substantiate these constructions as scientific facts regarding the person's experience. These constructions are comprehended as defensive and distinctive of the state of psychopathology.

I have discussed conceptions of defense in the context of differing theoretical definitions of psychopathology. Relativists hold that the "germ" of pathology is a conflict of motivation that is experienced as being unbearably intense. The person is unable to tolerate the experience of unpleasure, and it is then regarded as pain. Defensive attitudes are then instituted and maintained as a "psychological retreat" from this painful experience.

As an analogy to defensive attitudes, consider the situation in which a burglar alarm has been set off. The person may experience the noise of the siren as being unbearable. Then, nothing is more important to that person than reducing the painful experience of the noise. Resuming a game that was interrupted, protecting one's possessions, or catching the burglar all become less important. Instead, the person is now primarily motivated to lessen the painful experience and moves always from the source of the noise. The person will stop at that distance where the noise is attenuated to a bearable degree.

Defensive attitudes are the "place" to which the person psychologically "retreats," where the distance from what is painful has made it bearable. Because these attitudes are adopted to lessen the painful experience, any costs are tolerable as the lesser of two evils. Relativists define defense always with the connotation of defense against painful experience.

Split Attitudes

Split attitudes have been identified in which the S–O–A constellations are antithetical, particularly in the specific qualities of idealization–devaluation and good–bad. These are defensive positions against painful experience. The generality of defensive attitudes may be distinguished in two classes—disavowal and denial—each with a variety of forms of manifestation.

I have detailed how these two general classes of defense are identified in various manifestations both in everyday life and as transference resistance. It is useful but insufficient to recognize these forms of transference resistance. It is necessary to identify their classification as either a disavowal or denial of painful experience.

Among the forms of idealization–devaluation, those in which the summation of the self-image is either positive or zero are classed as denials. The summation of the self-image as negative is classed as disavowal. Among the forms of good–bad, those in which the summation of the self-image is either positive or zero are classed as denials. The summation of the self-image as negative is classed as disavowal.

Disclaimer

In accord with the relativist conception of psychopathology, relativist analytic psychotherapy aims at reducing the patient's need to maintain defensive attitudes. Because defenses deal with pain according to the categorical differences of disavowal and denial, a term is necessary to represent the generality of this construction of the patient's experience in the performance of defense. Constructions of experience both as disavowal and denial may be termed under the general heading of *disclaimer*. I take the term from the suggestion of Schafer (1976, p. 130) and use it as a general reference to a person's methods of dealing with psychological pain. The centrality of the realist conception of psychotherapy may be expressed as dealing with a patient's disclaimers that appear in the form of a disavowal or denial of psychological pain.

REFERENCES

Abraham, K. (1953). The psychosexual differences between hysteria and dementia praecox. In D. Bryan & A. Stracey (Trans.), *Selected papers* (pp. 64–69). New York: Basic Books. (Original work published 1908)

American Psychiatric Association. (1980). *Diagnostic and statistical manual of mental disorders* (3rd ed.). Washington, DC: Author.

Brenner, C. (1974). On the nature and development of affects: A unified theory. *Psychoanalytic Quarterly, 43*, 532–556.

Brenner, C. (1975). Affects and psychic conflict. *Psychoanalytic Quarterly, 44*, 5–28.

Brenner, C. (1976). *Psychoanalytic technique and psychic conflict*. New York: International University Press.

Brenner, C. (1987). Working through: 1914–1984. *Psychoanalytic Quarterly, 56*, 88–108.

Brodsky, B. (1967). Working through: Its widening scope and some aspects of its metapsychology. *Psychoanalytic Quarterly, 36*, 485–496.

Coleman, J. (1972). *Abnormal psychology and modern life*. Glenview, IL: Scott, Foresman.

Ferenczi, S. (1950). Stages in the development of the sense of reality. In E. Jones (Trans.), *Sex in psychoanalysis* (pp. 213–239). New York: Basic Books. (Original work published 1913)

Fraiberg, S., & Fraiberg, L. (Eds.) (1980). *Clinical studies in infant mental health: The first year of life*. New York: Basic Books.

Freud, A. (1946). *The ego and the mechanisms of defense*. New York: International University Press.

Freud, S. (1957a). Mourning and melancholia. In J. Strachey (Ed. & Trans.), *The standard edition of the complete psychological works of Sigmund Freud* (Vol. 14, pp. 237–258). London: Hogarth Press. (Original work published 1917)

Freud, S. (1957b). Remembering, repeating, and working through. In J. Strachey (Ed. & Trans.), *The standard edition of the complete psychological works of Sigmund Freud* (Vol. 12, pp. 145–156). London: Hogarth Press. (Original work published 1914)

Freud, S. (1964). An outline of psychoanalysis. In J. Strachey (Ed. & Trans.), *The standard edition of the complete psychological works of Sigmund Freud* (Vol. 23, pp. 141–208). London: Hogarth Press. (Original work published 1938)

Freud, S. (1959). Inhibition, symptoms, and anxiety. In J. Strachey (Ed. & Trans.), *The standard edition of the complete psychological works of Sigmund Freud* (Vol. 20, pp. 77–175). London: Hogarth Press. (Original work published 1936)

Glenn, J. (1978). General principles of child analysis. In J. Glenn & M. Scharfman (Eds.), *Child analysis and therapy* (pp. 29–66). New York: Jason Aronson.

Greenson, R. (1953). On boredom. *Journal of the American Psychoanalytic Association, 1*, 7–21.

Greenson, R. (1965). The problem of working through. In M. Schur (Ed.), *Drives, affects, behavior:*

Vol. 2. Essays in honor of Marie Bonaparte (pp. 277–314). New York: International University Press.

Greenson, R. (1967). *The technique and practice of psychotherapy*. New York: International University Press.

Grinberg, L. (1977). An approach to the understanding of borderline disorders. In P. Hartocollis (Ed.), *Borderline personality disorders* (pp. 123–142). New York: International University Press.

Jones, E. (1950). Fear, guilt and hate. In E. Jones (Ed.), *Papers on psychoanalysis* (pp. 304–319). London: Bailliere, Tindall & Cox.

Kernberg, O. (1975). *Borderline conditions and pathological narcissism*. New York: Jason Aronson.

Kernberg, O. (1976). *Object relations theory and clinical psychoanalysis*. New York: Jason Aronson.

Schafer, R. (1976). *A new language for psychoanalysis*. New York: Basic Books.

Sedler, M. (1983). Freud's concept of working through. *Psychoanalytic Quarterly, 52*, 73–98.

Taylor, S. (1983). Adjustment to threatening events: A theory of cognitive adaptation. *American Psychologist, 38*, 1161–1173.

Weinshel, E. (1984). Some observations on the psychoanalytic process. *Psychoanalytic Quarterly, 53*, 63–92.

19

Treatment of Disavowal

CLARIFICATION OF DISAVOWAL

In performing the process of clarification, the analytic psychotherapist will notice departures from the personal norm of the patient's defensive attitudes. Some of these transference resistance departures will be recognized as part of the category of disavowal. Observation will establish that the patient is able to tolerate a particular quality of psychological unpleasure by presenting an avowal of that experience in regard to the material.

Clarification of Avowal

The presentation by the patient of the subjective experience of a quality of psychological unpleasure is a part of the therapist's manifest data of observation. That, together with other considerations, is used by the therapist in arriving at valid and reliable inferences in the form of constructions of fact. The process of clarification is the method used by a therapist to clarify his or her understanding of facts about the patient.

The patient's avowal of psychological unpleasure is usually presented in terms of socially conventional meaning with biological, sociological, and psychological assumptions. These include anger, frustration, jealousy, fear, sadness, shame, depression, guilt, envy, and anxiety. These avowals represent the patient's impression of the quality of a negatively summated experience.

Clarification seeks to elicit further data of observation that will allow the ordering of the data in the form of unequivocal constructions of S–O–A constellations. This method is used to clarify the patient's self-experience of the event, arriving at a labeling of experience. Labeling is the result of clarifying the patient's avowal of an experience of psychological unpleasure.

Relabeling of Avowal

In the clarification of labeling, the therapist may note that the pattern of behavior is unsuitably described by the patient's presented label. A more apt relabeling should be presented cautiously by the therapist because it may be evocative of resistance.

Manifestations of resistance to relabeling avowals serve to identify the perimeter of the patient's sore spot. The content of the patient's labeling and the therapist's relabeling constitute the material used for interventions in disavowal.

Palpation of the patient's avowal of psychic unpleasure in other life areas allows the accumulation of other material useful for intervention. Those avowals of unpleasure that resist relabeling may be referred to as *claimers*.

Construction of Disavowal

The observation of resistance to relabeling is indicative of the patient's inability to tolerate particular qualities of psychic unpleasure. Those qualities that are avowed are demonstrably tolerable regardless of the degree of manifest intensity. In planning for intervention in this resistance, it is desirable to ascertain those qualities of unpleasure that are experienced as painful.

Relativist theory has defined the elements of unpleasure experience as fear, sadness, guilt, and depression. These elements have been specified as relating to particular conflicts regarding the pleasure principle, reality principle, and narcissism. With these concepts, it is possible to conduct clarification in order to identify the specific quality of unpleasure that meets with resistance to acknowledgement. The data of observation from clarification will support a construction of disavowal of pain. A construction of disavowal represents that quality of unpleasure experience that the patient finds too painful to recognize. The clarification of disavowed qualities of unpleasure should be carried out with the same regulation as in any examination of psychic pain.

INTERVENTION TOWARD DISAVOWAL

A construction of disavowal establishes the particular quality of psychological unpleasure that the patient regards as intolerably painful. Interventions toward disavowal aim toward provoking in the patient a small dose of that particular unpleasure. Any activity of the therapist that results in the patient's experience of that quality of unpleasure is a disavowal intervention, whether intended or not.

The performance of certain symptoms may be regarded as being similar to the performance of disavowal transference resistance. Both cultivate an attitude of experiencing one quality of unpleasure as an avoidance of the experience of another particular quality of unpleasure. The cultivation of fearfulness in phobias may be used defensively against the experience of sadness, guilt, or depression. This distinction would be useful in diagnosis for the purpose of analytic psychotherapy.

In the "palpation" of the patient's avowal of psychic unpleasure, the material eliciting departures from transference resistance have been noted. When the therapist decides to intervene toward disavowal, some "piece" of this material is chosen to be presented because it is judged as able to be tolerated by the patient. The method of "injecting" this dosage of the material is similar to the medical procedure of inoculation. There are several useful guides in judging tolerability.

Memory

The tendency toward an automatic inhibition of the faculty of memory in the face of unpleasure is useful in testing the effective degree of dosage of an intervention. A dosage that is experienced as too much will not receive the patient's cooperation with memory. Therefore, an initial presentation of intervention could be directed toward the patient's memory regarding the piece of material.

Because memories that are distant in time tend to be recollected less well, it is best to direct the patient's attention toward memories of the distant past. As these interventions prove more tolerable, the dosage can be increased by directing attention to the more recent past, the present, and then current experience in the treatment situation.

Sensations

One of the elements in the experience of an event is the observation of physical sensations. Directing the patient's attention to sensations that accompany the experience of the presented material may sufficiently dilute the dosage to tolerability. This mode of intervention may be formed by asking, "When you felt afraid at that time, where in your body did you especially feel it?"

This method serves as a probe of tolerability because it allows the patient the option of a softer, indirect participation. For example, the observation of a sensation of heat at the shoulder can be reported as an itch. Because "itch" implies an externally caused irritation, it is available as an indirect report of sensation.

Activities

Another element in constructing the experience of an event is the observation of activities. Directing the patient's attention to his or her activities during the experience of the presented material may dilute the dosage of the intervention. This may be formed by asking, "What were you doing just before you felt afraid at that time?" or "What did you do when you felt afraid?" and "What did you do after that?"

Avowal

I have stated that the defensive attitude avowing a particular quality of unpleasure experience has an antithetical relationship to the quality being disavowed. This antithetical connection can be exploited as an indirect intervention. If "black" is too touchy for the patient to deal with directly, there may be sufficient comfort to deal with "white." Therefore, interventions aimed at expanding avowed unpleasure serve to provoke indirectly a diluted dose of the disavowed unpleasure.

This mode may be formed by asking, "Can you tell me more of what it was like to have that feeling of fear?", "When else have you had that feeling of fear?", and "What seems to make the fear more or less?"

Object-Images

Attributes of one's self-image may be supplementarily or complimentarily ascribed to attributes of object-images. Both self- and object-images are elements in experiencing an event. Therefore, directing the patient's attention to an object-image within the experience of the presented material may dilute the dosage of intervention toward the self-images. This mode may be formed by asking, "What was there about the dark room that seemed most fearful?" and "Of what are you most afraid that she might do?"

Tolerance

The essence of disavowal is the patient's inability to tolerate an aspect of un-pleasure. This disability of toleration may be referred to indirectly by directing the patient's attention to his or her ability to tolerate an avowed unpleasure. This mode of intervention is a diluted dosage because a piece of the material is selected that can be presented in a positively summated manner. This mode may be formed by stating, "You seem able to stand considerable fear" and "Other people might have avoided even getting involved at all" or "How do you manage continuing a rela-tionship with such a fearsome person?"

Summary

The goal of these indirect modes of intervention in disavowal is to assist the patient in developing the ability to tolerate the recognition of a disavowed unplea-sure. The appearance of this achievement may be marked by some general and partial acceptance such as the patient's comment, "You know, I also felt a little sad at the same time."

WORKING THROUGH DISAVOWAL

According to the relativist theory of psychotherapy, the goal of treatment is to develop the patient's ability to tolerate that quality of the psychological unpleasure experience that is disavowed. According to the relativist theory of psychology, any experience of psychological unpleasure is the negative summation of motivations. Qualities of unpleasure experience are distinguished according to the chief motiva-tion that is evaluated negatively. Therefore, there are qualitative motivational dif-ferences in achieving the working through of the particular unpleasure that is intolerable.

Sadness

When the construction of disavowal specifies that a sadness experience is intol-erable, there is a negative summation according to the pleasure principle. The essence of this summation is the person's perception that some activity is costing a loss of satisfaction and happiness and should reasonably be curtailed. The condi-tion for such a judgment is the perceived gain in other pleasures that are contingent but inimical. These pleasures may be positive summations of the reality principle and narcissism. Despite the person's best judgment that a particular enjoyment should be curtailed, the prospect of the loss of that satisfaction is sometimes expe-rienced as painfully intolerable.

The best but painful resolution of this motivational conflict is postponed by the adoption of disavowal. A disavowal of sadness allows the indirect continuation of the enjoyment but requires withstanding the accompanying indirect suffering of negative summations.

Working through of sadness disavowal entails the recognition of all costs ac-cording to the pleasure principle, reality principle, and narcissism. Working through also entails the recognition of the particular pleasure with the sadness experienced in its curtailment. Working through is complete only when the patient has developed the ability to tolerate all elements of unpleasure in the motivational conflict.

The therapist presents all of these unpleasure elements to the patient using various modes of intervention in carefully chosen dosages. Although some element of unpleasure may be particularly sensitive for an individual patient, it is expected that the most sensitive element will be the sense of loss in the curtailment or relinquishment of that satisfaction.

Working through the intolerable pain of sadness that is represented by disavowal enables the patient to conduct life in what is to his or her self-judgment the best and most reasonable manner. This achievement may be referred to as self-actualization, sublimation, adaptation, or restoration of the self.

Fear

When the construction of disavowal specifies that a fearful experience is intolerable, there is a negative summation of the body-image according to the reality principle. The essence of this summation is the person's perception that some ability is noxious to healthfulness and should reasonably be curtailed. The conditions for such a judgment are the recognition that the activity is injurious to the body and that the activity is inimical with the pleasure principle, reality principle, or narcissism. Despite the person's best judgment that caring for the body-object is served by a curtailment of that activity, that prospect is experienced as painfully intolerable.

A best resolution of the motivational conflict is precluded by the painfulness of the negative summation, and its postponement is effected by the adoption of disavowal. Disavowal of fear allows the continuation of the activity by withstanding the contingent but indirect suffering.

Working through of disavowed fear entails the recognition of all costs according to the pleasure principle, reality principle, and narcissism. Working through also entails the recognition of the injuriousness to the body-object of the behavior. Working through is complete only when the patient has developed the ability to tolerate all elements of unpleasure in the motivational conflict.

The therapist presents all of the elements of unpleasure to the patient using various modes of intervention in carefully chosen dosages. Although some element of unpleasure may be particularly sensitive for an individual patient, it is expected that those related to narcissism will be the most sensitive. Although one's body is regarded as a "most favored object," this concern is superceded if it is necessary to be protective of a sorely injured narcissism.

Working through an intolerably painful fearfulness, represented by its disavowal, enables the patient to conduct life in what in his or her self-judgment is the best and most reasonable manner. This would be an achievement of self-actualization.

Guilt

When the construction of disavowal specifies that an experience of guilt is intolerable, there is a negative summation of social objects according to the reality principle. The essence of this summation is the person's perception that some activity is immoral and should be met with social rejection. It appears reasonable that this activity should be curtailed. The conditions for such a judgment are the recognition that the activity is socially objectionable as well as inimical with the pleasure principle, reality principle, or narcissism. Despite the person's best judgment that curtailing the activity would significantly reduce the social unpleasure of guilt, that prospect is experienced as painfully intolerable.

A best resolution of the motivational conflict is precluded by the painfulness of the negative summation and is postponed by the adoption of a disavowal of guilt. Disavowal of guilt allows the continuation of the activity by withstanding the contingent, indirect suffering.

Working through disavowal of guilt entails the recognition of all costs according to the pleasure principle, reality principle, and narcissism. Working through also entails the recognition of the sense of social immorality of the behavior. Working through is complete only when the patient has developed the ability to tolerate all elements of unpleasure in the motivational conflict.

The therapist presents all of the elements of unpleasure to the patient using various modes of intervention in carefully chosen dosages. Although some element of unpleasure may be particularly sensitive for an individual patient, it is expected that superceding considerations in the hierarchy of motivation will be the most sensitive. Superceding considerations toward social objects are those having to do with the body-object and narcissism.

Working through an intolerable pain of guilt that is represented by a disavowal type of attitude enables the patient to conduct life in a self-judged best and reasonable manner. This allows the achievement of self-actualization.

Depression

When the construction of disavowal specifies that an experience of depression is intolerable, there is a negative summation according to narcissistic motivation. The essence of this summation is the person's perception that in the performance of some activity, his or her sense of self-esteem is appreciably lowered. It appears reasonable that this activity should be curtailed. The condition for such a judgment is a significant loss of both pride and the sense of specialness, as well as the activity being inimical with the pleasure and reality principles. Despite the person's best judgment that curtailing the activity would reduce significantly the unpleasure experience of humiliation, that prospect is experienced as painfully intolerable.

A best resolution of this motivational conflict is precluded by the painfulness of the negative summation, and it is deferred by the adoption of a defensive attitude of disavowal. Disavowal of depression allows the continuation of the activity while withstanding the contingent, indirect suffering.

Working through the disavowal of depression entails the recognition of costs according to the pleasure and the reality principles. Working through also entails the recognition of the sense of self-debasement in performing the behavior. Working through is complete only when the patient has developed the ability to tolerate all elements of unpleasure in the motivational conflict.

The therapist presents all of the elements of unpleasure to the patient using various modes of intervention in carefully chosen dosages. Although some element of unpleasure may be particularly sensitive for an individual patient, it is expected that basic narcissistic unpleasure will be the most sensitive. The greatest unpleasure is that associated with the "taming of the sense of grandiosity," which I discussed in chapter 11.

Working through an intolerable pain of depression that is represented by the adoption of a disavowal defense enables the patient to conduct life in a self-judged reasonable manner. This allows the achievement of self-actualization.

DISCUSSION

Working Through Denial

Defensive attitudes of denial are characterized as positively or zero summated experiences. Working through denial increases the patient's ability to tolerate a negatively summated experience, or experience of anxiety.

The achievement of the ability to tolerate anxiety experience allows the cessation of the necessity to perform unreasonable activities in order to institute and maintain a denial attitude. The cessation of unreasonable activities provides relief from the irritation to self-esteem that is an inevitable consequence of denial attitudes. In addition, the achievement of the ability to tolerate an anxiety experience enables the patient to take a reasonable attitude toward the manifestations of anxiety. When the manifestations come to be regarded as merely unpleasant, not painful, they can be reasonably considered.

One frequent outcome in a reasonable consideration of observations that one is upset, anxious, or nervous is the decision that nothing needs to be done. These manifestations may be judged as not significantly hampering a satisfactory conduct of life, such as, "After all, no one is perfect." This is similar to learning that what one feared was an omen of cancer turned out to be merely a pimple. With that psychotherapeutic outcome, the treatment can be considered to be successfully completed.

On occasion, however, the patient may decide that it is unsatisfactory to conduct life with a "pimple." From some psychological positions, this is regarded as the completion of one psychotherapeutic contract and the engagement of another contract for service. The new contract may be seen as an educational undertaking for improvement and not found reimbursable as a medical expense by insurers of disability.

From the relativist position, the patient's decision to invest considerable time, money, and effort in order to have a pimple treated is regarded as manifestly unreasonable. In this case, an experience of unpleasure is presented as an avowal of trivial intensity. That is apparently contradictory to an intensity justifying investment in treatment. The analytic therapist may conclude that the patient is presenting a defensive attitude of disavowal and that this is an indication of psychopathology. The achievement of the ability to tolerate a previously intolerable general unpleasure may represent the ability to recognize the tip of an iceberg of a disavowed psychological pain.

This instance demonstrates that working through a denial defense can expose the presence of a disavowal defense. The successful treatment of the presenting psychopathology has revealed a deeper structure of psychopathology that the patient is now presenting for treatment in a guarded manner.

Working Through Disavowal

The same considerations I discussed in working through denial are applicable to working through disavowal. In the process of working through the disavowal of a quality of painful psychological unpleasure, enough tolerance might have been developed to enable the patient to present a previously concealed defensive disclaimer. The newly presented disclaimer may appear as either a denial or a different type of disavowal. The disclaimer may be presented either during the course of working through a disavowal or on its completion.

GENERAL CONSIDERATIONS

I have discussed how modulated therapeutic interventions tend to develop a general improvement in the ability to tolerate unpleasure. As the patient's tolerance increases, the presented defensive attitude may shift among the varieties of denials and disavowals. Consequently, the course of psychotherapeutic activity may be marked by shifts in the aim of the work currently at hand.

When a departure is presented from the disclaimer being worked through, there is the question whether to regard this as an increase in resistance to that process or as an expansion of the ability to deal with unpleasure. Theoretically, the departure may represent either condition.

The clinical wisdom to deal with the surface would direct one to shift attention to the presenting departure. Relativist theory agrees with this wisdom but with differing signification. Not only is attention shifted, but it is shifted from performing intervention to performing clarification.

The palpation of the new presentation will provide data of observation as to its defensive use by revealing manifestations of transference resistance. In that case, methods of reducing transference resistance are applied so that the plan for previous interventions can be resumed with a reduced dosage. In the event that clarification results in the avowal of new aspects of unpleasure, clarification can be continued in the usual manner.

During the course of psychotherapy, even after the patient has settled down into a general pattern regarded as his or her personal norm, many instances of departure can be observed. Some of these departures may appear to the therapist as reasonably related to events reported by the patient. Other departures may appear unreasonable and manifestly indicative of increased disturbance. Therapists are concerned with the patient's status of mental health, and departures are taken in the context of whether the patient is getting better or worse.

Relativists regard it as a basic error to use manifest data of observation as a basis for inferences as to this question, or any question. The procedure just cited contains another basic error, that of using what is called "normality" and "adaptation" as a standard for mental health.

Relativist theory sets the standard for mental health as the capacity of the individual to tolerate experiences of unpleasure without recourse to defensive alterations of attitude. As I have discussed, manifest departures may arise within the context of both increased and decreased ability to tolerate unpleasure. It is necessary to apply the method of clarification of experience to the person performing the departure in order to obtain scientific facts about mental functioning that can sustain a valid and reliable conclusion on the question.

All too often, therapists jump to the conclusion that presentation by a patient of increased subjective distress is indicative of a worsening in their condition. In supervising psychotherapy, an examination of the therapist's attitude has often revealed the presence of anxiety in observing the patient's presentation of distress. The countertransference issue in those cases has been the therapist's delimitation of the ability to tolerate viewing the patient's distress.

Consider an example of this instance. A patient and I were considerably along in working through a disavowal of sadness when crying became clinically frequent and copious. Although I was disturbed by the crying, the patient reported that she never had seen things more clearly than through her tearful eyes.

With the relativist definition of psychopathology and psychotherapy, I have discussed the components of the analytic attitude that are desirable for psychotherapists. I have also discussed in some detail the clarifying and intervention methods in the conduct of analytic psychotherapy. It may be noted that the conditions for performing relativist psychotherapy are not identical with those assumed by orthodox psychoanalysis.

Among others, Rangell (1988, p. 331) has reported satisfactory treatment outcomes despite variation from the orthodox conditions of using the couch and infrequency and discontinuity of treatment appointments. He considered that successful treatment was not dependent on those particular conditions but on a sound theoretical basis.

With the greater precision in definition afforded by relativism as to the nature of psychopathology and its analytic treatment, it would be profitable to reconsider those conditions that facilitate psychotherapy.

REFERENCE

Rangell, L. (1988). The future of psychoanalysis: The scientific crossroads. *Psychoanalytic Quarterly,* *57*, 313–340.

20

Treatment of Denial

I have described the general conduct of the analytic psychotherapist as performing the method of clarification. It has been noted (Schafer, 1983, p. 31) that the scientific principle of participant observation makes it clear that every activity of the therapist is an "intervention" in the patient's life. For example, the inquiry "What were you thinking while you said that?" is an intervention. It is a scientific fact that asking this question is an intervention.

The intervention is an objectively established scientific fact. However, under the relativistic theory of psychology, this objective fact is part of the data of observation. Observations of scientific facts about a patient do not constitute psychological facts. These are facts that concern the individual's experience of a scientific objective event. Thus, an objective intervention by the therapist is not necessarily experienced as an intervention by the patient.

Objective intervention is a scientific fact for the science of sociology. The subjective experience of intervention is a construction of scientific fact for the science of psychology. In psychology, any activity of the therapist may be experienced by the patient in a summation of positive, zero, or negative evaluations. Therefore, only those activities of the therapist that are negatively summated by the patient are termed *interventions* by psychologists.

In performing clarification, the therapist notes indications of the patient's negatively summated experience as transference resistance and backs off from that angle. Therefore, the process of clarification may also be described as the conduct of examination under the delimitation of avoiding the provocation of negatively summated experience.

These considerations bring me to the relativist definition of psychological interventions as those activities that are deliberate departures from clarification. Interventions are presentations by the therapist with the scientific expectation that the patient will experience them with a negative summation. Areas of the patient's negatively summated experience are identified by the method of clarification as disclaimers.

INTERVENTION TOWARD DISCLAIMERS

The identification of a patient's attitude as a disclaimer is the recognition of a clinical manifestation of resistance. As I have discussed, the greatest treatment gains are in the reduction of resistance (Schafer, 1983, p. 13) and disclaimed actions (Schafer, 1983, pp. 146–147).

Interventions by the analytic therapist that are deliberate activities have been termed *interpretations*. This term refers to the aim of conveying new information so that a patient comes to know himself or herself better (Brenner, 1976, p. 43).

The new information is selected by the therapist with the aim of bringing the patient toward recognizing himself or herself as an active agent (Schafer, 1983, p. 107).

The chief connotation of the term *interpretation* relates to learning, and the presentation of an interpretation is a method of teaching. At the same time, interpretation is also represented as a psychotherapeutic method. However, the only pathology that teaching can "remedy" is that of ignorance. Ignorance may be a consequence of psychological disorder, but it is not its cause. Therefore, whatever therapeutic effect is consequent to the presentation of an interpretation, it is not due to its informational quality. The informational value of a therapist's intervention is not relevant to its value as an active treatment of psychological disorder. Consequently, it is erroneous and misleading to refer to psychotherapeutic interventions as interpretations.

Relativists recognize that the presentation of information, whether new or not, may be experienced in summation as positive, zero, or negative. These are all possible consequences of an interpretation. However, it is a significantly different matter to present an interpretation that is expected to be summated negatively. A deliberate attempt to provoke an experience of anxiety or pain is better referred to as an intervention.

In the process of clarification, the therapist often offers new information. From the data of observation, the therapist's knowledge of the general principles of psychological functioning allows the probable inference of aspects of the patient's experience that are unreported by the patient. These inferences are interpretations of data of observation in the form of constructions of the patient's experience. In clarification, those interpretations that are judged to be received by the patient as either positive or zero are considered for presentation and use in labeling or relabeling. Those interpretations that are judged to be received negatively by the patient are withheld until the time when they will be used as therapeutic interventions. It is useful to consider a medical analogy. The presentation of an intervention is similar to an incision made by a surgeon. The process of clarification is similar to the surgeon's preparation of the patient for the operation.

The careful relativist distinction between interpretations that do or do not provoke resistance is recognized in the literature of clinical wisdom. Treatment often requires the presentation of interpretations that are regarded by the patient as "ego-alien" (Greenson, 1967, pp. 37–42). Presentations of information that go one step beyond the observations of a patient (Kernberg, 1976, p. 179) do sometimes provoke an intense reaction of anxiety (Kernberg, 1976, p. 23). The presentation of information that goes that step is regarded as a confrontation of the patient's contradictions or delimited recognition of reality (Kernberg, 1977, p. 95).

Clinical wisdom recognizes that it is no easy matter for a patient to become aware of what has, for his or her whole life, been regarded as intolerably painful (Brenner, 1976, p. 121). The presentation of an intervention is as necessary to achieve a successful treatment as is cutting the patient to perform an operation, and both must be done carefully.

I now depart from the surgical analogy because it is inapt in reference to the cause of illness. In surgery, the patient's sensitivity to being cut is tangential to the pathology and may be circumvented with anesthesia. Sensitivity is anesthetized to enable a more direct access to the cause of illness. In contrast, the cause of psychological illness is the patient's sensitivity. Because of the sensitivity, the patient's behavior is delimited. An anesthetizing of psychological sensitivity may enable the patient to expand the range of behavior, at least as long as the anesthetic is effective. However, the essence of being sensitive persists, as does its capacity to handicap behavior.

The relativist conception of psychopathology is that of a state in which certain conflicts of motivation are experienced with painful sensitivity. The relativist conception of psychotherapy aims at reducing this painful sensitivity. Therefore, relativist psychotherapeutic methods are aimed at desensitizing anxious and painful experience, regardless of whether the patient is subjectively aware of the unpleasure. The specific technique of relativist desensitization of unpleasure is the careful application of interventions. The aim of intervention is to provoke just enough unpleasure that the patient can tolerate.

The relativist conception of the presentation of doses of intervention as steps in desensitization is recognized in clinical wisdom. It is advised that interventions should be presented gradually and with frequent repetition, that no single dose is as important as the general plan (Brenner, 1976, pp. 50–51). Successful doses of intervention result in the patient's becoming able to tolerate that which was so painful that it had to be avoided (Brenner, 1976, p. 73).

INTERVENTION TOWARD DENIAL

Those clinical manifestations of transference resistance that are termed *disclaimers* have been distinguished in the categories of denial and disavowal. An attitude of disavowal indicates that the patient has a partial ability to tolerate some aspect of psychological pain, either the generality of anxious anticipation of unpleasure or some partial quality of psychic pain. In an attitude of denial, the patient demonstrates an inability to tolerate even anxious expectation. Interventions toward denial aim at provoking in the patient a small dose of anxious experience, or anxiety. Any activity of the therapist that results in the patient's experience of anxiety is a denial intervention, whether intended or not.

The performance of denial transference resistance is regarded in the same way as the performance of certain symptoms. Both patterns serve to avoid an experience of anxiety (Freud, 1926/1959, pp. 88–89), as in the case in which manifestations of conversion hysteria are regarded by the patient with indifference. This understanding suggests the usefulness for psychotherapy of distinguishing symptoms as to denial or disavowal because symptoms replace anxiety (Freud, 1933/1964, p. 63).

In the treatment situation, these general considerations are brought to bear in a singular clinical consideration. During clarification, the patient's departures from the personal norm of defensive attitudes will have been noted. The therapist will also note the aspect of interpretation that has been experienced as an intervention. The denial or disavowal quality of the departure will also have been noted. Thus, the therapist accumulates considerable evidence of what has been provocative of denial or disavowal transference resistance.

When the therapist decides to intervene in denial, there is abundant material to use for this purpose. This is one of those occasions in which it is a good technique to direct the patient's associations (Brenner, 1976, p. 101). However, there are several considerations in choosing how to direct the patient in denial interventions. It is first necessary to direct the patient's attention to the area that is chosen. That may be done by representing again the original interpretation that provoked denial. Freud (1926/1959, p. 151) did this as a "cathartic" method under the theory of abreaction, but he abandoned it when that proved insufficient. Relativists understand that the reevocation of an intolerable unpleasure is untherapeutic. It is a case in which the "medicine" both tastes bad and does not work.

The relativist method presents some "piece" of the intolerable entirety of the material with the expectation that the piece can be tolerated by the patient without recourse to the defense of denial. Therapists attempt to evoke some small aspect of anxiety that can be tolerated. This method is an analogy to the medical procedure of inoculation.

Denial indicates that the patient cannot tolerate the magnitude of an experience of anxiety and that any situation evocative of that magnitude must be regarded as a danger. This conception of perceptions regarded as "inner dangers" is similar to that proposed by Freud (1933/1964, p. 94). The art in this aspect of psychotherapy is in finding an intervention provocative of a piece of anxiety that the patient can tolerate. There are several useful guides to this goal.

MEMORY

It is a well-known observation that unpleasant memories are difficult to recall. Therefore, the recollection of a piece of anxiety is evidence that it is tolerable in that particular form. The initial form of intervention is to direct the patient to remember and to describe an event related to the denied material. This may be performed by asking, "What can you remember about our discussion of your father's operation?" This intervention may be too strong and may meet with denial of that event. A weaker form of memory intervention—directing attention to the dimmer recollections of past experience—may be successful. These may be formed as "What can you remember about your father's health last year or when you were in high school or when you were a child?"

SENSATIONS

The intervention is aimed at bringing the patient from the position of denial of anxiety to that of an experience of anxiety. Studies of the state of psychological anxiety indicate that the ideational component is denied, although the recognition of physiological excitation is tolerated (Freud, 1933/1964, p. 63).

In the case of a subjective denial of anxiety, an application of the sophisticated equipment of biofeedback could amply demonstrate a state of seething physiological arousal. The therapist may also observe the denying patient to be grasping the arms of a chair with white knuckles. Although physiological hyperactivity can be objectively demonstrated, this fact need not be subjectively recognized or "felt."

Patients may deny feeling the feeling of physiological sensations. More exactly, these sensations are acknowledgeable as long as they are not experienced with a negative summation. The method of intervention in this form of denial may be performed by asking, "While you are thinking about this matter, what bodily sensations do you notice?" This intervention may be too strong and may meet with a continuation of denial of sensations. Intervention in denial of sensations may be softened by reference to dimmer past experience.

ACTIVITIES

The physiological hyperactivity in objective states of anxiety also has consequences of motor tension (Freud, 1933/1964, p. 82), such as impediments of speech and foot shaking. Perception of these activities is acknowledgeable in other than a negative summation. Intervention in this form of denial may be performed by remarking, "That's a hard word to say when you're trying to talk rapidly" or "Your foot shaking suggests to me that there's more you wish to say on the subject."

EMOTION

Anxiety is a form of emotional state and, as such, it is an individual experience as the vector outcome of the pleasure principle, the reality principle, and narcissistic motivations. A negative summation of anxiety may receive its chief contribution from any of those contexts. I hold that these particular motivations are acknowledgeable in other than a negative summation. Even in instances of denial as zero summation, interventions of motivation may be tolerable in zero or positive form.

Interventions using the pleasure principle may be formed as "That might feel nice to many people" or "That seems to have nothing to do with fear." Interventions using the body-object of the reality principle may be formed as "That may be a healthy thing to do" or "It's not likely that will be harmful." Interventions using other objects of the reality principle may be formed as "You seem to have solved that situation well" or "It is not likely most people would notice that." Interventions using narcissism may be formed as "It would be natural to take pride in that" or "That seems to have nothing to do with self-esteem."

SELF-IMAGES AND OBJECT-IMAGES

The experience of anxiety, like all experience, is constructed by using S–O–A constellations. In denial, what is denied may be the negative summation of self- and object-images. I hold that self- and object-images are acknowledgeable in other than a negative summation.

Interventions toward the self-image may be formed as "That seems to say something about you're being a nice person" or "Any type of person may have done that." Interventions toward the object-image may be formed as "You make her seem like a kind person" or "I don't know what sort of person that is."

ATTITUDE

The attitude component in the S–O–A constellations of the experience of anxiety is fearfulness. In anxiety, this lacks connection to a definite object (Freud, 1926/1959, p. 105) and is a fearful attitude toward an unknown danger (Freud, 1926/1959, p. 165). In denial, what is denied is the attitude of fear. I hold that an intervention suggesting an attitude other than fear is able to be acknowledged if presented in other than a negative summation.

Interventions toward a fearful attitude may be formed as "Your leaving at that time seems a kindness since he was disturbed by your presence" or "There was no reason to stay when it became uninteresting."

UNPLEASURE–PAIN

It has been noted that a fearful expectation of unpleasure is often "realistic" (Freud, 1933/1964, p. 81). The expectation of injury that is judged about a particular situation may be normal and shared by reasonable people (Freud, 1926/1959, p. 165). In the neurotic form of a fearful expectation of unpleasure, the "realistic fear" is repressed (Freud, 1933/1964, p. 62). However, relativists note that the institution and maintenance of repression is indicative that the sense of unpleasure is perceived as painful and intolerable. In denial, what is denied is the intolerable painfulness of the unpleasure.

Avoidance is performed with an experience of unpleasure. I hold that interventions indicating unpleasure are tolerable if they are not sensed painfully. An unpleasure experience leads to avoidance based on judgment and taste. Painful unpleasure leads to avoidance based on powerlessness, inability, and loss of mastery (Freud, 1933/1964, p. 93).

Interventions presenting tolerable self-unpleasures may be formed as "It was wise to remove yourself from that insult" or "If it tastes terrible, why put up with it?"

ANTITHETICAL SELF-IMAGES AND OBJECT-IMAGES

Denial, like all defenses against painful experience, are formed by the institution and maintenance of split attitudes. One aspect of splitting is the adoption of antithetical self- and object-images. In that form of denial, what is denied is a negative attribution to the self-image. Any negative attribution to the object-image will be tolerable when it is experienced as unpleasant but not painful. This is similar to those considerations referred to by the term *projection*. Thus, intervention in denial may present an unpleasant characteristic of the object-image that will be experienced as tolerable.

Interventions presenting tolerable unpleasant characteristics of the object-image may be formed as "That appears to be a formidable situation" or "He seems to be a powerful person."

RELIEF PLEASURE

Denial maintains attitudes about pleasure experiences that are summated as either positive or zero, whereas negative summations are not tolerable. There are two different categories of the experience of pleasure: those consequent to either gratification or relief. An example of relief is the pleasant interpretation of sensations when removing a pair of tight shoes. In the case of denial, what is denied is the unpleasure of the sensations in wearing tight shoes. The other side of the coin, an experience of relief, is tolerable. Interventions toward the denial of unpleasure may be tolerated when presented as the converse experience of relief.

Interventions in denial presenting tolerable relief experiences may be formed as "It must have been quite a relief to get out of that situation" or "You seem to have been more relaxed that time."

Summary

When the therapist decides to intervene in one of the patient's denial manifestations of transference resistance, treatment presents a piece of the material that was denied. The same material may be viewed partially from the multiple angles of memory, sensations, activities, emotion, self- and object-images, unpleasure–pain, antithetical self- and object-images, attitude, and relief pleasure. These angles have proved useful both in personal work with patients and by therapists in supervision. Other useful aspects may come to light in further studies.

The choice of which aspect to present as an intervention is a matter of the therapist's judgment based on a general knowledge of the patient and an understanding of the patient's defensiveness at the moment. The analogy between denial and the patient's sore spot is useful in guiding that choice. The therapist wants to touch the perimeter of the sore spot as precisely as possible. He or she does not wish to be so indirect that the patient experiences no discomfort, nor does he or she wish to be so direct that the discomfort will lead to defensive intolerance. The art is to produce a degree of discomfort that the patient can tolerate.

Presentations of the material that originally met with denial may be formed from any of the aspects discussed. All of them have been designed to produce a small experience of discomfort for the patient and do not theoretically necessarily provoke defense. These modes are theoretically correct as interventions in denial. However, the sensitivity of the patient to the therapist's intervention is also contingent on many circumstances outside of the office, and these may be difficult to detect and to assess. For example, the patient may be subject to current physical, financial, or social stress. In the light of knowledge about the patient's current stresses, it may be apparent that certain aspects are likely to be experienced with particular sensitivity. Nonetheless, the considerable variety of angles that may be taken toward the material should allow the selection of those that are suitable for the moment.

Although carefulness in selecting the form of intervention is clearly indicated, the possibility of intolerability cannot be ruled out. Thus, it is wise to present interventions in a tentative manner in order to test the patient's sensitivity at that particular moment. The therapist must be prepared to withdraw that angle if it should prove to be intolerable.

WORKING THROUGH DENIAL

Experience of Anxiety

I have used the term *working through* to refer to the therapist's presentation of interventions in the patient's experience of painful unpleasure. Denial may defend against the painful feeling of anxiety. Denial has been worked through when the patient is able to tolerate the unpleasant recognition of being in a state of anxiety.

The presence of denial establishes that the patient finds the state of anxiety too painful to recognize. Consider what "too painful" means in the experience of the patient. As I have discussed, there is the usual assumption that the unpleasure of anxious anticipation can become so quantitatively intense that it is experienced as painful. However, there are two main objections to this quantitative assumption. First, there are many observations in which people recognize experiencing objectively intense anxiety and undertake emergency activities. Second, there are many observations in which people deny experiencing anxiety, when this can be demonstrated to be objectively mild, and they undertake no corrective action. These observations demonstrate that the denial of anxiety is not connected with the intensity of unpleasure.

The institution and maintenance of denial has no effect on the intensity of unpleasure that is objectively suffered by the person. In fact, denial ensures that no remedial action will be undertaken and that the suffering will be unabated. Denial only serves to refuse recognition of the state of anxiety and the person is prepared to pay the price of unremedied suffering. A person may deny recognizing a state of anxiety regardless of its intensity.

The experience of a state of anxiety is denied because of what it means to the person. In relativistic psychology, the meaning of an event for a person is comprehended by the concept of emotion as the vector summation in experience of motivational principles. From this point of view, denial is maintained despite its costs to the pleasure and reality principles. Only narcissistic considerations can supercede these motivations. Thus, the theory of relativism posits that the denial of anxiety is motivated by narcissism.

The presence of denial indicates that anxiety is experienced as an intolerable narcissistic insult. What denial denies is the experience of narcissistic insult. The patient's problem in granting recognition to being in a state of anxiety is that it is perceived as antithetical to the maintenance of a sense of self-esteem.

The experience of anxiety has been described as a "nameless fear." This refers to the fact that the person has perceived things about himself or herself that connotes fearfulness and that nothing is perceived that is regarded as fearsome. In experiential terms, people observe that they are acting in a nonsensible manner. They conclude that they are not in control of their mental faculties and that these faculties are functioning with disorder. They observe itching with no sign of a rash, the inability to recall a detail from a pleasant experience, the sensations of tiredness after a good night's sleep, a tremor of the fingers when the rest of the body feels relaxed, a feeling of aversion toward someone who is liked, the temptation to do something known to be ineffective, the failure to perform intended kindness, the avoidance of things that are usually desirable, or the inability to concentrate when that is desired. These observations may be regarded with the attitudes "I guess I'm upset about something" or "I must be nervous." In this event, the observation of one's imperfection is unpleasant but acceptable to one's self-image, and a sense of self-esteem can be maintained. However, if one's ego is already in a shaky condition, there is the connotation that "I must be getting worse." In any case, an experience of anxiety that is tolerated is represented by the attitude "I am upset."

Working Through Anxiety Experience

In denials of an anxiety experience, the totality of observations that "I am upset" is experienced as inimical with the maintenance of a sense of self-esteem (e.g., "I can't be that upset"). The threatened loss of self-esteem is experienced as painfully intolerable and leads to the adoption and maintenance of denial. The psychotherapy of denial is by interventions that provoke a little experience of being upset. The correct dosage of being a little upset is that which can be recognized by the patient while still maintaining the sense of self-esteem (e.g., "I may be a little upset, but at least I'm not crazy").

The art in the treatment of denial is the introduction of interventions that are tolerable provocations of anxiety. The working through of denial is the presentation of interventions from various angles. This process allows the patient to develop an increasing tolerance for the self-esteem implications of each little bit of anxiety experience. The treatment is complete when anxiety experience is no longer painfully intolerable. There is no longer recourse to denial, and the patient is able to recognize anxiety experience as unpleasant but tolerable.

Overdose of Intervention

Despite the therapist's care in selecting low doses of intervention in treating denial, there is the possibility of provoking too much anxiety. It has been noted that too direct of a confrontation of patients with their contradictory behaviors tends to evoke intense anxiety reactions to such an extent that the defensive attitude of denial cannot be maintained. Patients may back away from such excessive interventions by instituting further defensive attitudes or withdrawing from treatment.

The evocation of exacerbated anxiety reactions makes it impossible for the patient to maintain a positive or zero attitude in the face of his or her obviously distressful activity. The attitude of "being anxious" is not tolerable, and the patient may adopt attitudes of fear, sadness, guilt, or depression as additional defenses. The new attitude will be recognizable as a transference resistance departure from the patient's personal norm of denial. The new attitude of psychic pain is understood as a defense against the more painful experience of anxiety (Brenner, 1974, p. 551).

When attitudes of unpleasure are defensive of anxiety experience, they may be treated by special interventions called *interpretations of anxiety*. The patient's presentations of depression, fear, sadness, or guilt are countered by an interpretation of the patient being in a state of anxiety. Interventions by the presentation of interpretations of anxiety are chosen carefully as to dosage. These interventions may be formed as "You seem to be more agitated than fearful," "You look more confused than sad," "You're not describing guilt but frustration," or "I think you're not feeling small but upset." The administration of interventions in the form of interpretations of anxiety is subject to the same regulation as any intervention toward denial.

Forming Denial Interventions

Understanding the use of attitudes of unpleasure as secondary defenses of denial leads to an appreciation of a refinement in the general presentation of interventions toward denial. Their formulation should exclude any specification of a particular quality of unpleasure. To do so would constitute an invitation to the patient to use that as a secondary defense and avoid the development of the ability to tolerate a state of anxiety. To avoid an intolerable experience of anxiety, patients may rush to present unpleasures that they already can tolerate. The experience of unknown apprehension is better presented in interventions by deliberately vague formulations, such as anxious, confused, agitated, upset, nervous, and frustrated.

REFERENCES

Brenner, C. (1974). On the nature and development of affects: A unified theory. *Psychoanalytic Quarterly, 43*, 532–556.

Brenner, C. (1976). *Psychoanalytic technique and psychic conflict*. New York: International University Press.

Freud, S. (1959). Inhibitions, symptoms and anxiety. In J. Strachey (Ed. & Trans.), *The standard edition of the complete psychological works of Sigmund Freud* (Vol. 20, pp. 77–176). London: Hogarth Press. (Original work published 1926)

Freud, S. (1964). New introductory lectures on psycho-analysis. In J. Strachey (Ed. & Trans.), *The standard edition of the complete psychological works of Sigmund Freud* (Vol. 22, pp. 141–208). London: Hogarth Press. (Original work published 1933)

Greenson, R. (1967). *The technique and practice of psychotherapy*. New York: International University Press.

Kernberg, O. (1976). *Object relations theory and clinical psychoanalysis*. New York: Jason Aronson.

Kernberg, O. (1977). The structural diagnosis of borderline personality. In P. Hartocollis (Ed.), *Borderline personality disorders* (pp. 87–122). New York: International University Press.

Schafer, R. (1983). *The analytic attitude*. New York: Basic Books.

21

Psychodiagnosis

CURRENT STATUS

As I discussed in chapter 14 on the relativistic theory of psychopathology, there is no substantial theoretical justification for distinguishing mental disorders in the absence of an acceptable theory about the nature of those disorders. Nevertheless, practical exigency impels those with a professional responsibility to care for people with mental disorders to do the best they can in a responsible manner.

The construction of diagnostic schemes has been a response to demands for help from individuals suffering from these disorders, as well as to the needs of concerned social agencies. The absence of a theoretical standard to validate diagnostic distinctions has led to the regular use only of criteria of reliability despite the limitations of such an objectivist procedure. It is hoped that the diagnostic discriminations arrived at by groups of experts will result in a pool of clinical wisdom with implications for validity.

The *Diagnostic and Statistical Manual of Mental Disorders, Third Edition* (*DSM-III*; American Psychiatric Association, 1980) represents the best that the pool of clinical wisdom is currently able to do. At the same time, it is explicitly recognized that the observation of psychobehavioral patterns is not necessarily indicative of a type of discrete disorder (Blum, 1978, p. 1020; Pelz, 1987, p. 709). Nonetheless, such diagnostic schemes attempt to distinguish patterns of disorder (Schafer, 1983, p. 11).

RELATIVIST THEORY OF PSYCHOPATHOLOGY

Relativists hold that the essence of psychopathological states is the person's inability to tolerate an experience of unpleasure without a defensive alteration of attitude. Therefore, the factors making for any particular pathological state are tolerance of unpleasure and defensive alteration.

Sources of Unpleasure

The sources of unpleasure experience are distinguishable as primarily biological, sociological, or psychological. Therefore, psychopathological states are diagnosable according to the source of unpleasure that is regarded as intolerable. This diagnostic distinction is useful in distinguishing important differences in modes of planning for the treatment and social management of persons in psychopathological states.

Tolerance of Unpleasure

It seems reasonable to assume that all people are born with a mental faculty for tolerating unpleasure. I hold the corollary that the innate endowment with this faculty varies among individuals. I also hold that this endowment is subject to both maturational and developmental processes. Therefore, psychopathological states are diagnosable according to an assessment of both endowment and current development of the ability to tolerate unpleasure. This diagnostic distinction is useful in distinguishing important differences in modes of planning for the treatment and social management of persons in a state of psychopathology.

Defenses

Defensive attitudes are distinguishable in classification as to denial or disavowal, and different types of therapeutic intervention are required. Furthermore, denial defenses and disavowal defenses occur in distinguishable types, each of which requires a specific mode in the type of intervention. Therefore, psychopathological states are diagnosable according to the category and type of defensive attitude that constitutes the patient's personal norm. This diagnostic distinction is essential in distinguishing differences in modes of planning the analytic psychotherapy of persons in a state of psychopathology, regardless of whether the treatment is performed in a private setting or within a social agency.

Consequences of Defense

The institution of defensive attitudes is expressed in the development of patterns of avoidant behaviors. The maintenance of defensive attitudes is expressed in the development of insistent patterns of behavior. The performance of both avoidant and insistent patterns has necessary consequences of a physiological, sociological, and psychological nature. The consequences of each mode in each of the three areas may be assessed as being mild, moderate, or severe. Therefore, psychopathological states are diagnosable according to an assessment of the consequences of instituting and maintaining defensive attitudes. This diagnostic distinction is useful in distinguishing important differences in modes of planning for the treatment and social management of persons in a state of psychopathology.

RELATIVIST DIAGNOSIS

My concept of diagnosis is developed from the relativist theory of psychopathology. Four factors are identified that have bearing in making decisions about both psychotherapeutic treatment and social management of persons with states of psychopathology. Relativist diagnosis is a judgment that comprehends the assessment of the patient as to the source of intolerable unpleasure, the degree of tolerance of unpleasure, the defenses used, and the consequences of defenses.

By construction, relativist diagnosis would be immediately useful for analytic psychotherapeutic and social management purposes. Its usefulness for legal and educational purposes may be contingent on its relation with the concerns of other professions as well as political factors. Standards for the assessment of the elements of relativist diagnosis have yet to be developed.

REFERENCES

American Psychiatric Association. (1980). *Diagnostic and statistical manual of mental disorders* (3rd ed.). Washington, DC: Author.

Blum, J. (1978). On changes in psychiatric diagnosis over time. *American Psychologist, 33,* 1017–1031.

Pelz, M. (1987). Psychoanalytic contributions to psychiatric nosology. *Journal of the American Psychoanalytic Association, 35,* 693–711.

Schafer, R. (1983). *The analytic attitude.* New York: Basic Books.

Index

Abnormal, defined, 109
Abraham, K., 84
Activity, energy and, 62
Aggressiveness, 42–44, 187
Alcoholism, 124
American sign language (AMESLAN), 89
Anaclitic evaluation, 151
Anger, 187
Antithetical attitudes, 162
Anxiety, 160, 175, 202–203, 207–209
Archaic experiences, 8
Arousal, 107
Artistic activity, 90
Associative connection, 127
Astronomy, 9–10
Attitude, defined, 161, 205–206
Authority figures, 145, 149–150
Autoerotic behavior, 47, 93
Avoidance, 206

Bandura, A., 94
Behavior, 25
  behaviorist theory, 33, 119
  cognitive factors, 119
  disorders in, 115
  emotional, 107–108
  instinct and, 36
  need and, 40
  phenomena of, 34
  psychology and, 25, 27
  (*See also specific types, concepts*)
Behaviorism, 33, 119
Biological cause, 42
Birth, 67–68, 94–95
Body-image, 83, 177–179
Brain, 26
Brenner, C., 128, 175

Breuer, J., 145
Burnout, 123–124

Cannon-Bond theory, 106
Caretaking, 69
Cathartic method, 204
Cathexsis, 164
Causality:
  instinct and, 36–39
  knowledge of, 18, 23–29
  need and, 40
  realism and, 12, 35–36
  transcendental, 7, 12–13
  types of, 24, 42
Chaos theory, 8
Children, 55
  aggressiveness in, 44
  authority and, 149–151
  masturbation and, 54–55
  mother and, 79
  narcissism and, 93
  parents and, 145, 149–151
  reality principle and, 98
  self-concept of, 120
  temper of, 101
  (*See also* Infants; *specific behavior, problems*)
Chirality, 12
Chomsky, N., 8
Circularity, 8
Claimers, defined, 191
Clarification, method of, 148
Clinging behavior, 137
Cognition, 105–107
Cognitive theory, 119–120
Coitus, 56–58
Collective figures, 90